on writing
horror

revised edition

A Handbook by
The Horror Writers Association

EDITED BY MORT CASTLE

WRITER'S DIGEST BOOKS

www.writersdigest.com
Cincinnati, Ohio

Visit our Web sites at www.writersdigest.com and www.wdeditors.com for information on more resources for writers.

To receive a free weekly e-mail newsletter delivering tips and updates about writing and about Writer's Digest products, register directly at our Web site at http://news letters.fwpublications.com.

12 11   7 6 5

Distributed in Canada by Fraser Direct, 100 Armstrong Avenue, Georgetown, ON, Canada L7G 5S4, Tel: (905) 877-4411; Distributed in the U.K. and Europe by David & Charles, Brunel House, Newton Abbot, Devon, TQ12 4PU, England, Tel: (+44) 1626 323200, Fax: (+44) 1626 323319, E-mail: postmaster@davidandcharles.co.uk; Distributed in Australia by Capricorn Link, P.O. Box 704, Windsor, NSW 2756 Australia, Tel: (02) 4577-3555

Library of Congress Cataloging-in-Publication Data
On writing horror / by the Horror Writers Association ; edited by Mort Castle. -- 2nd rev. ed.
     p. cm.
   Includes index.
   ISBN-13: 978-1-58297-420-0 (pbk. : alk. paper)
   ISBN-10: 1-58297-420-9
   1. Horror tales--Authorship. I. Castle, Mort. II. Horror Writers Association.
   PN3377.5.H67W75 2006
   808.3'8738--dc22
                              2006019465

Edited by Michelle Ehrhard
Designed by Claudean Wheeler
Production coordinated by Mark Griffin

Permissions

Acknowledgments

Many, many thanks to all who contributed to *On Writing Horror*, but "super special oh yeah many thanks" to the trademarked Harlan Ellison®, who is the benchmark for quality, integrity, and intelligence; and to Bob Weinberg, who might not know everything about horror—but then again, he just might.

This book is dedicated to J.N. Williamson, aka "Avuncular Jer," aka "Big Guy," aka "The Hoosier Sage of Horror," aka my friend, my teacher ... .

We miss you, Big Brother, and we remember and honor you.

MORT CASTLE
May 2006

About HWA

The Horror Writers Association is a worldwide organization of writers and publishing professionals dedicated to promoting the horror genre. Formed in the late 1980s, it is the oldest and most respected organization celebrating the writers who revel in bringing sleepless nights to readers. Find out more at www.horror.org

Table of Contents

Part Four: Horror Crafting

Part Five: Horror, Art, Innovation, Excellence

Part Six: Tradition and Modern Times

Part Seven: Genre and Subgenre

Part Eight: Horror Business: Selling, Marketing, Promoting

Afterword

Foreword: The Horror Writers Association: A Shockingly Brief and Informal History of the HWA

—Stanley Wiater

As with most great ideas, the concept for a horror writers' association originated in the fevered imagination of one individual—in this instance, one Robert R. McCammon. In an interview with *Publishers Weekly* in 1984, the author (who had already published six horror novels) first publicly expressed his desire for a professional organization specifically geared to the needs of fellow writers of fear. At that point, however, his decidedly colorful name for the then-nonexistent organization was HOWL, Horror and Occult Writers League. Even so, reasoned McCammon, mystery writers had their professional organizations, as did science fiction writers. Wasn't it past time that the equally honorable genre of terror, fright, and the supernatural be formally recognized?

Perhaps more than anyone, McCammon was shocked at the subsequent— and often sincere—interest of the media in his remarks, including *The New York Times* and *The Washington Post*. Then the B. Dalton and Waldenbooks chains wanted to know more. Horror writers began to "hear the HOWL" and wrote McCammon to ask where to sign up, although it had always been his intent to survey every writer he could contact first before ever making a formal announcement about the proposed organization. Nevertheless, McCammon was deluged with still more letters of support from writers, editors, and scholars— both stateside and overseas—my own enthusiastic response as a self-styled "horror journalist" included.

Before long, McCammon enlisted the support of two colleagues who were instrumental in bringing the concept of HOWL snarling into reality: Texas author Joe R. Lansdale and his wife, Karen. They, in turn, sent out a formal letter of invitation to some 177 writers, 88 of which responded with suggestions or a willingness to join.

Working by phone and letter with McCammon, the trio committed themselves to the insane task of creating what they believed could be a nationally, perhaps even internationally, recognized writers' organization. Thanks primarily to Karen's unflagging energy, they then drew up the constitution and bylaws, formulated mailing lists, ran ads, issued press releases—whatever it took to ensure that, from the outset, HOWL would be recognized as a professional writers' organization, not a "fan club" for sideshow horror buffs.

Other new volunteers contributed in numerous ways, most notably in the production and content of the early newsletters. We took our organization seriously right from the bloody start. Why not? Stephen King and Peter Straub, among others, were becoming increasingly known as "brand-name writers." For the first time, "horror" was being labeled as a separate category in most bookstores. The entire field was riding a growing wave of popularity in the 1980s; it was only logical that those of us exploring this increasingly recognized genre would desire to have our own legitimate organization.

The goals of HOWL were stated simply and directly in the preamble to its constitution and bylaws:

> Be it known that the Horror and Occult Writers League is a non-profit organization of professional writers of fiction and nonfiction pertaining to or inspired by the traditions, legends, development, and history of horror and occult. Its members are together for their mutual benefit in an earnest effort to further a more widespread publicity, promotion, distribution, readership, and appreciation of the literature of horror and occult.

The lack of high-profile authors like King was one of the stumbling blocks early on, even as the organization was searching for recognition by its peers precisely among those most successfully working in our genre. (Dean Koontz and Robert Bloch were among the first to respond favorably to the concept and to volunteer their aid and reputations.)

Regardless, new members from all across the country and overseas were being added to the growing roster. It was obvious from the burgeoning newsletters that, for many writers, editors, and critics, the fledgling organization was being taken quite seriously.

Unfortunately, HOWL was not being taken seriously by some colleagues … or by much of the mainstream media, for that matter. (If even I can easily poke gentle fun at the acronym "HOWL," just think how anyone less than sympathetic would describe the virtually unknown group and its membership.)

Nevertheless, history was made when the first formal meeting took place on November 3, 1985, at the World Fantasy Convention held in Tucson, Arizona. (Subsequent meetings have taken place at both the World Fantasy Convention and the World Horror Convention.) No more than two dozen people attended that fateful meeting, led informally by founder Robert R. McCammon and Joe R. and Karen Lansdale. Outside this fledgling meeting, of course, there were hundreds of writers, agents, and other professionals at the convention.

Dare I say it: There, yours truly took note of the small number of "the faithful" in attendance that glorious Sunday morning. And so I made a brief-yet-heartfelt speech, imploring those present to change the name from the undeniably memorable "HOWL" to, say, the Horror Writers of America (HWA) ... with the obvious intent to bring our name recognition to the public more in line with such well-established groups as the Mystery Writers of America and the Science Fiction Writers of America (which became the Science Fiction and Fantasy Writers of America, Inc. in 1992). By unanimous vote, my suggestion was approved.

After that initial gathering, others were inspired to make our new organization truly viable and far more visible. McCammon formed a steering committee with Melissa Mia Hall and Joe R. Lansdale to tackle (as described in an open letter to members) "the toughest part of putting the HWA together—the trial by paperwork, if you will—and after these hurdles are overcome with your help and support, we'll have a stronger organization that will benefit authors in our field for generations to come."

Dated July 1986, Volume 1, Number 1 of the first Horror Writers of America (HWA) official newsletter appeared. Entitled *Our Glass* (after a famous medieval statue in which a corpse is admiring itself in a pocket glass), the professionally printed first issue was eight pages long.

It featured timely news items, a letters page, a market report, the first ballot for the formal election of officers, and brief interviews with artist Phil Parks and founder Robert R. McCammon. Only two issues appeared with this title, even as a search was launched for a permanent organization logo. (While the admiring corpse was suggested as one possibility, the logo would ultimately be a tastefully stylized haunted house.)

Later that year, early supporter Dean Koontz was chosen as the organization's first president. In a statement to the membership, Koontz declared his belief that the HWA could "add dignity and publicity to the field, as well as giving horror fiction a focus." Koontz further suggested an annual anthology to be composed of contributions from the membership ranks. The first of several such anthologies to subsequently appear would be *Under the Fang*, edited by Robert R. McCammon.

Through the volunteered legal counsel of Sheldon R. Jaffery, the HWA was legally incorporated in March 1987. The initial board of trustees was also in place, which, at that time, included McCammon, Lansdale, and Koontz. The HWA was formally on its way, anxious and ready to make its unique voice heard.

Koontz furthered, fostered, and promoted the idea that the HWA was a serious organization for writers, and damn well should be taken as such by all concerned. Before he left office, there were some three hundred members, many of them among the most popular and respected authors in the business. As many are aware, the most recognized horror authors in the world have become members, including Ray Bradbury, Stephen King, Peter Straub, Clive Barker, Richard Matheson, and Ramsey Campbell. The membership of the HWA today numbers over six hundred and is growing. Various regional affiliate chapters have been formed and are also thriving.

It was under Koontz's administration that the formation of an annual award for "superior achievement" was initiated. At the time, Koontz was chief among those who believed the award should be named after a famous (and deceased) writer. His short list of dead-on recommendations: Mary Wollstonecraft Shelley, Edgar Allan Poe, H.P. Lovecraft, and Bram Stoker. The membership ultimately voted on the "Bram Stoker Award," to be issued in the form of a magnificently wrought haunted house designed by Stephen Kirk.

In 1988, the first Annual Bram Stoker Awards Banquet and Business Meeting took place in New York City. Since then, the officers have attempted to satisfy both the West Coast and East Coast members by swapping coasts from time to time.

In 1993, to further involve its international membership, the name was changed once again, from the "Horror Writers of America" to the "Horror Writers Association." Whatever the name, the horror genre it proudly champions continues to be more widely recognized and increasingly appreciated in this new millennium, as the HWA continues to flourish and be taken seriously by both publishers and the public alike.

If I may close on a personal note, it's been my singular pleasure to be a dues-paying member from the earliest origins of the HWA. My highest honor in the literary field undoubtedly has been winning the Bram Stoker Award in 1991. Without the HWA, it's difficult to say where the career of at least one writer might have ended up. In fact, one might be sorely tempted to say it's too frightening to even contemplate ....

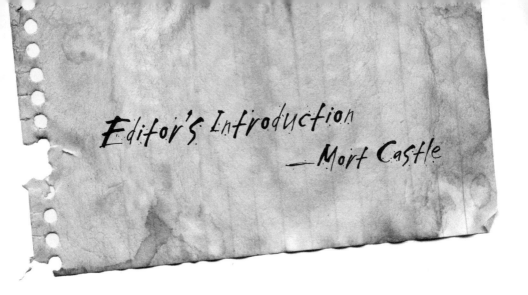

Editor's Introduction
—Mort Castle

I began the 1997 first edition of *Writing Horror: A Handbook by the Horror Writers Association* with the stated or implied questions you hear about horror fiction:

Horror? What—exactly—do you mean by that?

Where do you get ideas?

Why do you write such—*horrible/horrifying/horrific*—stuff?

There were the questions, too, directly related to the craft of writing horror:

But how can you make credible what is plainly incredible?

If you are creating mood, how can you keep the story's plot moving briskly?

How do you make your horror story characters act right, talk right, think right, respond to demeaning, spiritually destroying, agonizingly messy, maiming deaths right?

That first compilation by the talented members of the Horror Writers Association attempted to provide answers, often quite personal in nature, or at least to give hints to answers for these questions and many others. All the contributors and I are gratified that the book became the essential text on writing horror and has served as an inspirational touchstone for many writers who entered the horror field (some of whom are represented in this new edition).

But the horror genre has changed in numerous and significant ways:

1. In 1997, the horror field was emerging from a decade-long slump/disappearance. Today, horror is commercially viable once again, with a horror imprint to be found at most major publishers of fiction, and horror a virtual "sure sell" for youth-oriented films, television programs, and video games.

2. Small-press publishers were struggling or dying in 1997; now there's a vigorous "small and specialty press" with an enthusiastic and inventive e-publishing arm.

3. Above all, horror in 1997 was seen almost exclusively as "category fiction," unworthy of serious literary consideration or critical comment, whereas today it's transcended labels: Writers like Stewart O'Nan, Chuck Palahniuk, Mark Z. Danielewski, Joyce Carol Oates, and 2003 National Book Award winner Stephen King (the latter two sharing their thoughts in this book) have legitimized the field in a way that is not likely to happen for other brands of "category fiction" such as romance, fantasy, or even mystery-thriller.

That means, then, as the HWA and Writer's Digest Books realize, there are new questions posed by the contemporary horror reader and would-be writer:

What does the *informed* new horror writer need to know of the field's history and its contemporary state to be successful at the craft?

What possibilities and problems, as well as resources, are provided by new and emerging communications technologies and media?

What are the special concerns of the horror writer that are unique to his chosen literary venue?

You'll find that these questions and so many others (and questions *prompted* by these questions!) are dealt with in this new edition of On *Writing Horror*, as are those yet relevant topics covered in the previous book.

Horror, publishing, and the world have changed dramatically since the last book. (Why, back in 1997, not everyone carried a cell phone—and if the cell phone itself isn't the springboard to at least a dozen horror stories, then Frankenstein forgot to pay his electric bill!) One aspect of this book, however, is exactly the same as it was for its predecessor: the motivation of the fine people who've made this book happen.

That is, each of the contributors to *On Writing Horror* has made a serious time, energy, and creative commitment to sharing with you the *whys* and *hows* of horror. They have done so because they literally and openly declare their *love for* "this horror thing" of ours and genuinely want to communicate that love and their knowledge to you.

So, welcome to our (and your!) horrific world of wild imaginings, dark desires, and enlightening realities. Come in, and we, all of us together, will explore the strange art and demanding craft of ... *Writing Horror*.

—MORT CASTLE
July 2006

Part One

Horror, Literature, and Horror Literature

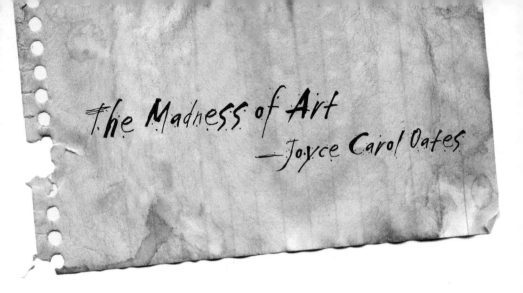

The Madness of Art
—Joyce Carol Oates

When you consider what a slight part the weird
plays in our moods, feelings, and lives, you
can easily see how basically minor the weird
tale must necessarily be. It can be art, since
the sense of the uncanny is an authentic human emotion, but it is obviously a narrow and
restricted form of art. . . .

—H.P. Lovecraft

The Brain, within its Groove Runs evenly—and
true—But let a Splinter swerve—'Twere easier
for You—To put a Current back—When Floods have
slit the Hills—And scooped a Turnpike for
Themselves—and trodden out the Mills.

—Emily Dickinson (no. 26, 1890)

Since the start of my writing career as an adult—I should acknowledge that
before I published my first short stories in national magazines, let alone my
first novel, I'd written literally thousands of pages of prose fiction—I have been
fascinated by the fluid and indefinable boundaries between "realism" and "surrealism." What are the "Gothic," the "grotesque," "horror"—as literary genres?
What is the distinction, if there is a distinction, and if it is significant, between

the art of Franz Kafka—that extraordinary tale of unspeakable horror, "In the Penal Colony," for instance—and the art of H.P. Lovecraft—that extraordinary tale of unspeakable horror, "The Shadow Out of Time," for instance? Is there any significant distinction, in terms of depth of perception or quality of vision, between Henry James's *The Portrait of a Lady* and *The Turn of the Screw* by the same author? Is Edgar Allan Poe, our most martyred American Gothicist, now a "mainstream" writer, as a consequence of the literary canon that has enshrined him as a "classic"? Perhaps, to transcend categories others have invented for us, we have to be both dead—long dead—and "classics."

In art, such extravagant, experimental movements as expressionism, symbolism, surrealism, and Dada, freely obliterated restraining and defining categories. The numinous and frequently nightmarish image lay at the core of the artist's inspiration.

Consider such work as *The Rape* by the Belgian surrealist Magritte, which combines features of the female anatomy and the female face in a nightmarish conflation that possesses its own logic, and other works of Magritte's in which the human form is distorted or dismembered, or melted into other, inanimate objects; or those most powerful horror images of Egon Schiele in which the human figure, Schiele's own in some paintings, is imagined as a living skeleton, an animated embodiment of Death; or the flamboyantly decadent art of Aubrey Beardsley, in which sexual organs seem to have acquired sinister lives of their own; and works of Klimt and Munch in which Death cavorts with life in scenes of arresting visual beauty.

The visual arts are perhaps the most radical of arts, for there seems to be no mainstream, no "convention," exerting its gravitational pull upon individual artists, at least since the time of Cézanne. In music, the "great, abiding classics" of Mozart, Beethoven, Brahms, et al, continue to be played incessantly, to the despair of contemporary composers who are forced, however against the grain of their ideologies and temperaments, to compete for a relatively small, conservative audience. In literature, the canonization of "classics" has resulted in the relative demotion of other writers and other kinds of writing; the elevation of "mainstream" and predominantly "realistic" writing has created a false topology in which numerous genres are perceived as inferior to, or at least significantly different from, the mainstream. If Edgar Allan Poe were alive and writing today, he would very likely not be accorded the acclaim given the putative "serious literary writer," but would be taxonomized as a "horror writer." Yet talent, not excluding genius, may flourish in any genre, provided it is not stigmatized by that deadly label "genre."

Speaking as a writer predisposed to reading and frequently to writing what I call "Gothic" work, I should say that this so-called genre fascinates me because it is so powerful a vehicle of truth-telling, and because there is no wilder region for the exercise of the pure imagination. The surreal is as integral a part of our lives as the "real," although one might argue that, since the unconscious underlies consciousness, and we are continuously bombarded by images, moods, and memories from that uncharitable terrain, it is in fact more primary than the "real." The Gothic work resembles the tragic in that it is willing to confront mankind's—and nature's—darkest secrets. Its metaphysics is Plato's, and not Aristotle's. There is a profound difference between what appears to be, and what is; and if you believe otherwise, the Gothicist has a surprise for you. The strained, sunny smile of the Enlightenment—"All that is, is holy;" "Man is a rational being"—is confronted by the Gothicist, who, quite frankly, considering the history and prehistory of our species, knows better. That there should be a highly conscious, rigorously crafted art of the grotesque, in the very service of such painful revelations, seems to me a tribute to our species, a check to the homogenization of culture, in which a single vision—democratic, Christian, liberal, "good"—has come to be identified with America generally.

Of course, horror fiction has its weaknesses. But so does "serious, literary" fiction. If there is any problem with the Gothic as an art, it is likely to lie in the quality of execution. In the literature of horror, a handicap has frequently been that of verisimilitude, the relative weakness or flatness of character. H.P. Lovecraft spoke of the "weird" rather than the Gothic, which seems to me, for all my admiration of Lovecraft's masterly work, unnecessarily restricting. To Lovecraft, too, "phenomena" rather than "persons" are the logical heroes of stories, one consequence of which is two-dimensional, stereotypical characters about whom it is difficult to care. Situations and plots may be formulaic, language merely serviceable, and not a vehicle for the impassioned inwardness of which "weirdness" is one attempt at definition, but only one. The standards for horror fiction should be no less than those for "serious, literary" fiction in which originality of concept, depth of characters, and attentiveness to language are vitally important.

Gothic fiction is the freedom of the imagination, the triumph of the unconscious. Its radical premise is that, out of utterly plausible and psychologically realistic situations, profound and intransigent truths will emerge. *And it is entertaining; it is unashamed to be entertaining.*

Those of us (how many of us!) who have given our souls to the activity of writing are obviously engaged in a lifelong quest. Perhaps, though we experience ourselves as individuals, our art is communal, like our language and our histories. We write in order not just to be read, but to read—texts not yet written, which only we can bring into being. Is this quest quixotic, perverse, or utterly natural? Normal? Do we have any choice? Henry James, one of our exemplary beings who understood the lure of the grotesque, the skull beneath the smiling face, as well as any writer, has characterized us all in these words:

> We work in the dark—we do what we can—we give what we have. Our doubt is our passion, and our passion is our task. The rest is the madness of art.

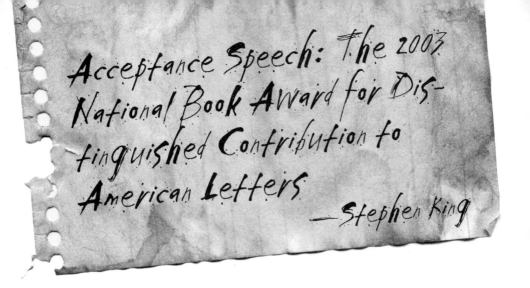

Acceptance Speech: The 2003
National Book Award for Dis-
tinguished Contribution to
American Letters
—Stephen King

Thank you very much. Thank you all. Thank you for the applause and thank you for coming. I'm delighted to be here but, as I've said before in the last five years, I'm delighted to be anywhere.

This isn't in my speech, so don't take it out of my allotted time. There are some people who have spoken out passionately about giving me this medal. There are some people who think it's an extraordinarily bad idea. There have been some people who have spoken out who think it's an extraordinarily good idea. You know who you are and where you stand, and most of you who are here tonight are on my side. I'm glad for that. But I want to say it doesn't matter in a sense which side you were on. The people who speak out, speak out because they are passionate about the book, about the word, about the page and, in that sense, we're all brothers and sisters. Give yourselves a hand.

Now as for my remarks. The only person who understands how much this award means to me is my wife, Tabitha. I was a writer when I met her in 1967, but my only venue was the campus newspaper where I published a rude weekly column. It turned me into a bit of a celebrity but I was a poor one, scraping through college thanks to a jury-rigged package of loans and scholarships.

A friend of Tabitha Spruce pointed me out to her one winter day as I crossed the mall in my jeans and cut-down, green rubber boots. I had a bushy black beard. I hadn't had my hair cut in two years and I looked like Charlie Manson. My wife-to-be clasped her hands between her breasts and said, "I think I'm in love" in a tone dripping with sarcasm.

Tabby Spruce had no more money than I did but with sarcasm she was loaded. When we married in 1971, we already had one child. By the middle of 1972, we had a pair. I taught school and worked in a laundry during the summer. Tabby worked for Dunkin' Donuts. When she was working, I took care of the kids. When I was working, it was vice versa. And writing was always an undisputed part of that work. Tabby finished the first book of our marriage, a slim but wonderful book of poetry called *Grimoire*.

This is a very atypical audience, one passionately dedicated to books and to the word. Most of the world, however, sees writing as a fairly useless occupation. I've even heard it called "mental masturbation" once or twice by people in my family. I never heard that from my wife. She'd read my stuff and felt certain I'd some day support us by writing full time, instead of standing in front of a blackboard and spouting on about Jack London and Ogden Nash. She never made a big deal of this. It was just a fact of our lives. We lived in a trailer and she made a writing space for me in the tiny laundry room with a desk and her Olivetti portable between the washer and dryer. She still tells people I married her for that typewriter, but that's only partly true. I married her because I loved her and because we got on as well out of bed as in it. The typewriter was a factor, though.

When I gave up on *Carrie*, it was Tabby who rescued the first few pages of single-spaced manuscript from the wastebasket, told me it was good, and said I ought to go on. When I told her I didn't know how to go on, she helped me out with the girls' locker room stuff. There were no inspiring speeches. Tabby does sarcasm; Tabby doesn't do inspiration, never has. It was just "this is pretty good, you ought to keep it going." That was all I needed and she knew it.

There were some hard, dark years before *Carrie*. We had two kids and no money. We rotated the bills, paying on different ones each month. I kept our car, an old Buick, going with duct tape and bailing wire. It was a time when my wife might have been expected to say, "Why don't you quit spending three hours a night in the laundry room, Steve, smoking cigarettes and drinking beer we can't afford? Why don't you get an actual job?"

Okay, this is the real stuff. If she'd asked, I almost certainly would have done it. And then am I standing up here tonight, making a speech, accepting the award, wearing a radar dish around my neck? Maybe. More likely not. In fact, the subject of moonlighting did come up once. The head of the English department where I taught told me that the debate club was going to need a new faculty advisor and he'd put me up for the job if I wanted. It would pay $300 per school year—which doesn't sound like much—but my yearly take in 1973 was only $6,600, and $300 equaled ten weeks worth of groceries.

The English department head told me he'd need my decision by the end of the week. When I told Tabby about the opening, she asked if I'd still have time to write. I told her not as much. Her response to that was unequivocal: "Well then, you can't take it."

One of the few times during the early years of our marriage I saw my wife cry really hard was when I told her that a paperback publisher, New American Library, had paid a ton of money for the book she'd rescued from the trash. I could quit teaching, she could quit pushing crullers at Dunkin' Donuts. She looked almost unbelieving for five seconds and then she put her hands over her face and she wept. When she finally stopped, we went into the living room and sat on our old couch, which Tabby had rescued from a yard sale, and talked into the early hours of the morning about what we were going to do with the money. I've never had a more pleasant conversation. I have never had one that felt more surreal.

My point is that Tabby always knew what I was supposed to be doing, and she believed that I would succeed at it. There is a time in the lives of most writers when they are vulnerable, when the vivid dreams and ambitions of childhood seem to pale in the harsh sunlight of what we call the real world. In short, there's a time when things can go either way.

That vulnerable time for me came during 1971 to 1973. If my wife had suggested to me, even with love and kindness and gentleness rather than her more common wit and good-natured sarcasm, that the time had come to put my dreams away and support my family, I would have done that with no complaint. I believe that on some level of thought I was expecting to have that conversation. If she had suggested that you can't buy a loaf of bread or a tube of toothpaste with rejection slips, I would have gone out and found a part-time job.

Tabby has told me since that it never crossed her mind to have such a conversation. You had a second job, she said, in the laundry room with my typewriter. I hope you know, Tabby, that they are clapping for you and not for me. Stand up so they can see you, please. Thank you. Thank you. I did not let her see this speech, and I will hear about this later.

Now, there are lots of people who will tell you that anyone who writes genre fiction, or any kind of fiction that tells a story, is in it for the money and nothing else. It's a lie. The idea that all storytellers are in it for the money is untrue, but it is still hurtful; it's infuriating and it's demeaning. I never in my life wrote a single word for money. As badly as we needed money, I never wrote for money. From those early days to this gala black-tie night, I never once sat down at my desk thinking: "Today I'm going to make a hundred grand." Or "This story will make a great movie." If I had tried to write with those things in mind, I believe I would have sold my birthright for a plot of message, as the old pun has it. Either way, Tabby and I would still be living in a trailer or, an equivalent, a boat. My wife knows the importance of this award isn't the recognition of being a great writer or even a good writer, but the recognition of being an honest writer.

Frank Norris, the author of *McTeague*, said something like this: "What should I care if they, i.e., the critics, single me out for sneers and laughter? I never truckled; I never lied. I told the truth." And that's always been the bottom line for me. The story and the people in it may be make believe, but I need to ask myself over and over if I've told the truth about the way "real people" would behave in a similar situation.

Of course, I only have my own senses, experiences, and reading to draw on, but that usually—not always, but usually—usually it's enough. It gets the job done. For instance, if an elevator full of people, one of the ones in this very building—I want you to think about this later; I want you to think about it if it starts to vibrate and you hear those clanks—this probably won't happen but we all know it has happened; it could happen. It could happen to me or it could happen to you. Someone always wins the lottery. Just put it away for now until you go up to your rooms later. Anyway, if an elevator full of people starts free-falling from the thirty-fifth floor of the skyscraper all the way to the bottom—one of those view elevators, perhaps, where you can watch it happening—in my opinion, no one is going to say, "Goodbye, Neil, I will see you in heaven." In my book or my short story, they're far more apt to bellow, "Oh shit!" at the top of their lungs because what I've read and heard tends to confirm the "Oh shit!" choice. If that makes me a cynic, so be it.

I remember a story on the nightly news about an airliner that crashed killing all aboard. The so-called black box was recovered and we have the pilot's immortal last four words: "Son of a bitch." Of course, there was another plane that crashed and the black box recorder said, "Goodbye, Mother," which is a nicer way to go out, I think.

Folks are far more apt to go out with a surprised ejaculation, however, than an expiring abjuration like, "Marry her, Jake. Bible says it ain't good for a man to be alone." If I happen to be the writer of such a deathbed scene, I'd choose "Son of a bitch" over "Marry her, Jake" every time. We understand that fiction is a lie to begin with. To ignore the truth inside the lie is to sin against the craft, in general, and one's own work in particular.

I'm sure I've made the wrong choices from time to time. Doesn't the Bible say something like, "for all have sinned and come short of the glory of Chaucer?" But every time I did it, I was sorry. Sorry is cheap, though. I have revised the lie out if I could, and that's far more important. When readers are deeply entranced by a story, they forget the storyteller completely. The tale is all they care about.

But the storyteller cannot afford to forget and must always be ready to hold himself or herself to account. He or she needs to remember that the truth lends verisimilitude to the lies that surround it. If you tell your reader, "Sometimes chickens will pick out the weakest one in the flock and peck it to death," the truth, the reader is much more likely to go along with you than if you then add something like, "Such chickens often meld into the earth after their deaths."

How stringently the writer holds to the truth inside the lie is one of the ways that he can judge how seriously he takes his craft. My wife, who doesn't seem to know how to lie even in a social context where people routinely say things like, "You look wonderful, have you lost weight?" has always understood these things without needing to have them spelled out. She's what the Bible calls a pearl beyond price. She also understands why I was, in those early days, so often bitterly angry at writers who were considered "literary." I knew I didn't have quite enough talent or polish to be one of them so there was an element of jealousy, but I was also infuriated by how these writers always seemed to have the inside track in my view at that time.

Even a note on the acknowledgments page of a novel, thanking the this-or-that foundation for its generous assistance, was enough to set me off. I knew what it meant; I told my wife. It was the Old Boy Network at work. It was this, it was that, on and on, and blah, blah, blah. It is only in retrospect that I realize how much I sounded like my least favorite uncle who believed there really was an international Jewish cabal running everything from the Ford Motor Company to the Federal Reserve.

Tabitha listened to a fair amount of this pissing and moaning and finally told me to stop with the breast-beating. She said to save my self-pity and turn my energy to the typewriter. She paused and then added, *my* typewriter. I did because she was right and my anger played much better when channeled into about a dozen stories which I wrote in 1973 and early 1974. Not all of them were good, but most of them were honest, and I realized an amazing thing: Readers of the men's magazines where I was published were remembering my name and starting to look for it. I could hardly believe it, but it appeared that people wanted to read what I was writing. There's never been a thrill in my life to equal that one. With Tabby's help, I was able to put aside my useless jealousy and get writing again. I sold more of my short stories. I sold *Carrie* and the rest, as they say, is history.

There's been a certain amount of grumbling about the decision to give the award to me and since so much of this speech has been about my wife, I wanted to give you her opinion on the subject. She's read everything I've written, making her something of an expert, and her view of my work is loving but unsentimental. Tabby says I deserve the medal not just because some good movies were made from my stories or because I've provided high motivational reading material for slow learners; she says I deserve the medal because I am a, quote, "damn good writer."

I've tried to improve myself with every book and find the truth inside the lie. Sometimes I have succeeded. I salute the National Book Foundation Board, who took a huge risk in giving this award to a man many people see as a rich hack. For far too long, the so-called popular writers of this country and the so-called literary writers have stared at each other with animosity and a willful lack of understanding. This is the way it has always been. Witness my childish resentment of anyone who ever got a Guggenheim.

But giving an award like this to a guy like me suggests that in the future things don't have to be the way they've always been. Bridges can be built between the so-called popular fiction and the so-called literary fiction. The first gainers in such a widening of interest would be the readers, of course, which is us, because writers are almost always readers and listeners first. You have been very good and patient listeners and I'm going to let you go soon, but I'd like to say one more thing before I do.

Tokenism is not allowed. You can't sit back, give a self-satisfied sigh, and say, "Ah, that takes care of the troublesome pop lit question. In another twenty years or perhaps thirty, we'll give this award to another writer who sells enough books to make the best-seller lists." It's not good enough. Nor do I have any patience with or use for those who make a point of pride in saying they've never read anything by John Grisham, Tom Clancy, Mary Higgins Clark, or any other popular writer.

What do you think? You get social or academic brownie points for deliberately staying out of touch with your own culture? Never in life, as Capt. Lucky Jack Aubrey would say. And if your only point of reference for Jack Aubrey is the Australian actor Russell Crowe, shame on you.

There's a writer here tonight, my old friend and sometime collaborator, Peter Straub. He's just published what may be the best book of his career. *Lost Boy, Lost Girl* surely deserves your consideration for the NBA short list next year, if not the award itself. Have you read it? Have any of the judges read it?

There's another writer here tonight who writes under the name of Jack Ketchum and he has also written what may be the best book of his career, a long novella called *The Crossings*. Have you read it? Have any of the judges read it? And yet Jack Ketchum's first novel, *Off Season,* published in 1980, set off a furor in my supposed field, that of horror, that was unequaled until the advent of Clive Barker. It is not too much to say that these two gentlemen remade the face of American popular fiction, and yet very few people here will have an idea of whom I'm talking about or have read the work.

This is not criticism; it's just me pointing out a blind spot in the winnowing process and in the very act of reading the fiction of one's own culture. Honoring me is a step in a different direction—a fruitful one, I think. I'm asking you, almost begging you, not to go back to the old way of doing things. There's a great deal of good stuff out there, and not all of it is being done by writers whose work is regularly reviewed in the Sunday *New York Times* Book Review. I believe the time comes when you must be inclusive rather than exclusive.

That said, I accept this award on behalf of such disparate writers as Elmore Leonard, Peter Straub, Nora Lofts, Jack Ketchum, whose real name is Dallas Mayr, Jodi Picoult, Greg Iles, John Grisham, Dennis Lehane, Michael Connelly, Pete Hamill, and a dozen more. I hope that the National Book Award judges, past, present, and future, will read these writers and that the books will open their eyes to a whole new realm of American literature. You don't have to vote for them, just read them.

Okay, thanks for bearing with me. This is the last page? This is it. Parting is such sweet sorrow. My message is simple enough. We can build bridges between the popular and the literary if we keep our minds and hearts open. With my wife's help, I have tried to do that. Now I'm going to turn the actual medal over to her because she will make sure in all the excitement that it doesn't get lost.

In closing, I want to say that I hope you all find something good to read tonight or tomorrow. I want to salute all the nominees in the four categories that are up for consideration, and I do, I hope you'll find something to read that will fill you up as this evening has filled me up. Thank you.

Why We Write Horror
—Michael McCarty

I'm having a great time at one of my book signings; people are asking for autographs, taking photos, shaking hands, talking about the latest scary best-seller.

Then the question gets asked: "Why do you write horror?" Romance, mystery, or science fiction writers sometimes hear a similar "Why do you write _____ (fill in the blank)?" but it is not meant in the same way. The query posed to horror writers more properly translates, "Why do you *think* this way?"

Below, some of the movers and shakers, the giants of our genre, share their responses to the question.

J.N. Williamson: A few years ago, Leisure Books published a story collection of mine called *Frights of Fancy*. The title says a lot about the approach I take to writing. The tales I chose to reprint are from all over the commercial and small presses and reflect dozens of shades of mood and style of not just horror, but *occult* horror, *crime* horror, *psychological* horror, *end-of-the-world* horror, *whimsically classic* horror, *erotic* horror—plus dark fantasy and a *Sherlock Holmes* pastiche!

I think life is often full of frightening challenges and that, frequently, people's beliefs add to the mysterious nature of what we confront and can either assist us in finding solutions or lead to our destruction.

Peter Straub: To me, mystery and suspense are very much the same thing. My mystery novels aren't really like the crime novels that anybody has written. When I called my novel *Mystery*, it never occurred to me that everybody in the world would look at it and say, "Oh, that's like *Ghost Story*, he's referring to the genre." I was referring to *Mystery* with a capital M, the mysterious realm that we sometimes apprehend around us, with a sense of the numinous, with a sense of things unknown …. It is very important to me to keep building up a gathering head of steam so the reader does really wonder, "What will happen next?" There is very little difference between the way that feels in the basic crime or spooky context. It's the same sense of anxiety, uncertainty, facing the unknown, being puzzled—in short, a layer of suspense.

Ray Bradbury: It's pure genetics. It's the way I was born. I was curious about the theatre, curious about writing poetry, curious about essays. I have always loved the mystery field, the science fiction field, and the horror field. A lot of writers in my field don't care about theatre and I grew up in the theatre. They didn't care much about radio either, but I started my career acting on it when I was twelve years old. (Bradbury sold his first script for radio to the *George Burns and Gracie Allen Show* at the age of fourteen.)

I wrote for a lot of the radio shows in my twenties. It's natural for me, to do all these things. I have loved poetry all my life, so I've written twelve books of poetry. Other people in my field simply don't do those things.

Gerard Houarner: Growing up, I was asked why I never wrote about nice things. Simple answer: "That's not the way I'm tuned." I'd like to write about nice things, but the dark won't let me. Look: I laugh; have a sense of humor; seek out and appreciate the wonders and glories of the world and its people. But the cold, harsh cruelties of everyday existence, and in everyday people, remain as obvious as sharp stones in a clear pool. They are a part of reality, and ignoring reality hurts too much.

Basically, I'm one of those weird folks who can hold two or more seemingly opposing facts, or opinions, or perceptions, in my mind and not go fundamentalist. I don't see dead people. I see monsters—and angels—frequently in the same individual, which not only makes me a dicey conversationalist, but fuels my creative life as well.

Michael Romkey: Why do I write horror?

To begin, note the verb *write* precedes the adjective *horror*. This is not a chicken-and-egg distinction. My main impulse is to write, and it doesn't especially matter what I write. E-mails. Grocery lists. Letters. Angry indictments of grievous injustices. The opening lines of poems never completed. Novels whose main characters happen to be vampires. A writer writes. *Period.* My first novel, *Fears Point*, is about a coven of witches that takes over a small town. It is also, in a way that I hope is not painfully pretentious, an allegory of small-town paranoia.

Which brings me to my second point: For me, writing category fiction is not so much about living up to the expectations someone would have picking up a book about vampires; it is, rather, the context wherein I write about the sorts of things writers always write about. You'll find the same themes in all horror writing. You'll find them in a good mystery, a romance, or "serious" fiction. I'm talking about the *big issues*: good, evil, love, envy, betrayal, trust, faith, hope, and, perhaps above all else, our need to find redemption.

David Niall Wilson: I don't consciously set out to write horror, but I set out to slice at the inner thoughts of readers and cause a reaction and, quite often, darker subjects and stories accomplish this most thoroughly. I have said that what I want most is to write things that leave people momentarily dazed, or even stunned, when they've finished reading. I want to make people involve themselves so deeply in the words that they stare at the wall and then go away for a little while when it's all over. The best way to know you've cut into an emotional cord like that is if the cord you cut is your own.

Harry Shannon: I remember reading years ago that most serial killers are not sociopaths, and often have a very punishing conscience. At first that floored me, but it makes sense. Imagine an endless war between sadistic, violent urges and a relentlessly judgmental, highly critical parent voice. It's the human condition, but squared. The resulting cognitive dissonance is so overwhelming it cannot be contained and must be acted out to gain even a brief respite from the pain. To paraphrase Carl Jung: *I had to try to gain power over my fantasies, for I realized that, if I did not do so, I ran the risk of their gaining power over me.*
That's perfect.
For me, reading and writing horror is about eating my own shadow so it won't eat me.

Mark Mclaughlin: When I was young, I used to spend hours reading horror anthologies at the library. I loved short stories and eventually started writing them myself. In time, so many stories of mine were out in the world, publishers started asking to release collections of my work, like *Hell Is Where the Heart Is*, *Motivational Shrieker*, and *Slime After Slime*. I love the craft of creating bizarre characters and setting them loose in exotic settings to live out astounding plots. I'm sure there will be novels in my future, but I'll never give up writing short stories. My horror stories are like my children, and I'm a very fertile parent.

C. Dean Andersson: When I was a boy, I gave a speech complete with crayon drawings to my grandmother's church group to WAKE THEM UP! by scaring them with stories of how flying saucers *are* real—so they would KEEP WATCHING THE SKIES!—because I'd read a book on UFOs and seen *The Thing From Another World* on TV, and they hadn't. When I got older, the trait that motivated my anti-complacency attack on the space alien threat-awareness-challenged/church-going grandmothers of Little River, Kansas, population five hundred, stayed with me.
I write horror because I still want to scare sleeping minds awake and expose readers to things they don't already know, so they'll see things they've never seen from viewpoints they've never experienced, and question assumptions they've never questioned. As Tristan Tzara said in his 1918 *Dada Manifesto*, "... [A]rt should be a monster which casts servile minds into terror ...."
Of course some people get grumpy when you wake them, angry when your stories don't validate their beliefs, and uncomfortable if they see something of themselves in the monsters you create. But as Marquis de Sade wrote in response to his critics, "Evil recognizes evil, and the recognition is always painful."

Part Two
An Education
in Horror

5:00

What You Are Meant to Know: Twenty-One Horror Classics
—Robert Weinberg

Breaking into the horror field isn't easy. Even if you use every tip, every suggestion in this book, there is no guarantee you'll make it. Markets expand and contract, change and disappear, all the time. Still, it's always toughest for a beginning writer to sell that first story. There's lots and lots of competition. Plenty of people want to become rich and famous like Stephen King and Anne Rice. Others just want to see their name in print.

No matter your answer to the question *Why do I write horror?* you need to convince an editor to buy your masterpiece.

And to accomplish that, you need to be original.

When editors say they're looking for the next Stephen King or Anne Rice or Dean Koontz or John Saul, they don't mean they want to find someone who writes exact imitations of those authors' works. Instead, they're hunting for authors who bring that same spark of originality and excitement to their work.

Anne Rice writes about vampires and witches—such monsters have been a popular staple in fiction for a hundred years. John Saul writes about children in dire peril—another oft-used theme since fiction was invented. Both of these authors, though, have given new life to old concepts. They've taken basic themes and ideas and looked at them in different ways. Creativity sells.

The biggest problem faced by many new writers is not lack of skills. They've learned how to write, know the basic structure of a story, and understand the rules of grammar and punctuation. However, there is one area of their education that has been sorely neglected. They don't know much about their subject. It's difficult—nearly impossible, actually—to be original if you do not know what else has been written.

Horror fiction did not begin with Stephen King. There's no doubt that he is the most popular practitioner ever to write in this particular field. But there are plenty of other important and influential writers, too.

Here is a checklist of twenty-one books that anyone who wants to write horror should read. It's not everything worth studying. There are books aplenty; and plenty more. This list is just a starting point. The more familiar you are with your subject, the better. But without these books, you're beginning the race a lap behind the competition. (This list is roughly arranged in chronological order.)

1. *Frankenstein* by Mary Wollstonecraft Shelley

Forget the Boris Karloff movies and the Hammer adaptations. Read the book itself to see what it says and does not say about the meaning of being human. At least one major critic has called *Frankenstein* the first science fiction novel. It may be that, but it is also a horror novel that has endured for over 150 years. This book raises important questions about life and death, and good and evil, that are still being debated today. Though slow-moving by today's standards, *Frankenstein* remains one of the cornerstones of horror fiction.

2. *Dracula* by Bram Stoker

Again, no on the movie versions—all of them. They are distinctive and flashy and reflect various directors' and actors' interpretations of the novel. Seeing a film is like getting your news secondhand. If you want to be a horror writer, you *must* go to the source material: the horror writing. Anyone who dreams of being a horror writer must read *Dracula*. The book, though overwritten and melodramatic, is filled with powerful images. Action scenes are fast and furious, the horror intense and replete with strong descriptions. *Dracula*, though written a century ago, still moves well. It stands as the most important book ever written in the horror genre.

3. *The Ghost Pirates* by William Hope Hodgson

Hodgson was a sailor before he became a writer. His promising career was cut short when he was killed in a major battle in World War I. Much of his reputation rests on his short stories of the sea, which are atmospheric and filled with menace. He wrote four novels, three of which are more fantasy than horror (*The House on the Borderland, The Night Land,* and *The Boats of the Glen Carrig*)—all of them are worth reading. Hodgson had a gift for describing ominous, gruesome monsters that few writers today can match. However, his novel *The Ghost Pirates* is not about monsters but about ghosts. It tells in straightforward, almost journalistic manner how a ship is overwhelmed by ghostly invaders. Hodgson makes no effort to identify the menacing figures—they could be the ghosts of dead pirates or beings from another dimension. All that counts is their gradual capture of the boat. It is one of the finest examples of the "tightly written" novel ever published.

4. *The Collected Ghost Stories of M.R. James*

Montague Rhodes James was a don at Oxford University who delighted his friends by telling old-fashioned ghost stories. When put down on paper, these tales formed the most popular collection of ghost stories ever written in the English language. While not the first English ghost-story writer, James is the most famous and perhaps the best. His stories are meticulously crafted, building slowly but steadily to the inevitable climax. James never failed to deliver, and his tales are filled with malevolent ghosts, ancient curses, and demonic creatures. James's fiction influenced numerous writers and, for decades after the publication of his work, most ghost stories were written in his style.

5. *Burn, Witch, Burn!* by A. Merritt

Abraham Merritt's roots were in the pulp magazines of the 1920s and 1930s, which shows in his fiction. He was one of the most famous writers of those publications, and his novels were extremely popular. Though regarded as a fantasy author of "lost race" adventures, Merritt wrote several novels that crossed over into the horror field. Of these, *Burn, Witch, Burn!* was the most successful and important. It deals with an evil crone who turns people into demonic dolls to commit crimes for her. What raises the book above standard pulp fare is that the witch's nemesis is a crime kingpin, a typical gangster of the 1930s, and his band of hoodlums. In an interesting reversal, a lesser evil battles a greater evil as the modern world fights a menace from ancient times. Merritt knew more about pacing and narrative than just about anyone. This novel sweeps the reader along in the best pulp tradition.

6. *To Walk the Night* by William Sloane

In the 1930s, genre fiction was not so clearly defined and writers were more willing to bend the rules for the sake of a good story. Think Dean Koontz and Stephen King were the first to write science fiction novels that were also horror stories? Read Sloane's *To Walk the Night*. This book combines horror, science fiction, and mystery into one of the smoothest presentations ever set on paper. The secret at the heart of the story is no surprise now, but in its time the book set the pattern for all those that followed. The author's other horror novel, *The Edge of Running Water*, is equally recommended.

7. *The Dunwich Horror and Others* by H.P. Lovecraft

Lovecraft turned horror fiction away from the ghosts of M.R. James and focused attention on the huge, unknown universe that surrounds us. The concept of "cosmic horror" perhaps was not invented by Lovecraft, but he certainly popularized it. His stories work best at novelette length: "The Dunwich Horror," "The Thing on the Doorstep," "The Call of Cthulhu." But all his fiction is worth reading. Lovecraft had his weaknesses (lack of characterization and dialogue are the worst), but his talent at hinting at the monstrous horrors lurking in the dark corners of our world remains unmatched more than a half century after his death.

8. *Fear* by L. Ron Hubbard

Many newer writers believe psychological horror was invented just a few years ago. Not true. Back in 1940, L. Ron Hubbard wrote this short novel about a professor searching for an hour of time he cannot remember—and the dire consequences of his actions. Is this the story of a man haunted by demons of the supernatural or by the demons within his own mind? *Fear* is overwritten in spots but still packs a real punch. It is one of those trendsetting novels that helped redefine modern horror.

9. *Darker Than You Think* by Jack Williamson

Werewolves are the stock and trade of horror fiction. There have been numerous werewolf movies, even werewolf comic books. But most people can't name the great werewolf novels because, in a field filled with memorable vampire books, horrific serial killer novels, and terrifying visions of cosmic horror, memorable werewolves are in woefully short supply. The title that stands above the rest is Jack Williamson's *Darker Than You Think*. It brought werewolves into the twentieth century and is filled with dark, powerful images. It first appeared in 1940 and remains *the* definitive werewolf novel.

10. *Conjure Wife* by Fritz Leiber

In the early 1940s, the pulp magazine *Unknown* (later titled *Unknown Worlds*) pulled horror out of the English manor house and into mainstream, urban America. *Fear* and *Darker Than You Think* both appeared first in *Unknown*, as did this novel by Fritz Leiber, who was one of the first authors to postulate that ghosts and witches would change with the times. His short story "Smoke Ghost" told of new spirits and unfriendly spooks that haunted big cities. In *Conjure Wife*, he mixed witchcraft and black magic with college campus politics. It remains one of the most influential novels ever written.

11. *I Am Legend* by Richard Matheson

Matheson is one of the true giants in our field. Though known primarily for his short stories, his few novels are equally well crafted and important. This tale, a blend of science fiction and horror, could be labeled the ultimate vampire novel as the entire population of the Earth is turned into monsters. It demonstrates that a horror novel can be more than just a series of shocks. Matheson explores the importance of legends and horror in a manner unique to the genre.

12. *Rosemary's Baby* by Ira Levin

Horror broke out of the pulp ghetto due to the popularity of several books. This novel, by a writer not previously associated with genre fiction, was one of the works that led the escape. It is subtle, well written, and quite frightening. The movie made from the book is excellent, but the novel stands nicely on its own. Again, it takes horror out of the countryside and haunted manors and puts it right in New York high-rise apartment buildings.

13. *Richard Matheson: Collected Stories, Vols. I, II, III*

Much of the finest horror writing is done in short story format. If you want to know how to do it, study two writers: Ray Bradbury and Richard Matheson.

This book, filled with startling images, horrific visions, and waking nightmares, is a textbook on how to write a horror story. Matheson can be subtle or shocking, but his work is always innovative, literate, and challenging. What makes it so spectacular is how often he is able to catch the reader completely off guard with his endings. Many people think Matheson is the finest horror short-story writer ever. This book offers strong evidence to support that claim.

14. *Hell House* by Richard Matheson

Haunted houses have been a standard device in horror and supernatural fiction for well over one hundred years. But a good writer can take a well-worn device and make it seem new. This book is very scary without being overly gory. Matheson knows how to push all the right buttons, and does exactly that in this modern horror thriller.

15. *The October Country* by Ray Bradbury

Yes, he has mellowed, but Ray Bradbury was one of the finest horror writers of the 1940s and early 1950s. He is unquestionably one of our finest living short-story writers. *The October Country*, a collection that includes many of his best pieces from his early days, is another sustained lesson on how to do it right.

16. *Something Wicked This Way Comes* by Ray Bradbury

Bradbury is much weaker as a novelist than as a short-story writer. But that does not mean he doesn't know how to write a long piece. This book, with its wonderfully evocative title (taken from Shakespeare's *Macbeth*) works on many levels. But most of all, it is scary and literary at the same time—a trick rarely accomplished.

17. *The Exorcist* by William Peter Blatty

This novel is credited with popularizing modern horror fiction. *The Exorcist* returned religious themes to horror and clearly defined the ongoing battle between good and evil. Though filled with shock after shock, the story primarily works because Blatty makes you care about the characters. As in all such novels, the evil proves to be much more cunning than first realized, and the menace is much greater than expected. The movie version of this novel helped make this one of the best-selling horror novels of all time.

18. *Falling Angel* by William Hjortsberg

Horror and mystery fiction are close companions. However, it is a rare conglomeration that combines supernatural horror with the private eye genre and makes it work. This novel takes some old ideas and twists them into something new and compelling. The horror is frightening; the mystery is well presented; the ending is both shocking and yet somehow logical. Perhaps the best hard-boiled horror novel ever written.

19. *Salem's Lot* by Stephen King

Undoubtedly, Stephen King is the most popular horror writer ever. His books have sold millions (and millions and millions) of copies and he is one of the favorite authors of this generation. King's success is no fluke. He writes books that people want to read. His characters are ordinary people facing extraordinary circumstances. How they deal with the nature of good and evil makes fascinating reading. In *Salem's Lot*, King employs a standard horror theme and combines it with mainstream fiction techniques. Instead of focusing on the monster, King presents many different stories. By shifting emphasis from one or two main characters to the entire community of the town of Salem's Lot, he makes the evil all-pervasive and much more believable. King knows that the more believable a horror novel is, the more frightening it becomes.

20. *The Stand* by Stephen King

The end of the world as envisioned by Stephen King. There were other horror novels before *The Stand* that described a global holocaust. Lots of science fiction novels did exactly that. But King was the first to link science fiction as the cause and supernatural horror as the aftermath. Again, mainstream fiction techniques are responsible for the book's success. Readers cared for the characters—whether they succeeded or failed, lived or died. The book was the first epic horror novel. It worked. There have been other epics since, but *The Stand* remains the best.

21. *Watchers* by Dean Koontz

Dean Koontz, over the course of several decades, took the horror thriller of the 1920s and 1930s and reshaped it into a product for modern readers. Tough, competent heroes and heroines engage in life-or-death struggles with sinister forces—from secret government agencies to science gone berserk—in a mad scramble that keeps readers flipping the pages of one best-seller after another. *Watchers*, though basically a science fiction story, works equally well as a horror novel. More importantly, it works as a gripping drama with characters readers care about. Those who think horror novels can't be anything more than light entertainment have not read *Watchers*.

There you have twenty-one books. Read them all and you'll have some idea of what horror fiction is all about. Not a complete grasp of the field, since there are plenty of writers who are extremely important and who don't have one defining book, but a whole body of work that should be read and studied. Robert Bloch and Harlan Ellison are two authors who immediately come to mind.

But this list serves as a good starting point. Read these books; see what the authors did to make them work. Then take that same drive, that same ambition, that same vision, and apply it to your own ideas.

The editors are waiting.

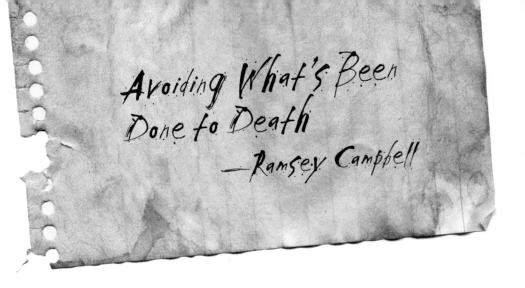

Avoiding What's Been Done to Death
—Ramsey Campbell

You can't avoid anything unless you know what it is. This idea alone would be sufficient reason for me to recommend that anyone who wants to write worthwhile horror fiction have a working knowledge of the tradition of the field. The finest single introduction to it is *Great Tales of Terror and the Supernatural*, edited by Wise and Fraser, and still, I believe, readily available. If you find nothing to enjoy and be awestruck by in that book, then it seems unlikely that you have any real feeling for horror fiction. On the other hand, you may be taken aback by how many of the themes in the book have recently been bloated into best-sellers. I would hope that realization may make you deeply dissatisfied, because that kind of dissatisfaction is the first step in creating something new.

Some people (generally critics with no fiction to their name and writers near the end of their careers) claim that there's nothing new in horror. In a sense, that may be true. More than sixty years ago, H.P. Lovecraft drew up a list of the basic themes of weird fiction, and I can think of very little that the field has added to that list since then. But that's by no means as defeatist as it sounds, because the truth is surely that many of the themes we're dealing with are so large and powerful as to be essentially timeless.

For instance, the folk tale of the wish that comes true more fully and more terribly than the wisher could have dreamed is the basis not only of "The Monkey's Paw," but of Stephen King's *Pet Sematary* and of my own novel, *Obsession,* yet the three stories have otherwise far more to do with their writers than with one another. That suggests (if I may be forgiven for emitting a homily now and then in the course of this essay) that one way to avoid what has already been done is to be true to yourself.

That isn't to say that imitation never has its uses. Here, as in any other of the arts, it's a legitimate and useful way to serve your apprenticeship. Though it may not be obvious to readers who know only my recent work, I began my career by imitating Lovecraft. No writer has orchestrated terror in prose more carefully than Lovecraft, but you certainly won't learn how to write dialogue or deal with character from him. Such skills are best learned by reading writers outside the field (in my case, Nabokov and Graham Greene, among others). If you're writing in a genre, it's all the more important to read widely outside it in order to be aware what fiction is capable of. It's less a matter of importing techniques into the field than of seeing the field as part of a larger art. Depending wholly on genre techniques can lead too easily to the secondhand and the second-rate. There's only one Stephen King, but there are far too many writers trying to sound like him.

It's no bad thing to follow the example of writers you admire, then, but only as a means to finding your own voice. You won't find that, of course, unless you have something of your own to say. I did, once I stopped writing about Lovecraft's horrors and began to deal with what disturbed me personally. I began to write about how things seemed to me, which was more important and, at first, more difficult than it may sound. I tried (and still do try) to take nothing on trust to describe things as they really are or would be.

I'm sure I don't need to tell you that the horror field is riddled with clichés. The house that's for sale too cheaply, the guy who must be working nights because he sleeps during the day (must be a handyman, too, judging by that big box he keeps in his cellar), the attic room the landlady keeps locked, the place none of the topers in the village inn will visit after dark—we can all have fun recognizing these and many others, which is by no means to say that they haven't been used effectively by masters of the craft. But I think there are more fundamental clichés in the field, and I think today's writers may be the ones to overturn them.

Take the theme of evil, as the horror story often does. Writing about evil is a moral act, and it won't do to recycle definitions of evil—to take them on trust. Horror fiction frequently presents the idea of evil in such a shorthand form as to be essentially meaningless—something vague out there that causes folk to commit terrible acts, something other than ourselves, nothing to do with us. That sounds to me more like an excuse than a definition, and I hope it's had its day. If we're going to write about evil, then let's define it and how it relates to ourselves.

All good fiction consists of looking at things afresh, but horror fiction seems to have a built-in tendency to do the opposite. Ten years or so ago, many books had nothing more to say than "the devil made me do it." Now, thanks to the influence of films like *Friday the 13th*, it seems enough for some writers to say that a character is psychotic; no further explanation is necessary. But it's the job of writers to imagine how it would feel to be all their characters, however painful that may sometimes be. It may be a lack of that compassion that has led some writers to create children who are evil simply because they're children, surely the most deplorable cliché of the field.

Some clichés are simply products of lazy writing. Tradition shouldn't be used as an excuse to repeat what earlier writers have done; if you feel the need to write about the stock figures of the horror story, that's all the more reason to imagine them anew. For instance, we might have believed there was nothing new to be written about vampirism until Karl Wagner wrote "Beyond Any Measure," whose stunningly original idea was always implicit in the vampire tradition, just waiting for Karl to notice. Again, generations might have thought that the definitive haunted house tale had been written, but it hadn't been until Shirley Jackson wrote *The Haunting of Hill House* (a statement guaranteed to make some of you try to improve on that novel, perhaps). Put another way: One reason some folks recoil from my own novel, *The Face That Must Die,* seems to be that it confronts you with what I imagine it might be like to be a psychotic killer, rather than keeping a Halloween face or ski mask between him and the audience, and depicting him as a bogeyman that we could dismiss as being nothing like ourselves. It's only fair to warn you that many readers and publishers would rather see imitations of whatever they liked last year than give new ideas a chance. But I've always tried to write what rings true to *me,* whether or not it makes the till ring. If you don't feel involved with what you're writing, it's unlikely that anyone else will.

There's another side to the field that is overdue for attack by a new generation— its reactionary quality. A horror writer I otherwise admire argued recently that "it has been a time-honored tradition in literature and film that you have a weak or helpless heroine"—implying, I assume, that we should go on doing so. Well, tradition is a pretty poor excuse for perpetrating stereotypes (not that the author in question necessarily does); time-honored it may be, but that certainly doesn't make it honorable. In fact, these days, so many horror stories (and especially films) gloat over the suffering of women that it seems clear the authors are getting their own back, consciously or not, on aspects of real life that they can't cope with. Of course, that isn't new in horror fiction, nor is using horror fiction to define as evil or diabolical whatever threatens the writer or the writer's lifestyle. But, at the very least, one should be aware, as soon as possible, that this is what one is doing, so as to be able to move on. I have my suspicions, too, about the argument that horror fiction defines what is normal by showing us what isn't. I think it's time for more of the field to acknowledge that, when we come face-to-face with the monsters, we may find ourselves looking not at a mask but at a mirror.

Workshops of Horror (and Seminars and Conferences)
—Tom Monteleone

The Why of Workshops

I am a firm believer in workshops, seminars, and conferences for writers ... for one good reason: They make you a better writer.

I sold my first short story more than thirty years ago because I attended a writer's workshop.[1]

Prior to getting that thirty dollar check (a penny per word for three thousand words), I had sent out twenty plus stories to every conceivable market from *Playboy* to the *Sewanee Review*. The process had consumed more than two years, a lot of postage, and had garnered me enough rejection slips to wallpaper my bathroom. In short, I was writing a lot, but I hadn't sold anything. During that time, writing had been a most solitary adventure for me. I sat in a room, finished a story, sent it out, and started on the next one.

The only feedback I ever got was the rejections slips—usually pre-printed form letters (notes, really), which never told me the reasons why my stories weren't selling. Eventually, as my writing improved, I began to get a few handwritten notes from editors who saw potential enough to at least tell me what I was doing wrong.

---

[1] *It was called the Guildford Writer's Workshop, conducted by the late Jay Haldeman and was held in Baltimore, Maryland, twice yearly. Some of the writers who attended were Jack Dann, Joe Haldeman, Roger Zelazny, George Alec Effinger, Ted White, and Gardner Dozois—all of whom went on to have solid careers writing genre fiction. Ted White, who was the editor of Amazing Science Fiction Stories, told me that if I revised the story I'd brought to the workshop along the lines that had been suggested by the group, he would buy it. I did; and he did, which was my first professional sale.*

But for the first year or two ... not a word.

That's the way it is for most writers: They work alone, in a vacuum, in which they have little to no idea (a) what they're doing wrong, (b) how to recognize their errors, or (c) how to fix them.

One of the best ways to rectify this is to get out from behind the keyboard once in a while and attend a writer's conference, a seminar on writing, or a real hands-on workshop. There's a sense of camaraderie at these gatherings, both undeniable and well-appreciated. Knowing there are so many writers *out there*, enduring the same problems and disappointments as you, makes for a surprisingly encouraging experience.

But the best thing about conferences, seminars, and workshops (hereinafter known as CSWs) is that you get insights and feedback on your writing. By attending a panel discussion that focuses on character or dialogue, you may recognize mistakes you've been inadvertently making, or perhaps learn techniques or tricks that will make your characters act and speak with what Poe called *verisimilitude*. By submitting your work to be analyzed and critiqued by your peers, and by forcing yourself to do the same to the work of others, you will learn two important skills: how to examine and deconstruct any piece of fiction, and how to employ those abilities to look at your own work more objectively—in other words, how to edit yourself.

In order to be a good analyst and editor, you will have to want to do it. You will need to be perceptive, patient, intelligent, and widely read (in a myriad of disciplines). Having a solid grounding in English grammar and usage, plus a masterful vocabulary, are also necessities. You should also have an extensive knowledge of the literature of your chosen genre: horror. If you are unfamiliar with the classic themes, plots, characters, and literary traditions of horror and dark fantasy, you won't have the critical ammo needed to know if you're evaluating a story that is innovative and wildly imaginative ... or if it's a tired cliché.

If you feel ready to start hitting the CSW circuit, here you have a few of the best ones currently operating in the horror community. They may differ widely in terms of availability, cost, duration, or methodology, but you can bet on them all sharing similar goals—the major ones being to make you a better writer and to ultimately get you writing material that will get professionally published.

The Workshops

International Conference on the Fantastic in the Arts (ICFA)

The typical writers conference will usually run for a day or so and basically offer a slate of guest speakers covering a variety of topics that will presumably touch many of the bases a new writer needs to visit.

The ICFA is different. It is a conference, but it also combines elements of the seminar and the symposium. Guests and participants are invited to submit and present serious, academic papers, which explore a diverse number of topics within the genres of horror, dark fantasy, suspense, mystery, and other types of fantasy as well. Each year, a particular *theme* is emphasized and all papers and presentations reflect and examine that theme.

Endowed by a grant from the mother of acclaimed fantasists, Thomas Burnett Swann, the conference was founded in 1980 by Robert A. Collins, a professor at Florida Atlantic University. It has grown so much since those early years, it is now administered by the International Association for the Fantastic in the Arts (IAFA), and is a highly professional operation.

To quote the Web site of the Association: "*Celebrating* its twenty-sixth year, the Conference on the Fantastic is one of the most diverse, energetic, provocative, and delightfully addictive interdisciplinary gatherings in the world. Its primary sponsor, the IAFA, maintains a listserv and publishes an annual membership directory and *The Journal of the Fantastic in the Arts.*"

One caveat: It is serious, and if you plan on attending, also plan on a rigorous weekend of revelation and assimilation. Web site: www.iafa.org Address: ICFA Registrar, P.O. Box 50517, Eugene, OR 97405

World Horror Convention Writing Workshop

Organized and conducted by Mort Castle, this workshop has been an extremely popular and successful gathering of never more than fifteen intrepid writers who want to learn how to create original and imaginative horror/dark suspense tales. I've had the opportunity to interview many of its past attendees, and every one of them had nothing but the highest praise for Mr. Castle and his methods.

It is conducted during the annual World Horror Convention, which is held in a different city each year, usually in April.

The cost is extremely reasonable—$35–$45 (depending on the city)—and with so few participants, every writer gets plenty of attention. The program last four hours, which is split into two (2) two-hour sessions. Mr. Castle reports that between two and ten hours of writing time are required between sessions, depending on the assignment and the abilities of each student.

The application process doesn't require students to send in writing samples. "Motivation always means more than talent," says Workshop Director Castle. "And laying out bucks says something about motivation."

Applications are sent through the staff of each year's World Horror Convention and passed along to Mort Castle. This is a well-respected and enjoyable writing and learning experience. A word to the wise: Apply as early as possible.

Information for signing up and attending can be found at http://whc2006.org.

Clarion Science Fiction & Fantasy Writers' Workshop

Don't let the name fool you. Although this workshop started out (thirty-nine years ago) with science fiction and fantasy being the primary focus, it has long since encompassed all types of imaginative fiction, from magic realism to dark suspense and flat-out horror fiction.

Held each summer, a manageable number of apprentice writers get together in a college dorm setting for a six-week workshop. Usually, the group has been selected on the basis of the quality of writing samples they submitted during the application process—the assumption being the more potential to be a successful, professional writer, the higher the chance of being selected to participate in the workshop. Most are novice writers and have not been previously published, but some may have already sold a story or two. Almost all are from the U.S. and range in age from late teens to those in mid-career. Their varied occupations give them a wide spectrum of skills and experiences.

For the first four weeks, a new instructor (usually a writer or editor of substantial reputation) conducts the workshop each week, giving the students a variety of styles, techniques, and assignments. The final two weeks are under the supervision of what Clarion calls a two-writer anchor team. The weekly writers are almost always available for one-on-one consultation. Each day is divided into morning sessions for group critiques and afternoons and evenings for writing assignments, individual conferences, and some social events.

In a workshop of this duration, the group has the potential to become a tightly knit community forged in the fires of honest opinion and mutual support.

Application information is available online at www.msu.edu/~clarion/, by e-mailing clarion@msu.edu, or by writing to Clarion Science Fiction & Fantasy Writers' Workshop, 112 Olds Hall, Michigan State University, Lansing, MI 48824-1047.

Odyssey-The Fantasy Writing Workshop (OFFW)

Since its inception in 1996, Odyssey has quickly become one of the most highly respected workshops for writers of fantasy, science fiction, and horror. Top authors, editors, and even agents have served as guests at Odyssey, and Director Jeanne Cavelos says 40 percent of OFWW's students have gone on to publish their work. The workshop, held annually on the campus of Saint Anselm College in Manchester, New Hampshire, runs for six weeks, featuring lots of on-site writing and a chance to learn from working pros who provide in-depth feedback on students' manuscripts.

Odyssey is for developing writers whose work is approaching publication quality, and who are serious about a commitment to getting published. Class meets for four hours in the morning, five days a week, and students use afternoons and evenings to write and read each other's work. College credit is available upon request.

Director Cavelos learned her craft as a senior editor at Bantam Doubleday Dell, where she won the World Fantasy Award for her efforts. She is the primary instructor and is aided each week by a visiting guest lecturer.

Guest lecturers come in once a week, for about a twenty-four-hour period, to add their own unique perspectives and give students feedback on their work. Every year, Odyssey features the top names in all the genre fields, each year bringing in a new group of working professionals. I had the privilege of guesting a week with the Odyssey students several years back, and it was grueling for me, so I know it was tough on the writers.

Students must apply for each year's workshop by April 14 of the workshop year. Those who apply by January 30 will be eligible for early admission, and applicants will be notified by February 27 whether they have been admitted under the high standards of early admission or whether their applications will be held over for consideration for regular admission. Applicants for regular admission will be informed of their status by May 1.

All applications must be accompanied by a fifteen-page writing sample.

Costs: application fee of $25; six week tuition of $1,600; optional college credit processing fee of $120.

Additional costs: shared apartment for $625, or a single apartment for $1,250. Participants can see to their own food or can take all meals in the college cafeteria for approximately $100 per week.

To get an application by mail, send an SASE to: Odyssey, P.O. Box 75, Mont Vernon, NH 03057, Attention: Applications; or apply online at www.sff.net/odyssey/apply.html.

Borderlands Press Writers Boot Camp

If you're looking for a weekend that packs as much learning and writing into its schedule as possible, this intense workshop might be for you. Held in Baltimore, Maryland, twice a year (January and July), it's sponsored by award-winning, specialty publishing house Borderlands Press and overseen by Elizabeth Monteleone, winner of the Bram Stoker Award for Editing.

The camp is divided into two *platoons*: Short Fiction and Novel. Twenty writers are selected for each platoon, and each is led by four different instructors (all successful writers or editors). Each instructor is responsible for covering one of four major writing topics: Characterization; Dialogue and Point of View; Plot and Setting; and Grammar, Syntax, and Style.[2]

---

[2] *Some previous instructors include Berkley Books Editor Ginjer Buchanan, David Morrell, F. Paul Wilson, Richard Chizmar, Tom Monteleone, Jack Ketchum, Beth Massie, and Tom Tessier.*

Borderlands calls it a boot camp because the writers who are accepted start working hard even before they show up. Each "grunt" receives a massive binder jammed with stories by everyone else in their platoon. By the time the grunts arrive for camp, they will have read all materials and compiled extensive critical notes on each manuscript.

The weekend is an intense combination of lecture (a little), spontaneous writing assignments, oral readings, two days of solid, almost continuous critical analysis, and exercises designed to develop better writing—and writers. Most grunts finish the camp in a state of near-exhaustion tempered by the joy of learning so much about their writing.

The atmosphere of Borderlands Press Writers Boot Camp is informal but intense; the criticism and feedback are constructive, sometimes brutal, but always honest. This is a chance to work in small groups with well-known, successful writers and editors practically one-on-one.

Applications for the January camp must be filed by October 15 of the previous year; for July, November 15 of the previous year. Elizabeth Monteleone reports a high volume of applicants for each session.

Short story applicants submit a piece of short, imaginative fiction up to three thousand words; for the novel, a sample chapter plus a synopsis of no more than five pages.

The cost is $500, which includes two breakfasts and a lunch on Saturday. Rooms at the Towson University Berkshire in Baltimore are extra. More Boot Camp info is available by mail, e-mail, or online. Address: BP Boot Camp, P.O. Box 660, Fallston MD 21047; Phone: 1-800-528-3310; E-mail: info@borderlandspress.com; Web site: www.borderlandspress.com.

That is a sampling of the best CSWs that can offer you the opportunity to learn how to write horror stories and novels that will sell. Most of them let selected applicants meet and talk with editors, agents, and writers who have the experience and the knowledge to help them attain success. All the programs I've discussed have great track records—the rest is up to you and what you bring to the table.

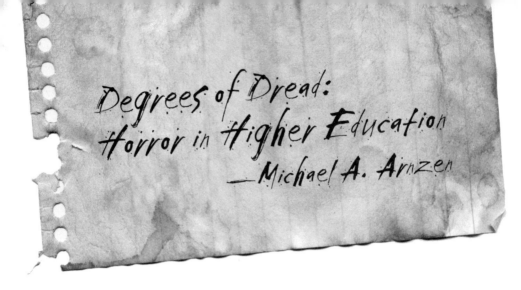

Degrees of Dread:
Horror in Higher Education
—Michael A. Arnzen

Ghoul School

If you want to be a professional, successful author in the horror genre, capable of landing publication and earning your audience's adoration … If you perhaps aspire to teach or edit someday, to make a living surrounded by the written word … If you want to be a better horror writer, and you are dedicated to the art of scaring people with your words, college has much to offer.

Given the realities of today's publishing world, going back to school might be more useful now than ever for the professional writer. There was a time when editors would collaborate with their writers in an informal apprenticeship—cultivating a relationship akin to teachers mentoring their students. Today, that's considered a charming bit of whimsy. The editors of the twenty-first century expect writers to already be savvy about their craft, providing well-polished content that needs little editorial advice. Competition is so fierce that you have to be a master before you can even get your foot in the door. So getting a good education *before* you submit can help you get your whole leg in (or is that a leg up?).

But before I tell you about the benefits, I want to make one thing perfectly clear: Simply having a diploma in your back pocket will never get you into the pages of *Cemetery Dance* or land you a contract from Leisure Books. Good writing sells itself, in any genre, and while a college class may improve your writing, it will never teach you *how* to write.

In a university, you'll learn plenty about the written word from books, teachers, and classmates, but as far as mastering the craft of writing goes, it always comes down to pounding the keyboard and running your ideas through a ritualized process of planning, writing, revising, and striving for publication over and over (and over) again.

College can humanize this process. When you go to school, you're joining a community of like-minded thinkers who openly share their ideas. A writing classroom is a social environment in which you are encouraged to intellectually collaborate with others, but you only learn by doing—by writing. A writing program gives you time to focus, resources to assist, and the motivation to improve. It can make you a more disciplined and thoughtful writer, but you still need to apply what you learn—on your own.

True, there is no substitution for the proverbial School of Hard Knocks—actual experience. But guess what? Education *is* an actual experience. Besides, if you want to write books, then it would seem there's no shame in a little "book learning." If you can afford the time and expense, college is an ideal place to practice your craft (without embarrassing yourself in the eyes of the public first), while picking up enough invaluable shortcuts and literary wisdom to save yourself many of the hardships that fledgling writers suffer.

Don't Knock Hard Knocks

In Tom Monteleone's chapter of this book, "Workshops of Horror (And Seminars and Conferences)," you'll find real-world possibilities for learning "horrorcrafting." Genre fiction communities, romance writers, mystery writers, etc., have developed a valid educational system all their own—it just isn't accredited as such. You can ostensibly cobble together your own writer's education, using informal workshops and trade seminars in consort with your own "syllabus" of how-to books, Internet research, and key titles in the field. In the process, you'll not only learn from the masters, but also have the opportunity to network in the industry, making invaluable connections with people who actually write and publish.

The Academy of Horror

So why bother with the snobbier halls of academe?

There's an old myth that says, "Those who can't do, teach." Wrong. Those who can teach, do teach. They have to do it well to keep their jobs. They also must publish. (Ever heard the expression "publish or perish"? It comes from academics who must sell a book if they hope to secure tenure.)

So if you do enroll in a college-level writing program, you can expect to study under expert teachers who have some knowledge of and experience in publishing—and you will get a degree for it.

Enrolling in a creative writing program in higher education allows you to concentrate your focus by offering a "safe haven" for you to develop skills over time, under the watchful eye of a wise professional. The workshop paradigm is central to a good college program. When I teach writing workshops at Seton

Hill University, I often introduce them with this important caveat: *A workshop doesn't teach you how to write; it teaches you how people read.*

Knowing how readers respond to your work helps you both revise your manuscripts and predict a reader's responses—because if you do that often enough, you'll start hearing critics' voices in your head. This will make you a better editor of your own prose.

Whether you're considering a bachelor's, master's, or doctorate degree, you will inevitably face a problem inherent to your genre: *Horror scares people.* Just because it is discomforting, it gets a bad rap. You may encounter academics and non-genre writers who unabashedly see no literary merit in horror. But don't let that get you down. Your job is to prove its merit through your writing, and to gently remind them that horror is an emotion that has been an element of the storyteller's art even before Homer's *Odyssey*.

You see, those who don't read horror only perceive it through a torrent of stereotypes that rain down from the mass media. To them, horror fiction is like a story dressed up in a cheap Halloween costume. But the truth is that death is a part of life, and it's probably been written about more often than love, class struggle, and all those other familiar tropes from mainstream fiction. There would be no "popular novel" without the Gothic. And if you go to college, I recommend you take as many literature classes as you can muster, to learn more about horror's literary history. From Middle English folktales to postmodern, existentialist literary criticism, you'll find horror everywhere across the English major curriculum. Take solace in that. And learn as much of it as you can; it will make you more savvy about the genre.

In fact, take advantage of every resource a college provides. Want to write about a psycho killer? Take a course in Freud or criminalistics. Master voodoo? Visit the anthropology professor. Invent a poison? Spend some extracurricular time in the chem lab.

Whatever you can't discover in the classroom, you can easily find in the college library—and if you've never been in one, you'll be blown away by how much more useful they are for writers than the local, downtown public library. If you're in a graduate program, you can check out most books for the whole term; you can even secure your own carrel, research room, or writing office. Imagine being a student at the University of Maine, where you could browse the donations from alum Stephen King. Or browsing at the University of Kansas, where fantasist Kij Johnson is building the Center for the Study of Science Fiction. Colleges can provide all the background research you'd ever need.

Finding Your Haunt

Given occasional academic bias against horror writing, you might be wondering which programs will be receptive to horror fiction and how to break in. This is the tricky part. You'll have to do some research and be willing to take risks.

The college where I teach, Seton Hill University, is unique in that it offers a program that most horror writers would probably find ideal. At Seton Hill, you can earn a Master of the Arts in Writing Popular Fiction.

For a thesis (about two years to complete), students write a market-ready novel manuscript in a genre of their choice, working under the advice of a published author who mentors them along the way. Authors and agents who have taught, mentored, or visited our program include Gary Braunbeck, Nalo Hopkinson, Tom Monteleone, Lawrence Connolly, Octavia Butler, Orson Scott Card, Donald Maass, and many more. Most of the program is conducted through distance learning—that is, online, via e-mail exchanges and participation in private chats and message boards—supplemented by attendance at two week-long "intensive residencies" per year (one summer, one winter) for workshops and classes.

In my opinion, the benefit of this program isn't just our emphasis on practical publishing matters and the expertise one develops in the genre, but also the feedback one gets from working with writers from such diverse genres. A romance writer might provide assistance with that troublesome love scene. A horror writer might help a mystery writer describe … "the body." Synergy and cross-genre feedback make our students better writers, on top of the unique faculty (published pros) who we "import" to help.

Although they may not focus exclusively on popular fiction, other colleges are receptive to it and some schools offer distance learning opportunities that make it easier to accommodate your writing schedule. Scour the programs that are out there to ferret out faculty who write in or on the field, schools that publish horror stories in their magazines, or who invite visiting writers who are best-sellers. You want to look for places like Columbia College Chicago, where *On Writing Horror: A Handbook by the Horror Writers Association* editor Mort Castle teaches, which offers distinctive BFA and MFA degrees, publishes *Spec-Lit* (a science fiction journal), offers a basic *and* an advanced course in writing science fiction in addition to offering classes in writing popular fiction, historical fiction, comic books, and graphic novels. This institution even sponsors a citywide Story Week festival, a yearly event that draws writers of all kinds to Chicago.

If "fine arts" isn't your bag, then the master's in professional writing program model (espoused by places like the University of Oklahoma and the University of Southern California) concentrates on crafting a novel-length thesis of publishable quality in practical ways (whereas many traditional MFA theses are short-story collections, rather than full-length works). Or, if you really want an inside look at the business side of publishing, you could enroll in a "publishing institute" like Denver University's or the Center for Publishing at New York University. If you work full-time or have family needs that prevent you from living on campus, a number of new "low-residency" programs for writers have sprung up over the past five years to accommodate today's hectic lifestyles—distance learning programs like Seton Hill University's MA in Writing Popular Fiction or the

University of Southern Maine's Stonecoast MFA in Creative Writing program, which offers an option to concentrate on popular fiction.

This is only a small sampling of what's available. When you search for schools (you can find them listed in the pages of trade magazines like *Writer's Digest, The Writer,* or *Poets & Writers*), try to read between the lines for "openness" to genre fiction. Consult, too, *The AWP Official Guide to Writing Programs,* published by the Association of Writers & Writing Programs, with its descriptions of programs including key faculty, course offerings, requirements, etc. Look for keywords like *professional, genre, popular,* and *novel.* Talk to writers in the Horror Writers Association (HWA) or other groups to learn more about their alma maters. Send an inquiry via e-mail to a faculty member. Such detective work can give you clues as to the best places for you.

When you apply, submit the best writing sample possible—and the most appropriate story in your repertoire. Do not try to "test" the admissions committee with some outrageous horror story. Although you want to find a horror-friendly program, learning is a two-way street; you must be willing to challenge yourself, test new boundaries, and be open to test-driving new literary techniques, even if they strike you as being foreign or alien to your genre aspirations. Most college professors believe that teaching you general literary strategies can make you a better genre writer, but not the other way around. When they sort through writing samples, they lean toward an appreciation of character depth over plot twists. Good genre fiction is a marriage of convention *and* invention—so in your writing sample—emphasize your inventiveness.

And, by all means, avoid stock subgenre icons of the supernatural (like vampires or haunted houses). Even though you might be offering an "escape" or doing something highly unique with your work, professors will only see the icon and assume you're unimaginative (perhaps because they haven't read as much horror as you have). Once you're in the program, tentatively test the waters with your more overt horror fiction and see if it flies. If it doesn't, either bail out and go write on your own, or stick around, suck it up, and commit to becoming a better writer—despite your affinity for the creeps. Think of it as an opportunity to discover new markets for your work.

Cringe Benefits

College isn't nearly as difficult to afford as people assume—and it can be downright lucrative. Educational expenses and college loans are tax deductible. Student loans have some of the lowest interest rates you'll find, so it's an affordable way to improve your lot in life. And if you're lucky, you might even get a teaching assistant's paycheck and a "free ride" tuition waiver—or even bonus grant and scholarship money—while you earn your master's. Assistantships are an excellent way to get teaching experience while working on your thesis, and most large universities offer them as incentives to promising new students. If you're already a published author, you bring a lot of clout to a program and can even help them teach their basic writing classes.

It happened for me; I essentially earned a living by going to grad school while drafting my second novel. My master's degree virtually paid for itself, and I did so well, I was subsequently swept up by a Ph.D. program that allowed me to study horror films for my doctoral work while I wrote and taught on the side. And now I've worked my way up to tenured professor. My trips to horror cons are paid by the school, and I get to work with young writers of talent on their horror stories full-time. My college bookstore stocks my work and the alumnae come to my readings. I even expect a sabbatical next year—time away from teaching to write my next book from home while drawing a full year's salary.

I'm happily living a life immersed in literature. I'm not a full-time freelancer, but then again, I get to choose my projects and not worry about how to pay the bills.

I'm very lucky, and my situation is certainly unique. But, I read once that every graduate degree you earn boosts your salary an average of ten grand a year. I doubt that's entirely true for creative writers, but many full-time writers consider attaining degrees because they want a teaching or editing gig to generate extra income while they write.

Without the MFA or Ph.D., they have a hard time finding even part-time or adjunct teaching opportunities because school administrators only count diplomas toward their accreditation—not publishing credits, unfortunately. And when given the choice of an MFA over a novelist, a publishing house seeking someone for an editorial position will likely choose the MFA because they'll assume they could work in any department, not just one narrow genre.

The final benefit of seeking education is not yours. It's ours. We learn much from you when we sit beside you in a college classroom or over a manuscript at the local pub, talking shop. We need more horror writers in the halls of higher ed in order to show the "lit snobs" just how talented and complex we really are. Plus, we can always use more educated writing published in the genre.

Horror loses its history when it isn't taught.

Horror loses its head when its writers stop learning.

Educational Online Resources

Workshops

Horror Writers Association: http://horror.org

Borderlands Press Writers Boot Camp: www.borderlandspress.com

Clarion Science Fiction and Fantasy Writers' Workshop: www.msu.edu/~clarion

Critters Workshop: www.critters.org

Odyssey—The Fantasy Writing Workshop: www.sff.net/odyssey

Online Writing Workshop for Science Fiction, Fiction, and Horror: http://sff.onlinewritingworkshop.com

World Horror Convention Writing for Real Workshop: www.worldhorrorsociety.org

Academic Programs

Seton Hill University: http://fiction.setonhill.edu

Columbia College Chicago: http://fiction.colum.edu/program/index.html

The University of Oklahoma: http://jmc.ou.edu

University of Southern Maine Stonecoast MFA in Creative Writing: www.usm.maine.edu/stonecoastmfa

Graduate School Programs in Professional Writing: www.gradschools.com/programs/professional_writing.html

The Association of Writers & Writing Programs: www.awpwriter.org

Part Three
Developing
Horror
Concepts

5:00

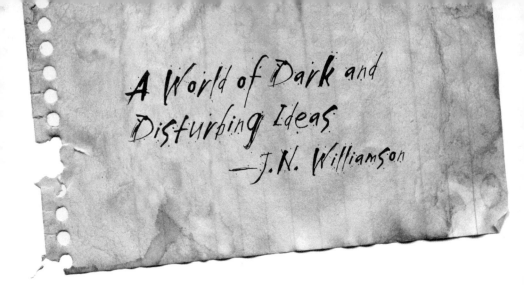

A World of Dark and Disturbing Ideas
—J.N. Williamson

Throughout my professional writing career, I have thought of an "idea" as a "useful premise," and my impression has a worthwhile history. Mary Wollstonecraft Shelley, in a dream influenced by a long, eerie conversation and perhaps John Milton's *Paradise Lost,* conceived the notion of a living human being created by a man. Bram Stoker remembered reading about people who genuinely believed in creatures called "vampires."

Because neither author actually became immortal on the strength of individual inspiration, the originality we respect in them resides in the uses they made of these concepts. Dr. Victor Frankenstein might instead have been a mere neurotic whose innocent, horrifying being existed solely in his mind. Dracula could have been an insane woodcutter or book editor whose only interest to readers depended upon his abnormal, but not supernatural, lust for human blood.

The numerous tales since then, in which writers have used man-made monsters or vampires in different forms with different agendas and a variety of endings, have been made possible by virtue of ideas.

But when dealing with the urge to create fiction that's a twist on what was already written—on primary conceptions existing before Mrs. Shelley or Mr. Stoker were born—the originality demanded of you or me is both centered on and discovered elsewhere: on the setting or date of the yarn, on new characters, on more modern science and contemporary beliefs, or on the opponents and pursuers of our particular versions of the monster.

Defining a Useful Premise

Why do I like the term "useful premise" instead of "idea"? Writers' ideas that won't sell are useful only as practice. I define a useful premise as a concept that (1) may be new or hasn't been developed into a plot for quite awhile, (2) the writer is comfortable with, and (3) for which, it can be reasonably assumed an accessible market exists.

These three numbers above correspond with the following clarifications below:

1. Entirely new ideas are as precious as gold and thus rarely discovered.

Most people argue with this; I know I did. But consider some of the alleged ideas annually developed by droves of new writers who haven't read nearly enough: people who are injured and find out they're man-made or from a different planet; mirror stories, magic and otherwise; vampires who have AIDS or steal blood from blood banks; little girls who turn out to be little boys, and vice versa; short-shorts written in one sentence; lovers who discover they are sister and brother; grandparent-ghosts who save a grandchild; sentient, malicious machines, and vicious vehicles; and, more recently, abused women who mutilate and humiliate men.

No, these are not new or original ideas; they have not gone undeveloped for a long period of time, and they decidedly are *not* useful premises.

2. Contrary to what college writing teachers once instructed, it is not necessary for new dabblers in the great fictive sandpile to make castles based on the backs of their houses and populated by characters who resemble the people who live inside them. If that were true, there would be precious little science fiction and, I think, not much horror fiction. Most of us aren't related to monsters of any kind, including the serial killer variety.

However, unless a writer has experienced an amazingly checkered life and held dozens of unrelated jobs—and unless said paragraph collector has the luxury of spending all the time required in extensive research—there are ideas for fiction that won't make the writer feel very comfortable in his or her development of a plot.

I've had a dozen or more appealing ideas I have sadly had to judge as "somebody else's," as if the mysterious creative process erred and got the imaginative right hemisphere of my brain confused with some other author's.

Are you ready, comfortably and credibly, to sustain characters of very different age, background, sexual lifestyle, and outlook on life long enough to write a commercial novel?

The question is particularly important in learning to write effective dark fiction, which is often fantastic, or at least improbable, and demands that a higher premium be placed on characterization than is required by mainstream fiction. When we ask readers to believe the impossible, we have a greater likelihood of cooperation if we're comfortable with our characters, and if they remind our readers of people they know.

3. Often, new writers, who are simply excited at getting a story idea, just sit down and see where the "story" takes them. Although spontaneity may be

underrated, impulse tales have a way of meandering out of the mood set at the start and wandering into other genres. The product is the most difficult of yarns to place: a mixed-genre or genre-straddling piece.

You see ... one of the criteria for creating fiction—the type that a writer can reasonably assume has a chance to sell—is honoring the demands of the kind of story being written. Clever endings that clash with the type of yarn one just wrote should be saved in a folder for use at the close of a new, appropriate tale.

Study the fiction currently being bought, and attune your imagination in those directions.

An accessible market might conceivably mean almost any active one, whether in books, magazines, television, or film. But reason tells us it is much more limited than that. With the exceptions of a few "name-brand" authors, I know only two who have sold to *Playboy*. The overwhelming majority of us begin with immeasurably smaller financial successes.

The accessible commercial market is one that reads your tale, likes it, and has the honest intention of doing something toward getting it into print, in return for a sum of money spelled out in a contract legally signed by you and the purchaser.

Engaging the Hypnagogic State

Everything you've read to this point is merely wrapping paper on the gift I'm about to give you. Under the heading of "How do you dream up all those ideas?" is my reply that I *do* "dream them up."

The somewhat pompous term for the source of my useful premises is the *hypnagogic state*. The gift you get is a description of how I first "visited" that state, what I took from it, what I've managed to do with it for two decades, and my belief that those of you, imaginative, talented, and ferociously wanting to write, can go there and find similar success.

In the mid-1970s, I'd had a few stories sell, but working as a sales manager and raising a large family, I was not writing at all. One night, I had a Mary Wollstonecraft Shelley-like nightmare and was up early, fascinated by its content. It may be important that I stayed put; rising might have chased it away. I was astounded to find that there was so much detail, I reconstructed it as a novel, laid out for me chapter by chapter! Oh, I didn't know the names of the children or the monster living down the hall from them, but I saw each of them, very clearly, as I lay on my side, remembering this strange intruder into my dreams.

I got up, located a notebook and pen, and began jotting down the whole nightmare, just as my unconscious mind had presented it. The first names of the girl and boy, Peg and Eric, leapt instantly to mind; otherwise, it was an exact replica of my dream, and I decided to start writing it that weekend. I named it *The Offspring* and, while the book didn't sell until I'd become the published author of seven other novels, the book won me my first agent, who did sell novel two.

That was the one in which I *consciously tried* to do what I'd done before—lie in bed and attempt to coax my creative right hemisphere into telling me, the author, a story. But there was a significant difference: I had seen the movie *The Omen* and liked it, but sensed that I had an entirely different "take" on the Antichrist theme. So my unconscious mind knew what I wanted—I had programmed it to that degree—and the magic happened again! I wrote several chapters plus an outline of what, once more, I had "seen" in my thoughts, and in 1979, *The Ritual* became my first published novel.

I had no idea that there was a name for what I was doing with my imagination, or that there was anything unusual about it, until my wife, Mary, gave me Colin Wilson's marvelous book *Mysteries* for my birthday in 1979. By then, I had visited the hypnagogic state often enough to have conceived all or part of the other seven novels, and even a few I eventually decided not to finish. Since novel eight, *The Offspring*, I've written and sold (as of this date) twenty-nine more novels as well as 126 of my 155 short stories.

In *Mysteries*, Wilson, arguably the most versatile writer of our time, wrote, "As you pass into unconsciousness, you linger briefly in a twilight realm that has been labeled the hypnagogic state." Apparently, "hypnagogy" also happens in such realms before you awaken; although for all I know, the basic seeds for *The Offspring* and *The Ritual* were "planted" as I fell asleep, my unconscious mind fertilized the plots while I slept, and they were just "there" in full bloom, warmed by the morning sun.

In my article "Releasing Creativity" (*The Inkling*, January 1984), I asked:

> Can you tap such an inexhaustible source? Read Wilson's next sentence: "Everyone has experienced these states, if only for a few seconds." They seem, he points out, independent of you, even thrown at you; they are often representational. He cites the psychologist, (Wilson) Van Dusen: "One doesn't explore these things for long without beginning to feel there is a greater wisdom in the inner processes than there is in ordinary consciousness."

Wilson also alluded to research at the Menninger Foundation suggesting that all "states of creativity" may involve theta brain rhythms produced by individuals having hypnagogic imagery. Perhaps the idea for any story you have written came to you this way.

For your voyage to the twilight realm, you need to arrange *not* to be disturbed even for the usual important call or visit. Unless you do it at night and your bunkmate is never restless, you'd be wise to choose a part of the day when your home and neighborhood are customarily quiet. A vital point: Never is this a case of forcing anything. Your conscious mind should be void unless your need is to get an original, useful premise for a specific "theme" anthology or issue, or to find a way to complete chapter six, or perhaps to begin a book or story for which you already have a basic concept. Wandering off mentally, in those instances, to

A World of Dark and Disturbing Ideas

43

thoughts on what to have for dinner or how well your team's draft choice will fit in, is the equivalent of inviting your neighbors over for a party!

But then, you surely know the world must seem still for you to write at all. Visiting the hypnagogic state calls for a serious approach, even if you appear to be staring into space.

It seems to me the proof is in the pudding, and in what I can draw from my right hemisphere for this chapter. Truth is, in recent years I have resorted to "hypnago-gis" mostly for short stories I was invited to create. Even when I wrote "Releasing Creativity," more than ten years ago, it had become possible for me to imagine novel ideas basically at will, sitting upright in my chair. *Bloodlines,* my 1994 hardcover, was born while my wife, Mary, and I were playing canasta late one night.

So, now—the man and his self-appointed challenge—ten ideas in twenty minutes!

I don't know if the ideas I'm about to seek while I sit before my typewriter will be good short story or novel ideas, or possibly just subtext (lesser ideas to be drawn from my file to make a more useful premise more substantial). All I can say beyond that is I wish the little girl speeding by my window on her tri-cycle would go home for dinner!

The clock is running:

1. A White House politician illegally requests files from the FBI detailing the private lives of more than one hundred people, including the President. Our pol discovers "facts" about the Prez, which he knows, for a fact, are lies! After some research, it becomes clear that the Chief Executive was replaced, at some point, by an impostor who has no past. Who and what is the President? Oh, by the way, because our pol has broken the law to obtain these files, he cannot tell the FBI—and certainly not the man in the Oval Office!

2. A meeting of the best meteorologists at the Weather Network. The newest and youngest scientist, a chic woman, rises to announce her findings: It's late winter, people want to know when spring is coming—but her readings show no sign of a warming trend anywhere. "Yet I have this memo saying I must say there are temps in the middle sixties due over the next ten days." Jane is told, "There are." She asks boldly, "By whose authority?" A white-haired weatherman murmurs, "The government of the United States." Honest, she says, "Gentlemen, my long-range readings indicate that spring may not come at all this year. Nor summer, for that matter. *Something's* wrong." The old weatherman says to an underling, "Willard, lock the conference room door until the Secretary arrives for our next briefing." Jane stares at them in shock. (Story might be called "Spring Will Be a Little Late This Year.")

3. A mid-teenage girl who has "felt funny" for weeks awakens in the hospital. Nurses treat her well but answer no questions, particularly the one about what

was wrong with her—and why she has a white bandage across her stomach. The nurses leave the fearful girl. She wants to see her boyfriend, Willie, and we discover that she is a virgin. She peels back the bandage and finds the remnants of an umbilical cord trailing from her navel. (No . . . I don't have a clue what this means.)

4. A man is trying to quit smoking. One morning he hungers badly for a cigarette and locates a pack of his brand, which he had concealed. Tearing off the cellophane, he tries to tap one cigarette into view. A creature never seen before, by any living man, crawls out and eats its way through his chest into the closest lung. The last thing the man sees is the warning label on the edge of his cigarette pack and the words: *May be hazardous to your health.*

5. Another man—Jack, that's what we'll call him—collapses in a seizure, then awakens to learn that he has a brain tumor. It's benign and it's operable; surgery is planned in a month. But when he next undergoes an MRI, the tumor hasn't grown and surgery is not needed. The same test result occurs six weeks later and then again in another eight weeks. Now, amazingly, the tumor is shrinking! The neurosurgeon tells Jack that what's happening is incredibly rare, but isn't it wonderful? Jack attempts to go on with his life, but the thought recurs and won't leave him: *What if I'm just imagining this and I'm actually in a vegetative state?* Everyone is thrilled for him but their reactions begin to seem abnormal to him. He wants to know, suddenly, where he really is. He starts to contact hospitals, and then tells people who care about him what he's doing. Afraid he will harm himself, Jack's wife puts him in a mental ward. Jack realizes that he has been a fool, but it may be too late. Then, a huge door is left ajar, and Jack escapes into a corridor to find himself outside a door with a window! Inside, in a bed, head swathed in bandages but with face exposed, lies ... Jack himself! Staring at nothing. Jack tiptoes back to the psychiatric wing, claims he's well now, and is ultimately released. He and his wife lead an idyllic existence, but sometimes Jack opens his eyes around 3:00 A.M. and imagines he's staring out a window at a hospital hallway.

6. A childproof lighter drives aging, rich Margaret into a screaming breakdown. Her younger husband (number four) takes control of her funds. He throws away the lighter in which he had substituted water for lighter fluid and orders a new car.

7. A small boy is always told he must eat all his veggies or he might "get like Uncle Sydney." The kid loathes green food but obeys. For the first time, he meets the great-great uncle, who comes for a holiday meal. The frail, emaciated man eats no turkey. Amazingly, he covers his plate with vegetables! Then he chokes, has a terrible coughing fit, and gasps his last words to the little boy: "I was as healthy as a horse till I turned ninety and your mother threatened to put me in a home unless I started eating more damn vegetables. As you value your life, boy, consume no more green food!" He dies with a racking cough, as

one new pea rolls from his lips. Come spring, the boy pulls up everything Mom plants, always looking at her sideways with suspicion. He stands a chance of growing up to become a veggie serial (not cereal!) killer.

8. *The Bully* (a novel). Prologue: A young, bright student is teased, then beaten, by the high school bully. Asked to identify his attacker, he refuses. Worse, the boy knows he wouldn't squeal because he wants personal vengeance on the huge kid someday. The novel takes place in the present and the bully hasn't changed, just grown. He beats his wife and child and commits crimes. Our protagonist, the ex-victim, is now a police detective. Evidence in a murder points to the bully; in an interrogation, the latter still verbally abuses the detective. Arresting the bully would be easy, but the detective is not convinced of his guilt. Knowing the cop's wife from school, the bully phones her to say "hi," beginning a sequence of taunts. Then the officer learns from Domestic that the bully battered his (the bully's) wife and she refused to press charges. Our hero goes to her in the hospital and begs her to file a complaint. In retaliation, the bully actually visits the cop's wife and, without touching her, says what he'll do to her "one day"—but it's his word against hers. This psychological thriller has the suspense note: Which of these former students will break first and physically attack the other? Each underestimates the other's commitment—to good and to evil. (I may just decide to use this useful premise!)

9. Just like in many old and extremely politically incorrect jokes, a southern Baptist, a Catholic priest, and a Jewish rabbi are on a plane when the pilot dies, and there is only one parachute. My creative right mind tells me this is a serious story that explores an interesting point: Having heard the jokes before, which man will bring them up first and (mainly this) will all three plunge to certain death instead of quibbling over who gets the parachute?

10. UFO aliens are actually vampires. They abduct people for their usual bloody reasons, and the experiments the people remember are merely false "screen memories" for the bloodlettings they suffered. The aliens are gray in color for the obvious reason that they are the "undead." They have no intention of taking over the world, beyond what they've already done, because nobody capable of stopping them believes in them, and their food supply is, with Earth densely populated, unlimited. But one of them, a leader, makes the mistake of falling in love with his abductee ....

Ten ideas!

But, one confession before closing this chapter ...

It took over an hour for these ten ideas—not all useful premises, to be sure—to appear on paper. In planning for twenty minutes, I did not allow for the time it would take to type my ideas into understandable form. Besides, by the time

I'd put down premises as lengthy as the fifth and eighth, it got harder to slide backwards into my unconscious thoughts.

What turned out to be most remarkable to me was the disappearance of the little girl who was riding past my window back at the beginning of this exercise.

Bonus time for you — and me:

11. Useful premise: A writer getting in touch with his creative side wants a child on a trike to stop disturbing his concentration and go home to eat. Next day, she has vanished.

She does not, however, stay vanished. He finds her, red ribbon in her hair and all, the next time he needs to write a story about a little girl who interrupts a writer busily getting in touch with ...

Mirror, Mirror
—Wayne Allen Sallee

There are no vampires or werewolves in my world. The terrors I create usually come from the boy/girl next door or from my own mirror.

Isn't this always the question—new writers approach me at conventions or book signings and ask where I get my ideas. Each and every time, I reply that I am fortunate to live in Chicago, where the most vile deeds do occur, and often for the most absurd reasons.

Where do I *not* get ideas?

But there are those writers who live in small towns or allegedly safe suburbs who do not have the benefit of witnessing odd characters acting out cathartic scenarios unless relatives are over for Thanksgiving dinner. (And, that is not to say that senseless crimes and squalor only occur in the Big City. In recent years, I have found increasing amounts of "fiction-fodder" in my father's hometown of Shelbyville, Kentucky, where several events rival any Chicago claim of a monopoly on wickedness.)

Newspapers are good sources, but television is even better. One local news station touted itself as "Your window to the world." I challenge you to watch any given edition (or episode, depending on your level of cynicism) of your local news, then stop and think about just how you can possibly startle someone with your prose when the anchorpersons at five, six, and ten o'clock are doing a bang-up job of it already.

Put Yourself in the Picture

I had never planned to look into the mirror and bastardize my own life experiences as a native Chicagoan. But it is the easiest groove to fall into, particularly because I choose, more often than not, to write in first-person-narrative point of view.

What I found difficult, though, was developing the story itself. I had the setting nailed down—the love/hate relationship every area writer has with the Windy City had long ago invaded even my dreams. My first dozen or so stories (written in about six months), I approached as if I were scribing a confessional (another mirror of sorts).

Going back to the evening news and its "if it bleeds, it leads" standards, I projected myself as an invisible bystander at actual occurrences in Chicago's passing parade. On paper, I let it all play out differently; the character's actions answering, or at least defining more clearly, my darkest questions about myself.

Only the fates have been changed to protect the innocent.

Those early stories, about a woman murdered beneath an elevated platform as one lone man looks on, a drunk who disappears from a strip joint and is found at the bottom of a quarry the next day, and several more from the vantage point of commuter and/or observer, were all heavy on atmosphere. In fact, my first three stories had *not one* line of dialogue. But the reader was given smells and sights, from the shape of the downtown skyline to the amount of dirt beneath a little boy's fingernails, to the manner of dress of the people on the street and the type of reading material each chose for the train ride home. Describing something as common as a man bending down to tie his shoelace or something as patently absurd—to some people—as a young woman applying mascara while sitting on a lurching bus.

My images from public transportation notwithstanding, each of the scenes I've just described can be dreamed up by a writer living in the smallest of towns, in which the skyline is merely a water tower set against a billion stars.

"Sometimes, people cannot detach themselves from the original circumstances and see the ways in which the writer has had to, for aesthetic reasons, transform not only the circumstances but also the characters." So says Richard Stern, a much-lauded novelist living in Chicago's Hyde Park neighborhood. I cannot agree more. Whether you are writing about your Uncle Vern and Auntie Nurleen, your first employer (only you changed his name to Jerry Mizel, see), or a camp counselor from your childhood, someone out there might take umbrage at being described as a tyrant or buffoon. You cannot let yourself think of these matters. There is a potential tale to be told in the eyes of each and every person you encounter. Life is a game that you learn as you go, even if the playing board is tattered and worn. If you can think of your writing in those terms, you will see we're *all* in the game, *all* on that same board.

And the thimble game piece is as intruiging as the top hat or the race car.

Getting in the Game

Carry a pencil nub and a notepad, or lug that laptop to the corner tavern or coffee shop and choose a "game piece." Write a thumbnail sketch about that figure, describing his appearance, mimicking his speech pattern, or making mention of his body movements. What is your subject eating or drinking? What song does he play on the jukebox?

Mentioning brand names or models of cars or rock groups indigenous to 1965, 1997, or 2006 America might get you labeled "contemporary," and there is nothing wrong with that. And do not think that using contemporary icons to describe your characters and their situations will soon make your work seem dated and muddled. This is not so. Lovecraft never gave us the exact address of his Shunned House, though the structure used as its basis does exist and is, in fact, part of the Providence, Rhode Island, guided tour. By contrast, Stephen King gladly tells us the beer of choice for every Maine inhabitant from the picture-perfect town of Jerusalem's Lot (also known as Salem's Lot) to Castle Rock.

I mention the icons of our everyday lives, I suppose, to give you a sense of something familiar. Surround yourself with the commonplace and the prosaic, and you'll find that replacing "fast-food restaurant" with McDonald's or WaffleSteak will give both you and the reader decidedly different settings.

Now, for the flip side of this advice—reasons *not* to use an actual place, be it a franchise or national chain. Simply put, if you invent your own commercial abattoir, anything and everything goes within its confines, with no threat of maligning a corporation or, even worse, fostering reader disbelief. All right, we know acts ranging from murder to embezzlement to the unimaginable have occurred at late-night mini-marts across the country, but it might still be in your best interest to make up a place if, say, it featured circus clowns wrestling Sumo-style with wagers taken on the side. The sole reason Chicago was never specifically announced as the setting for the 1980s cop show *Hill Street Blues* was that Police Capt. Frank Furillo's city was entirely corrupt. The network needn't have worried; come Election Day, our unofficial motto is "Vote early, and vote often!" If written distinctly enough, the fictitious can be made into an icon, too.

The icons, real or invented, are part of the ritual: the ceremonies of our workday and our nightlife.

In 1994, *Young Blood*, a horror paperback anthology of works by mostly first-sale writers under the age of thirty (edited by the late Mike Baker), was published. The book made me reminisce about my college writing workshops. *Young Blood* was filled with tales like the stories we shared in that University of Illinois classroom, mostly written by young writers who were working hard to bring readers into their—the writers'—familiar surroundings. Into the formalities of their—the writers'—lives. If the story focused on a clerk in a mail room, you could bet that the writer once held such a job, if he were not still employed as such. That held true in my 1982 workshops. The college stories were about frustrations with classes, the opposite sex, even tuition and the transit system.

Perhaps I had no social life back then, and certainly found no horrors in working for a retail clothing store, because my story was about the attack beneath the elevated tracks. The impetus for such a tale came equally from my habit of devouring the morning newspapers and from the fact that my father was a Chicago police officer. (Something to keep in mind: Close family members—or even co-workers—can provide a jump-start to your story, if you believe your own experiences to be less than spectacular.)

I said earlier that my first three stories contain no direct dialogue. I wanted the reader to be overwhelmed by the sputtering neon and angular shadows, the smells from the street mixed with the autumn air and the sounds of both impatience and complacency.

I guess this approach worked. The late Karl Edward Wagner chose that first story, "Rapid Transit," for DAW's *The Year's Best Horror Stories XIV* despite, in his words, "the less-than-polished writing," and because I had created (also in his words) "images that [he] could not get out of [his] mind."

Certainly, my approach to that story today would make it better constructed, but most new writers would agree that the impact of images that stay in an editor's memory is a necessary and great boon.

No, the murder of my fictitious victim, Quita McLean, never occurred—yet aside from her killing—every sight and sound that filtered through my protagonist, Dennis Cassady, was personally witnessed by me one October night in 1982. The descriptions you will create are always just an arm's length to infinity away.

The Horror of the Mind

I've mentioned characters and settings. I've talked about carrying those blank scraps of paper around, and the importance of writing everything down, no matter how seemingly banal. You can sort through it all later. But exactly what is it that you will be discarding? What truths will remain? What horrors will remain?

When asked why I write psychological horror, I always reply that this form is the most intimate way to reach a reader. Think about it.

Whether it is an aversion to spiders or a shadowy figure in the alley behind an apartment building, you've got your readers, and you've got 'em good—even if they have a "been there/done that/bought the T-shirt" feeling of superiority. The true and pristine horror is that of the unknown, and so those latter readers who look at the genre with condescension are still showing a reaction, be it in denial at being frightened or in ignorance of today's indignities.

Most of us write about what moves us most. And I believe that this is true particularly in the field of horror.

Horrors, real or imagined, are all around us. In an increasing number of instances, they can be both real and imagined. Welcome to the realm of the inner demons. With the increasing awareness of different behavioral traits, new writers may have a fresh angle on terror. Things that go bump in the night are no longer ghosts or succubae, but the heightened heartbeat of someone suffering from OCD (obsessive-compulsive disorder) and its attendant cousins; or, as at least one well-known horror novelist has written of, repeated alien abductions.

New Directions

Earlier, I mentioned the difficulties of coming up with more terrifying story ideas than the true-life incidents that can be virtually witnessed in television news programs. Think about it. With whom, or what, did Poe or Lovecraft have to compete? Perhaps I oversimplify the matter, but I might suppose the only competition for both were the public's memories of the War of 1812 and World War I, respectively. Even the infamous Jack the Ripper wasn't a terror to be reckoned with until the advent of the pulps, forty years after he murdered the women of Whitechapel.

Conversely, the world we now live in allows new writers to embrace a broader range of topics. At the turn of the century, Stephen Crane wrote on how he was too busy running from demons (he did this by making sense of his world through his prose) to attempt to find out why they'd singled him out in the first place. Now, in our time, those demons, or their hosts, are appearing on talk shows—daily.

My own ideas of horror have changed. I have accepted that there will always be the vampire, either romanticized or brutal, still as big a cash cow as the next installment of Must See TV. In the time I've been professionally published, vampire novels have consistently appeared, along with shared-world anthologies and role-playing game tie-ins. But, whereas my leanings are not toward vampires or anything supernatural, I do realize that to write successfully about the *undead*, I would have to treat each one as I would a living human being. In fact, giving your supernatural characters certain human traits or afflictions, as I did when I wrote of a werewolf with Huntington's chorea, may propel your story further, as well as make it more memorable.

On most any convention panel, the question will be raised regarding "the direction in which horror is headed." To concern yourself with this is as potentially destructive as equating the money you earn per story with the amount of time spent writing it. No matter "directions," categories, genres, subgenres, or whether your terrors are archetype or topical—your characters must be timeless.

As long as you can look into and then through the mirror, whether real or pretend, be it atop your dresser plastered with postcards and family photos or reflected in a bus or train window tagged with graffiti, if you can look and see the humanity, the common struggles and the little victories, then you will always be able to place your own signature, your style, on your work.

As Richard Stern said, "The best and worst readers of your work are those who provide stimulus, even partial models, for it."

If you want my spin on it, I recall Roy Scheider portraying Bob Fosse in *All That Jazz*. He'd take a long look in the mirror and say, "It's showtime!"

It's showtime!

Now go to it.

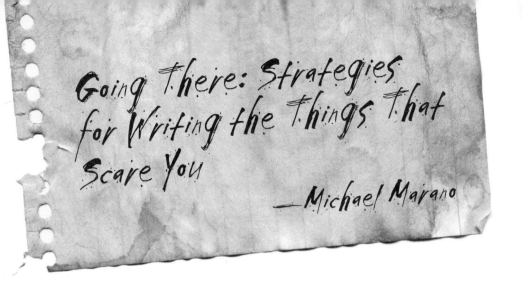

Going There: Strategies for Writing the Things That Scare You

—Michael Marano

The Fear of Going There

I feel it physically—half of me turns to smoke. The corners of the room go dim, and from about the rib cage down, my body feels as numb as the ghost limb of an amputee. It's what happens when I'm about to write something that frightens me. Freaking yourself out is an occupational hazard for a horror writer. It's also, if you rise to the challenges it presents, a great opportunity to hone your craft.

The first time I frightened myself was in 1989, when I felt this half-fading away and saw those midnight-colored shadows crowd the edges of my sight. I squinted at the monitor of what was, even then, an outdated computer, trying to give the bones and blood of syntax and grammar to a scene I'd hoped would have the same impact in prose that the infamous "exploding head" scene in David Cronenberg's film *Scanners* had. It was to be a scene of horror early on in the narrative that would blindside and keep the reader on edge throughout the work. It would be a gruesome moment, but would also be a description of something *spiritually* malignant: violent to bodies, but more importantly, to souls.

I was afraid of what I'd imagined. The fear wasn't like a wall. It was an acres-wide bramble I'd have to hack into. But I had to go there, into that wilderness. And I did. It was grueling to confront a thing out of my own mind that had frightened me, but I knew the effort was worth it when I showed the draft to a friend, and asked if she thought the scene "worked." Her wordless reply was to take my hand and press my fingers by her throat. Her pulse was racing. By going there, I'd taken her along.

Horror is more than what makes a pulse race. There are other sources of horror besides fear; some are far worse than fear, and far harder to write about. I spoke to a horror writer I admire about a scene he'd written that was so full of anguish and loss that it had made my wife cry. He told me that the scene had been so brutal for him to write, he had cried at his keyboard while writing it. It can be dangerous to capture in words what skulks in the Mirkwood of your head. The nineteenth-century French writer Guy de Maupassant was tortured by what he imagined, and died crazy ... a year and a half after trying to slit his own throat.

Dangers of the Wilderness

No two wildernesses are alike. Each has unique dangers. There's the wilderness of physical violence and gore, which made Jack Ketchum's *Off Season* a horror milestone. There's spiritual pain and doubt, like that of William Peter Blatty's *The Exorcist* or Gary Braunbeck's *In Silent Graves*. Sadness and loss create their own terrors, as Clive Barker showed us in "Coming to Grief." There's the terror of reality, breaking like a molar crunching down on a pebble—something Philip K. Dick repeatedly showed in his novels and stories. Consider Thomas Harris's bravery in depicting how killers like *The Silence of the Lambs'* Jame Gumb think. The total absence of morality can be horrifying: Popeye, the villain in William Faulkner's *Sanctuary*. Peter Straub's "The Juniper Tree" makes us feel the evil of child abuse. Franz Kafka's "In the Penal Colony" and Joseph Conrad's "Heart of Darkness" depict the terror of political and economic power gone amok. Nobel Prize-winner Elfriede Jelinek's *The Piano Teacher* is such a gut-punching portrait of psychological abuse, the book almost feels abusive to the reader.

It's useful to think of these dark places as wildernesses because, like wildernesses, you can understand them through a kind of mapping. Let me put a spin on advice for new writers that Walter Benjamin gave in his 1928 work, *One-Way Street*. Benjamin wrote metaphorically about texts being like country roads, and that " ... [t]he power of a country road is different when one is walking along it from when one is flying over it by airplane." He advised writers to write out passages from works they admire, because *to read* a passage is to fly over it, while *writing it out* is to walk the same path that the writer did. Writing out text is a way not only to learn the technique of another writer, but also to learn about yourself and what *you're* capable of as a writer: "Only he who walks the road on foot learns of the power it commands ...."

Hunt down a passage from a work of horror that didn't just get under your skin, but that rat-gnawed into your marrow. For me, this would be the climax of Ramsey Campbell's "Potential." When I read that story in high school, I was floored by its presentation of an almost Lovecraftian horror in such a mundane setting as a dank, old pub, and that the malevolent agencies of that story, through a few artful glimpses, could be given such a dreadful sense of purpose.

Study the passage that bothered you. Savor it. If you're inclined, read it out loud, to discover cadences you might otherwise miss. Then copy it out. Get your fingers into it. Walk the same path that the author did. Discover, at ground level, how he confronted and articulated the idea that wigged you out. It's empowering to see words that freaked you out flowing from your own pen. As Benjamin said: "Only the copied text thus commands the soul of him who is occupied by it, whereas the mere reader never discovers the new aspects of his inner self that are opened by the text ...." Once you've had the experience of putting into words a scene imagined by someone else that has frightened you, you'll have a sense of how to put into words the things hatched from your own imagination that frighten you.

The Thoughts of Monsters

Another way to "go there" is a method not strictly dependent on the written but the theatrical arts. At times, what can frighten you as a writer is not a horrific event, but horrific thoughts ... be they the thoughts of a human or an inhuman monster. I mentioned earlier the bravery of Thomas Harris in his depictions of the thought processes of human monsters. Look at Harris's *Red Dragon*, the definitive serial killer novel, written before the term "serial killer" came into common parlance. Study the artful way that Harris waltzes between the thoughts of *Red Dragon*'s killer, Francis Dolarhyde, and the thoughts of Will Graham, the FBI profiler who is, himself, terrified to think the way that Dolarhyde does, but who knows he must, in order to stop him.

It's uncomfortable and brutal to think and write the thoughts of monsters. In writing my own fiction, I've had to describe the thoughts of a succubus, a man whose mind is sundered by a demon, a child who is raised by corpse-eating monsters in a sewer, a homunculus who doesn't know he's been conjured as the unliving lover of a demented artist, among many other people, and things whose thoughts can be nasty to think—let alone express—through the written word. The best training I had for hacking into those dark places did not come from any writing class, but from the training I had as an actor.

The acting "Method" developed by Constantin Stanislavsky, and detailed in his book *An Actor Prepares,* trains actors to use their emotional memory, to reach back into their own experiences and pull forth feelings they can use to craft a "believable truth" while performing. Writing is a kind of performance. And when writing horror, is there anything more urgent than the creation of a "believable truth"? Stanislavsky felt an actor's own personality and emotional core were his most vital tools as an artist.

Think of your emotional memory as a kind of clay; you can change its shape and proportions through your craft. Stanislavsky offers strategies for developing this skill. I was not raised in a sewer by monsters and fed corpses. So, in order to write that particular story, to create a mental reality that most would prefer not to imagine, I used what I'd learned from Stanislavsky to reach into my own experience and exaggerate emotions that I have felt. If writing is performance, then writing about monsters is playing a specific kind of role. In this context, Brian Cox, the first actor to play Thomas Harris's killer Hannibal Lecter, said something kind of creepy and illuminating about the art of playing monsters: "The first profiler was Stanislavsky."

Finding Negative Space

Filmmaking offers another strategy for depicting things from your own imagination that frighten you. "Negative space" is a technique filmmakers use to define something important by surrounding it with emptiness, by letting the void around the important thing in a shot give it defining shape. How is this applicable to writing horror fiction? You can indirectly describe what frightens you by what surrounds it. Shirley Jackson's *The Haunting of Hill House* is one of the most frightening books ever written. Yet what does Jackson describe? Nothing, directly. She defines the malignance in Hill House by what surrounds it—not just through the house itself, with its odd angles and the uncomfortable furnishings that threaten to swallow up Eleanor and her fellow psychic investigators, but through the psychology and actions of the people who encounter that disease.

The late Hubert Selby, Jr., author of *Last Exit to Brooklyn*, is a master at describing terrifyingly spiritual sickness through the destructive thoughts that surround it. His novels *The Demon* and *The Room* overwhelm with the broken thoughts of their main characters. Yet, it's not these thoughts that are frightening; it's the *black hole* of emotional paralysis defined in vague outline *by* those thoughts.

Giving a strategic glimpse of what frightens you can lessen the effect of writing about *that thing*'s impact on you, and it can, at the same time, increase the impact of *that thing* (whatever it is) on your readers. Find the single facet of *that thing* that frightens you—that which most everyone can relate to—and use that one facet as a weapon to frighten your readers. It's a given in horror that the unknown is a great source of fear. But what's known, in the right context, can be much worse. The full scope of Nazi atrocity is hard for the typical modern North American to understand in a visceral way. It's because of this that I'll never forget a moment while seeing Roman Polanski's *The Pianist* in a packed theater. The audience watched the film, full of the horrors of oppression, in silence. Yet, one scene in which a Nazi knocks a frail old man to the ground wrung startled gasps and flinches from the audience. Knocking over the old man—that small glimpse of larger atrocity—commanded such a reaction because everyone could relate to and understand that one vile act, and thus understand a bit better and feel more fully the scope of what was being shown.

One last tip: When trying to write, in prose, something that scares me, I've found that writing it first for another medium (in screenplay format, as a radio drama, or in comic book script) lessens the difficulty of putting it in prose form.

The Opportunity of Fear

I mentioned that being frightened by what you've imagined is an opportunity. Think about it. You, as a horror writer, as someone familiar with the genre and maybe jaded to it, have discovered something that can affect you. How often does that happen to you as a reader?

If you've discovered something that frightens you, a horror fan and writer devoted to his or her craft, being able to blaze a trail into that unique wilderness is a true gift. By going there and writing about it, you can share that gift, to the benefit of yourself, your readers, and the genre as a whole.

Honest Lies and Darker Truths: History and Horror Fiction
—Richard Gilliam

Let us start with an observable tact: Many commercially successful novels and motion pictures pay only slight attention to historical accuracy. This is just as true in horror fiction as it is in other types of historical storytelling. Let us also observe that these inaccuracies are found in many outstanding works of literature and drama, and that faithfulness to history does not, by itself, create compelling stories.

This places me in somewhat of a quandary. I've always valued accuracy in writing and the skillful use of historic facts to enhance a story. Yet, I concede to being a fan of the motion picture *Braveheart*, which uses the names of actual persons and places but grossly violates both the facts and issues surrounding William Wallace. Neither do the events in the film conform to the known history of the era; nor was the historic Isabella the likable person found in the film. (She caused her husband, King Edward II, to be murdered and then, with her lover Roger de Mortimer, corruptly ruled England until her son, Edward III, overthrew them and assumed power in 1330 A.D.)

Accuracy vs. Relevance

Does it matter if *Braveheart* has only a tenuous relationship to the era of history in which it's supposedly set? What's more important is that *Braveheart* has relevance to today's world, and that its central issues resonate with current audiences. It's very likely that the film, historical inaccuracies and all, spurred a significant part of the recent increase in interest in Scottish history. It's probable that because of *Braveheart*, many more people have taken the time to read about William Wallace than would have done so otherwise.

And perhaps most importantly, particularly to us, as writers: As a story, *Braveheart* is outstanding. There has long been a place in literature for the "pseudo-historical" fable that tells its lies honestly, and *Braveheart* occupies that place well.

There is, though, a danger that the fictional image may overwhelm the historical one. Certainly there are many examples of inaccurate propaganda being advanced to further unworthy political or social agendas. It's a dangerous game to tamper with history for the sake of convenient storytelling. Still, every work of fiction in some way must deviate from objective history; it is the very nature of *fiction* to do so. Each writer must determine individually the standards and limits for abstractions from the objective world.

Researching Your Lies

What methods, then, should a writer use for historical research—assuming the writer is interested in an honest re-creation of a historical setting? There isn't any "one-size-fits-all" answer; you'll find a wide range of successful methods and successful authors. For whatever help it might be, here are some of my experiences in researching historical fiction.

The first historical fiction I attempted was "Caroline and Caleb," a twenty thousand-word novella written for the Civil War anthology *Confederacy of the Dead*, a book widely regarded as a model of "horror + history fiction." I primarily used the reference books in my personal library, supplemented with research at the public library in Clearwater, Florida, where I was living at the time.

The story is set in eastern Tennessee following the end of the U.S. Civil War. I grew up in northern Alabama, had visited eastern Tennessee often, and already had a pretty clear idea of what the geography was like; I didn't need a new research trip to the area. There were three primary areas of research I felt were needed for this project.

The Historical Setting

The first area, obviously, was the Civil War itself. For example, in today's military, recruits from all parts of the country serve together, but that wasn't the case in the 1860s. Individual states raised their own armies, which meant that most of the persons from a particular region of a state would likely be known to have fought in a specific set of battles and campaigns. Even though the story begins some months after the end of the war, that was the sort of historical detail I wanted to make the story more interesting. Most people are probably unaware that Tennessee raised armies for both the Confederacy *and* the Union. To get these elements and the characters introduced, I started the story with Caleb and his father attending a Sunday church service as part of a congregation whose members included both Northern and Southern veterans. Thus, I was able to get a good bit of the historical exposition out of the way early, which is often a good thing to do in storytelling: Once the setting is established, the writer can then get on with the task of building a strong narrative flow and sharpening character development.

The Environmental Setting

The second area that required research was plants, animals, and geology. This was pretty much a matter of going to the Clearwater library and using natural history books to verify information. Nonetheless, in early drafts, I made one mistake in flora and fauna—I had grizzly bears instead of black bears living in the Smoky Mountains. Fortunately, a friend caught the error while proofing the story and it's correct in all final print versions of the story. For reasons of storytelling, I made a deliberate decision to include a red wolf and a raven in the story, even though neither species is thought to have still inhabited eastern Tennessee by the 1860s. The reason I did this ties in with the third area of research.

The Religious Setting

A major theme of "Caroline and Caleb" is the contrast between the religious beliefs of the Cherokees, who were indigenous to eastern Tennessee, and those of the white settlers who displaced them. I knew plenty of Protestants, so researching that history was fairly easy—I called my sister and asked a few questions, mostly having to do with how the annual church calendar (Easter, Christmas, etc.) affected the themes of sermons. For the Cherokee religious beliefs, I turned to my friend Owl Goingback, whose story "Spoils of War" also appears in *Confederacy of the Dead*. Owl, who has lectured throughout the country on the customs and folklore of Native Americans, explained that not until the 1800s, after about three centuries of cultural contamination, did the Cherokee begin keeping written records of their ceremonies. That made its way into the story, both in an expository section that foreshadowed later developments and again symbolically through the Cherokee spirit the Raven Mocker, who is himself corrupted after being exposed to the Christian concept of damnation.

You may find interesting one small decision I made to deviate from Cherokee symbology. According to Joseph Campbell and other writers, the sun is primarily a female Cherokee symbol, though there are some examples of Cherokee representations of the sun as male; I used the sun as a male symbol for Caleb and plant life as the female symbol for Caroline. I probably would have been uncomfortable having one of my male Cherokee characters represented by the sun, but I think it was appropriate for the story and for Caleb.

How does all this historical background relate to horror writing? The plot of "Caroline and Caleb" is pretty simple: Boy meets girl. Boy marries girl. Monster threatens community. Monster is defeated.

My idea was to use *setting* and *background* to build up to a horrific event that could only be overcome by the defeating of the Raven Mocker. In Cherokee beliefs, the Raven Mocker tears people's *hearts* out. While many dark events are mentioned in the story, there's only one horrifically graphic portion of "Caroline and Caleb," and that occurs just prior to the final confrontation. Some people believe horror stories should maintain a horrific tone from beginning to conclusion and end on a downbeat note, and I'll certainly agree that many fine stories follow that structure. Even though by the end of "Caroline and Caleb" all the major characters have been killed, the story has a redemptive conclusion. If horror fiction tends to have unhappy endings, then, I suggest that horror fiction set during unhappy periods of history tends to have "even less happy" endings, and that the unhappy periods of history are often the most happily interesting.

The What-If Story

One form of historical story is the "what-if" story based on one single, deliberately selected deviation from history. The reader knows upfront that this is an "alternate history," that the writer is speculating on what *might have* occurred.

A possible problem with this structure is that the premise is often more interesting than the story. Another is that the personality of the subject may be at odds with the premise. I once proposed to Timothy Leary a story in which, instead of leaving the West Point cadet corps, Leary would remain in the military and become the commanding U.S. general during the Vietnam War. Leary loved the idea, and someday I may write the story—if I can figure out how to be faithful to the person Timothy Leary was while presenting the story as a credible premise. After all, Leary's conflicts with the inflexible rules at West Point and his later similar problems at Alabama and Harvard are central to why he became an icon of his era. Iconoclasm and civil disobedience are traits rarely sought in military commanders. Indeed, almost by definition, anyone who rises to command an army cannot possess them.

I had a much easier time envisioning an alternate history about the Roman emperor Caligula, in "Phantoms of the Night," for the anthology *Phantoms of the Night*. The "what-if" here is that, rather than being assassinated by his guards, Caligula escapes into hiding, returning to Rome only decades later, haunted by the ghosts of his past. The point gets back to honest lies—it's easily believable that Caligula might have escaped, and that he would continue to be ruthlessly insane, just as he was when he ruled Rome. Timothy Leary as a military commander would not be an honest lie. If that idea worked at all, it would most likely be at a gimmicky or exploitation level with the premise being more interesting than the story.

It's probably easier to write a credible "what-if" horror story about a horrible person, or perhaps about a nice person who lives in horrible times. While there have been several excellent horrific alternate-history stories and novels in recent years, it continues to be an underutilized form that is perhaps more popular with readers than with authors.

The Parable

Yet another sort of historical story is the parable that substitutes a historical situation for a contemporary one. For examples, we can look to the "McCarthy Era," that shameful period in the United States in the 1950s when accusing someone of being a Communist was sufficient evidence to ruin the person's career. Those who spoke out against McCarthyism were often investigated for supposedly being unpatriotic, or worse, sympathizers to the Communist cause. This created a chilling effect that stifled both political dissent and the creative arts. It was decades later before Hollywood was willing to make movies about the McCarthy Era. Nonetheless, some writers used historical stories to criticize the social and political climate. *The Crucible, Inherit the Wind,* and *High Noon* used historical events—the witch trials of Massachusetts, the 1925 Scopes Trial, the American West—to mirror the problems of the contemporary era. Such metaphoric stories are rare in horror fiction, perhaps because the genre is so seldom concerned with political events.

What About Gothic Horror?

I have, thus far, not discussed what is commonly called "Gothic" fiction, partly because entire books have been written on the subject, and also because Gothic fiction encompasses far more than historical fiction. (Other chapters in *On Writing Horror* do offer sometimes varying views of the Gothic aesthetic as well as the bizarre and surreal techniques associated with it.) It is worth noting, I think, that when Mary Wollstonecraft Shelley wrote *Frankenstein*, the setting was contemporary to her. Most commercially successful horror fiction has a contemporary setting, and this is true of both nineteenth-century and twentieth-century horror fiction. The primary current exception is Anne Rice, whose novels frequently use both historic and contemporary settings. Rice uses vivid historical detail to establish mood and draw the reader into the world of the protagonist. Creating that world for the reader is at the heart of good historical fiction writing.

Methods of Research

The methods writers use to conduct research vary drastically. The great "true adventures" writer Daniel Mannix felt that experiencing the event was an integral part of the process of writing. Thus, when asked to write an article on vampire bats, Mannix obtained several vampire bats and wrote about how it felt when they bit him and fed from his arm. On the other hand, Bram Stoker wrote *Dracula* without ever traveling to Transylvania—indeed, he seldom left Ireland during the period when most of his work was published.

It's also worth noting that authors often change methods of research. When writing *Memos from Purgatory*, Harlan Ellison joined a street gang so he could write about the subject convincingly. The result was one of the landmarks of Ellison's career, leading him to Hollywood as a writer for film and television. Some years later, when writing *Mephisto in Onyx*, he spent hours on the telephone interviewing the warden at Alabama's death-row prison and then wrote about the institution so convincingly that he continues to receive letters from inmates asking when he visited there. With all respect to the younger Harlan who rumbled in the Bronx and to Daniel Mannix and his vampire bats, there are easier ways than personal experience to research a story, particularly if you're writing about what it's like to be a death-row inmate. Raymond Chandler said it nicely: "There are only two professions where you need to know how to rob a bank—and one of them is being a writer."

Are there absolute maxims specific to the writing of historical horror fiction? I think not. The elements of good writing important to any form of fiction are important to all horror fiction, and to all historical fiction, for that matter. Readers want to be taken someplace they haven't visited—or perhaps someplace they've visited before and enjoyed. Writers create historical fiction for many of the same reasons. And horror writers? Creating horror from history takes us on an intriguing search for those darker truths that reside amidst the honest lies.

Part Four
Horror Crafting

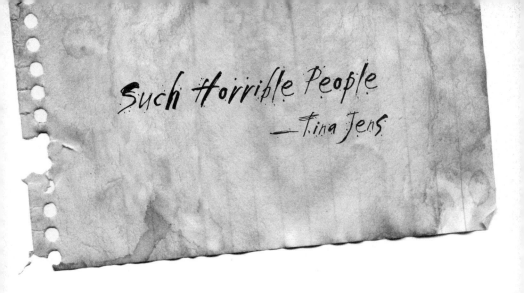

Such Horrible People
—Tina Jens

If you have carefully plotted your story from beginning to end and you are now planning to plug your characters into this ever-so-cleverly woven plot, you are doomed. That is, your story is doomed to failure.

But I'm the master puppeteer! I'll make my characters do whatever I want. I am in charge!

Wrong. Your people, the characters of your horror story, are not puppets. If you want to play with two-dimensional, paper-doll characters, you can force them to jump through your hoops. But, if you want three-dimensional, come-alive-on-the-page and grow-in-readers'-minds characters—no way.

Writing with three-dimensional characters is kind of like herding ducks. You can guide them in a general direction, but they're basically going to go wherever they want to.

That sounds like a lot of work. Why should I go to all the bother, if two-dimensional characters are so much easier to work with? After all, horror is about plot.

No, it isn't. Horror is about how people react *when they encounter* the plot.

Even the coolest monster gets dull fast without a protagonist we can really care about; someone who acts in an intelligent, realistic way.

Take the movie *Creature From the Black Lagoon*. The Gill-Man—one of the coolest monsters ever created—in one of the dullest movies ever made. Why? Because the supposedly intrepid and scientific exploration team was dull and dumb. They jumped through plot hoops instead of acting as individuals.

"Plot hoop"—a definition: When a character does something really dumb or so far "out of character" that the response is:

Yo! Why are you chasing the zombie motorcycle gang into the dark room by yourself when backup's on the way?

Why are you going into the vampire's lair at midnight when you could wait a few hours and do it safely in daylight?

Plot hoops are what make people put down your book and turn on the television, walk the dog, or call up Auntie Em for a long chat. No one wants to read about puppets jumping through plot hoops. So what can you do?

Find the Character First

Start by re-arranging the steps in your writing project. Don't plot, then create character. Start with your basic idea: Vampires invade small town. Man creates monster. Tornado carries girl to fantasy world.

Now, before you take your premise another step, find your characters. I like to start with "the bad guy." Put flesh on his bones, attitude on his lips, and a driving passion in his brain.

Okay, back to plot for a moment (exactly *one* moment). What is the monster's goal? To find a mother for the brood of teenage vampire boys? To seek revenge against an uncaring creator? To capture the girl with the magic shoes?

Time! That's plenty of plotting—for now.

Back to characters.

Who is this monster likely to run up against? Who's going to be brave enough, smart enough, likely to happen by in your story's particular geographic location or fantastic milieu?

If your vampires live under a 1970s seaside boardwalk, your choices for a hero or heroine are going to be very different than those you would encounter in seventeeth-century Rumania or the merry, old land of Oz.

But not all heroes are chosen by geography or historical era. Sometimes careers predetermine monster and hero. If your story takes place on another planet, you're probably going to be dealing with astronauts and aliens. If your tale involves a ghost riding the cyberwaves of the Internet, chances are there's a computer geek somewhere nearby. If the people in your story are being mugged in back alleys and their internal organs removed while they were still using them, you can bet there's a doctor on call.

You know where your hero lives. You know that person's profession. Ready to return to plotting?

Nope. Don't. Not quite yet.

It's time to make a new best friend. Actually, a couple. It's time to get to know both your hero and your villain—painfully, intimately, well.

Borrow From Life

There are several ways to do this. One is to borrow a character from real life: your step-mom, your husband's boss, your second cousin's mechanic. This is a quick and easy path to characterization, and one fraught with peril. If real-lifers recognize themselves in story characters, and do not like what they see …

Best case scenario: You have a rift in the relationship.

Worst case: A libel suit.

Generally, I only use this technique when I'm in a hurry or I want to give a "gift" to a close friend or relative. I follow two strict rules. I take bad habits or character flaws only from myself. If I'm borrowing from anyone else, I play up the good side. My friends and relatives are almost always cast as good guys.

I had a tight deadline and was dealing with a family crisis when I was trying to write a story for the anthology *The Secret Prophecies of Nostradamus*. I had problems bringing my heroine to life. So I borrowed, very liberally, from … myself—and then exaggerated the characteristics on loan. Agent Charlie (don't ever call her Charlene) and I have the same taste in wine (though I don't drink as much as she). We both hate housework (though my bedroom isn't quite as messy as hers). And while I can be, let's say, "outspoken," Charlie can be downright rude. Of course, she's probably a little smarter, a little funnier, and a little braver than I am, too.

As a Christmas gift to the family, I once "cast" two cousins as the fictional audience to an old woman's storytelling. "The Princess and the Frog," a modern re-telling of the Cinderella story, can be found in *100 Wicked Little Witches*. Cuz One and Cuz Two provided nice dialogue and added depth and ambience to the story. And, the family still likes me.

I suggest you do not cast your mother-in-law as the bitchy, old neighbor lady. Don't cast your pastor as a demon from hell. And just to be on the safe side, don't cast your hometown as a generations-old warren for mangy, man-eating dogs. Not if you want to stay on good terms with family, friends, and neighbors.

Start a Picture File

Another way I sometimes develop my characters is to pull out "the picture file." I clip interesting pictures of people, from magazines mostly. My best sources are *Rolling Stone* (really creative photographers!) and *People* (because of its profiles of such, ah, "odd" human specimens). But sales catalogs and *Newsweek* have provided interesting photos, too. Certain snapshots present a fully realized, flesh-and-blood, full-of-attitude character. If you look closely, you can almost see the lips move as the pictures talk to you and the photographees tell you all about themselves. When I need a character, I'll flip through the pictures until one stops me to say, "I can take on that monster. Just give me a chance."

Those are the fairly easy ways. But when they don't pan out …

Create a Character Sketch

A third and usually reliable way to create a living, breathing character is to create a "character sketch."

I generally start with basic personality type: Joker. Class clown. Optimist. Pessimist. Rebel. Eco-warrior. Artist. Musician. Activist. Politician. Worrywart. Ant-sized self-esteem. Hippo-sized ego. Paranoid. Schizophrenic. Lovesick. Sick of love. Power-hungry. Computer nerd. Bimbo. Beauty queen.

Next, the name. Names can convey a great deal about the character. You didn't have the choice of your own name (at least, not way back then!), but you can pick your character's name. Make the choice count. Don't name your hero John Smith unless he's a Pilgrim or wallflower. Give him a nickname. You may never use it in the story, but nicknames do a good job of highlighting the essence of the character.

What does the character look like? Tall, short, skinny, fat? Truly attractive or double-ugly? What does the character think about how he looks? Do others agree?

These choices can lead to excellent plotting possibilities for the story. The character stands four feet, eight inches tall, the antidote is on the top shelf, and there's no chair or ladder in the locked room. How does she get it down? Or does she die trying?

What mode of transportation does the character use? Bicycle, moped, skateboard, el train, chauffeured limo? He drives a car? What make and model? A backfiring beater (two-tone job, primer, and rust) or that near-silent purring Jaguar? Does it have a nickname? Is it clean or messy?

Clothing: New, used, wrinkled, or torn, starched and pressed? Designer boutique, outlet mall, Am-Vets resale shop, or Aunt Gertrude hand-me-downs? Fashion: Anne Klein, Gothic, punk, corporate, or grunge? How long does it take to get ready in the morning? Quick because "I don't care how I look"? Or "I am obsessively efficient and manage my time well, thank you"?

Family history: The character needs a mom and dad with full names and occupations, even if *mater* and *pater* won't appear in the story. How does the character relate to these parents?

Best friend.

Hometown.

Hometown ... Time to ask some questions: Did you grow up there or did you move away? How do you feel about that? In what religion were you raised? Do you have a job, or a career? Either way—what, exactly—is it that you do? When you were a kid, what did you want to be "when you grew up"?

More questions: Where do you live? An apartment, condo, halfway house, mental ward, retirement village, high-rise, beach shack, abandoned car, or treehouse in your aunt's backyard? Oh, you share a houseboat with a cousin? A college dorm room with your best high school buddy?

Do you own, rent, live on the street, or crash in the back room of a pool hall?

What are the character's political leanings? What political issues press the hot buttons? How do you feel about gun control, abortion, environmental protection laws, peacekeeping forces sent to fight in other countries, draft registration, drinking age, welfare, Social Security, gay rights, feminism, assisted suicide?

Hobbies? Talents? (The latter might not play a part in the former.)

What kind of pet do you own? Chia pet or pit bull? What kind of pet would you like to own? Why do you hate pets? Are you allergic to them?

A general philosophy of life: Don't worry, be happy. Don't sweat the small stuff. Details, details, details. Be prepared. Be kind to others. Beware of strangers. Never trust anyone over thirty. You can't always get what you want. It's only rock and roll (but I like it). When the going gets tough, the tough go shopping. The one who dies with the most toys—wins. The one who dies is dead ....

The character's favorite music is _____.

This is one of the first questions I answer for my characters. Often, I give them a theme song or "theme band." A character who likes only classical music may be quite different from someone who worships Aretha Franklin, Bob Dylan, David Bowie, Joan Baez, Joan Jett, Thelonius Monk, The Who, The Go-Go's, Guns N' Roses, Hootie and the Blowfish, the Kingston Trio, or Captain and Tennille.

Eating well—or ... Eating? Well ... How and when your characters feed themselves will tell you a lot about them. Do they count calories or grams of fat? Do they cook gourmet meals or order pizzas delivered?

What's their favorite junk food? Which vegetables do they hate? Do they binge when they're unhappy or starve themselves before a date? What do they drink? Are they caffeine addicts or alcoholics? Do they carry Evian everywhere they go or drink milk right from the carton?

What do they do when they're upset? This is an important question. If you're writing horror, we must assume your characters will be upset, scared, frightened, or ticked off on a fairly regular basis. Do they listen to music, exercise until they're exhausted, yell, cry, brood, shadow box, make crank phone calls, play video games, strum the guitar, slam dance, write nasty letters, call Grandpa, break pencils, smash dishes, punch holes in walls?

Now the fun part.

Give your characters flaws. Lots and lots of flaws. (Just like us real-lifers!)

Are they messy, neat freaks, grumpy in the morning, grumpy all the time? Can't remember names, always hopelessly lost?

You say you are jealous of others, you hate dogs, you're rude to strangers? You hang out in biker bars, read horror books instead of doing housework, have no table manners, burp in public, can't color coordinate your clothes. You're so clumsy that friends won't let you in the house. Why are you always losing your keys? You sing off key, snore, sleepwalk. You're stingy, always overdrawn, generous to a fault. You won't answer the phone and there is a stupid message on your answering machine.

What is the character's worst habit? What is the character's worst habit—in his own opinion?

What does he do that drives others crazy?

What is he afraid of: airplanes, heights, dogs, snakes? Enclosed places, exposed places, dying while asleep, dying while awake, dying and being dead? Monsters under the bed, monsters in the bed? The building collapsing in an earthquake, a meteor flattening the house, an inferno raging through a high-rise?

Be sure to spend as much time giving your bad guys *good traits* as you do giving your good guys *bad traits*. A bad guy with no redeeming qualities is no fun to beat. And a good guy who can't lose is no fun to root for.

By now, you should have a two- or three-page character sketch.

Am I going to use all this stuff?

Of course not.

So why'd I do all this work?

To get to know your character. At some point, you should have stopped making up random answers to those questions and the character should have started answering for himself. Your character has attitudes and opinions, a philosophy and bad habits, moods, and a physique.

Your character should be talking back to you by now, which is what character sketch work is all about.

Listen to Your Characters

That's a lot of work for one story!

Yes, it is. And in the beginning, I did it for each major character in every story I wrote. I don't have to do it for every character anymore because I'm now in the habit of asking those questions, almost subconsciously, so the details come to me without having to put it all down on paper.

But when I get stuck—when a character refuses to talk to me—I pull out that list and start interviewing the shy character.

And now, finally, back to plotting.

Only now, you aren't doing it by yourself. Your hero and your villain are sitting beside you. Your villain throws up an obstacle and your hero tells you how he will overcome it. Your villain observes your hero's weaknesses and fights dirty! Your hero cleverly finds a way to turn his own weaknesses into strengths, spies the villain's fatal flaw, and devises a plan that cannot be beat.

But your villain beats it.

Your hero learns from his mistake and comes up with an even better plan! As a writer, your job is not that of *master puppeteer*.

It's more like *office stenographer*.

Once you've created your characters, trust them. They will whisper in your ear and tell you what they need to do. Even if what they suggest wreaks havoc with all your plots and plans, listen to them!

For my story "Preacherman Gets the Blues" in the anthology *Phantoms of the Night*, I had carefully created a character sketch of: my heroine, a single mother who runs a haunted blues club; my anti-hero, a young and cocky guitar player; and my villain, a demon from hell. I listened to them as I plotted the story.

But as I was plotting "Preacherman," two minor characters—a grizzled, old, barfly used-to-be-musician and the ten-year-old daughter of the club owner—teamed up and told me they knew how to save the day. They were only supposed to have a couple lines each; I'd merely tossed them in for atmosphere and color. They took over the story—and wrote a far better one than I had outlined on paper.

Listen to your characters. It pays off.

Use Anecdotal Evidence

Once your plotting is done and it's time to start writing, you will, of course, refer to your character sketches. You're looking for voice and details. But don't drop chunks of your character sketch into the story like a brick into a fishbowl.

Yiri the vampire was a shy type whose motto was "never trust anyone over three hundred."

Don't tell us. Show us. That's why you did all that work—so you know your creations well enough to provide anecdotal evidence instead of surface observations.

To return to "Preacherman Gets the Blues:" Suzy establishes that she's ten years old, has blonde hair and blue eyes, and was raised in the night club, getting to know some of the greatest blues musicians in Chicago. Her nickname is Little Mustang. She's precocious and racially colorblind (her best friend is an old, black man who frequents the club). She helps her mom out in the bar and wants to be a blues musician some day.

But those are just surface observations. They have to be turned into anecdotal evidence. Here's how we first meet Little Mustang:

> Her daughter came bounding over to the waitress station and climbed up on a bar stool.
>
> "Hey, Little Mustang!" The grizzled patron winked at her over his snifter.
>
> "Hey, yourself, Old George!"
>
> Old George let out a laugh that was equal parts wheeze and chuckle.
>
> Sarah shook her head. "Sweetheart, put out the ashtrays will you?"
>
> "—kay, Mom."
>
> Sarah smiled as her daughter grabbed the stacks of ashtrays and started distributing them to each table, stopping to greet the regulars.
>
> At ten years old, Mustang's nose barely reached the rail of the bar when she stood up. Sarah had bought the club while she was pregnant. Unable to afford a sitter, she took the child to work with her. Mustang had grown up on the knees of the blues greats Buddy Guy, Koko Taylor, Son Seals, Junior Wells.

They'd played checkers with her between sets, sung her lullabies, even changed her diapers in an emergency. When the musicians weren't playing with Mustang, Jayhawk was. And if the baby started fussing in the middle of a set, all the band had to do was break into a rendition of "Mustang Sally." It calmed her down and put her right to sleep every time. Sarah had named her daughter Suzy, but she doubted if even Suzy remembered that.

If you do your research up front, getting to know your characters until they are truly living, breathing people, the rest of the writing process is easy.

Wooden puppets may seem easier to work with, but they're stiff and brittle, and they tend to break when it comes to issues of believability. That's when you lose your readers.

If you know your characters as well as you knew your best friend in high school, every secret dream and desire, every pimple, every wart, then your characters will be as loyal and devoted as your high school buddy. Trust them and there's no writing obstacle that they can't help you overcome. They'll lead you back to the plot when you wander off the trail; they'll lower a rope ladder to you when you paint yourself into a plot corner; and they'll goad you back to your computer and nag you to finish their story when you're being lazy and watching football on the couch.

Know and trust your characters. They will stick by you every step of the way.

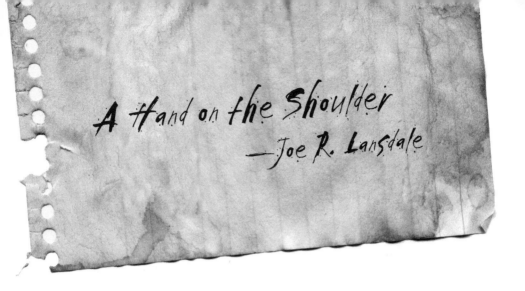

A Hand on the Shoulder
—Joe R. Lansdale

In writing, if you're truly connected to a region, sense of place is like a friendly hand on your shoulder.

Recently, I was on vacation in Aruba, an island off the coast of Venezuela, and I was working on a story in my head.

I was sitting on the hotel patio in the sunshine listening to the roar of the ocean, feeling the cool, blasting winds that constantly pummel Aruba, watching palm trees sway, and I was thinking about a hot, humid, pine-tree littered, sandy soil, clay road region back in Texas.

East Texas to be exact.

I was born and have lived in East Texas most all my life. (People from this region generally spell East with a capital instead of a small letter. It's almost like a separate state.) I haven't always written about East Texas, but mostly. And without a doubt, my best work has taken place there.

First off, it is so unlike most of Texas. More Southern in background, with tall trees, creeks, and rivers. It's a little like Louisiana in appearance; maybe not so swampy. There's something unique about it, mysterious even.

It's a land of people, black and white and brown—mixed cultures. East Texas, though Southern in nature with a strong influence of black culture and a way of talking more akin to Louisiana and Tennessee than Dallas or West Texas is also strongly influenced by Mexican culture, remnants of American Indian culture, Old Spain, and Cajun culture from across the Louisiana border. It's the home of country music and country boogie.

Hot country, where in the dead of summer, the heat falls down on your head like a wool sweater drenched in sweat and rests on your shoulders like an anvil. And when you walk, it's like wading through molasses wearing concrete boots. Air conditioners hum in homes and stores constantly, and East Texans air-condition with a vengeance. In an instant, you can go from feeling as if you're frying in lard to feeling like you're inside a meat locker.

It seeps into your writing. A land like this—thick in contrast, mixed with so many fine cultural wines and a strong sense of good ol' Texas individualism— produces a unique character for both region and individual. A land like this, a culture like this, can brighten or darken your writerly vision from one moment to the next.

East Texas is a place where hyperbole, wild metaphors, and bouncing similes spurt forth from the mouths of locals like the nasty matter that runs through a goose after it's had its dinner.

This is my region. A region the rest of our state refers to as being "behind the pine curtain."

Good and bad, East Texas has influenced the way I write.

My point is, I didn't know this until about ten years ago, and as I said, I've lived here all my life. Writers, most of us, really don't recognize the gold mine when we're in it. We stand there with our pick and shovel, we look about, and though the walls glow brightly with strains of gold, we squint our eyes against the light, reach down, and pick up iron pyrites instead of gold.

Finding a Unique Voice

So many beginning writers ignore their background and region and try to write about places far away: places that sound exotic. Places often written about, filmed, and glamorized.

I tried this myself. But what I soon realized was that while there's no crime in writing about places you don't know—I've done it and will probably do it again— there certainly is much to be gained by writing about what you *do* know.

When I sit down to write about East Texas, I'm comfortable that the language I use is correct. It's my language. It's unique to my region.

My descriptions reflect what I see every day. I don't need a research book to see what pine trees look like or to identify mockingbirds on a barbed-wire fence. My themes reflect what I see, what I feel, what I smell, what I touch every day—good and bad—and my writing glows with a brighter intensity than if I were writing about people in New York or Los Angeles or Ohio, those who talk differently than I do, have different daily experiences, and, for the most part, are culturally different.

I'm certainly not promoting division between regions. But I am trying to express the fact that whichever region you live in, that is your background and your voice, and I truly believe that is also your style—the one thing most writers find so elusive. It is my belief that the majority of writers never really find their true voices or their styles. Only the rare ones do. Writers like Ray Bradbury, Pete Hamill, Elmore Leonard, Harry Crews. They have voices unique to, not only their respective regions, but to themselves.

All writers are regional writers; we all come from some region. But not all writers recognize this. It might also be said that even those writers who do have the good fortune to spot this are not always able to open their eyes and ears enough to profit from their observation.

Think about it. Voice is found not only in your experiences, but where you live and how you live. You've got to get in touch with that. And when you do, the language leaps, the characters breathe, and themes run beneath the floor of your story like underground rivers.

If the land you live on is rolling hills, it affects the way you walk. If the weather is hot, making it necessary to move slowly, this affects how you walk and how you talk. There is evidence that linguistics affect how a person thinks because a word picture may not be the same to a Southerner as it is to an Easterner or a Northerner, even if the words used to create that picture are the same. The way words are spoken or employed changes the speaker's perceptions.

If the roads you drive down are bordered by tall, dark trees or by huge, concrete structures and shoulder-to-shoulder sidewalk traffic, this affects how you view the world and how you see yourself in that world.

Books as Characters

When you write, who you are invariably finds its way onto the page—not necessarily reflected in the nature of the characters, though that can certainly be true as well, but reflected instead in the character of the writing. Writers who are able to tap into their environment, their cultural roots, are generally those writers who actually turn the book itself into a kind of character.

Giving important, fine examples of how place affects style and description is James Lee Burke. When you read his books about Louisiana, you can taste the gumbo and the dirty rice, hear the rivers run, and smell the stink of dead fish, putrid swamp mud, and the scent of sweet flowers on the wind.

Even if the plot fades, you remember the characters, and I believe, even above that, you remember the character of the novel itself. Rank and ripe, sweet and sour.

Other examples: Neal Barrett, Jr. and his small communities and neighborhoods. Even when Barrett writes about cities, he has a small-town vision of those cities: a rubbernecker from the sticks who may not be as sophisticated as some, but, like Flannery O'Connor, still knows "weird" when he sees it.

And, of course, Flannery O'Connor, Faulkner, all the Southern writers I'm particularly fond of. You may well remember the characters in the works of all these writers, not simply because they are all masters of character, but because each has something very special and rare. They are masters at presenting *the book* as a character.

This particular trait comes out of a writer who is in touch with his or her environment. The land. The people. The weather. I suppose you might say, unlike so many books and stories, these writings don't have pages that stink of the library with the obvious feeling of research from afar.

In this respect, all great writers—regardless of what region they write about—are the same. They write best about what they know, where they live, or where they have been.

They bring to their books personal visions designed by different backgrounds. And consequently, due to this ability, their books become characters.

Telling the Truth

Let me mention another environment: the one inside your head. The one that's full of your life's experiences, your passions, your basic instincts. That ole primitive brain. Getting in touch with your internal environment, letting the delights and the disappointments of your life seep their way into your writing, personalizes it.

You don't necessarily have to tell the truth. As fiction writers, we're all liars. Tell the truth as you see it. Cut open the emotional apple and find the core, not the skin. It's not the event, it's how you feel about the event. If you can get there—to the inner core—you can interject these feelings into the work, even if the scenes you're writing have nothing to do with the actual incidents of your life.

This way, you're writing a lie, but you're telling a greater truth.

A truth nonfiction can't tell.

What I'm suggesting here is environment as writing teachers—both internal and external environment. Herein lies the secret to fiction that's chewable, inhalable (and not even illegal), in 3-D and Touchathon.

Words that glow. Sentences that writhe with excitement. Paragraphs that shine like the sun.

Think about it, and realize that your own region, as well as the region inside your head, is a wealth of ideas. The source for your voice and your individuality.

Write what you truly know.

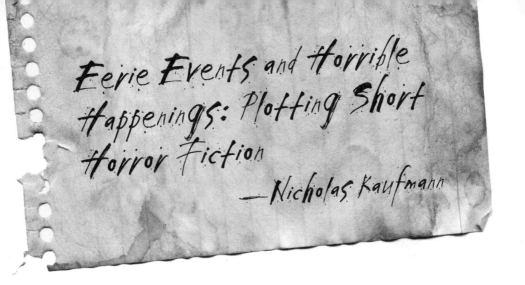

Eerie Events and Horrible Happenings: Plotting Short Horror Fiction
—Nicholas Kaufmann

What We Talk About
When We Talk About Plot

Ask a friend to tell you the plot of a favorite story, and what you're likely to hear is a sequence of the story's events, often boiled down to a sentence or two. "It's about this woman whose basement is filling up with mud, but it's not really mud, it's some weird creature that eats everything it touches. Only she can't get out of the house because ..." For the reader, that's a plot: the story's movement from point *A* to point *B* to point *C*, set-up from conflict to resolution. For the writer, though, there are mechanics involved that make plotting more complicated than a simple sequence of events.

Plot is comprised not only of *what* is happening but also *why* and *to whom.* With that in mind, let's cook a sample stew using these three different yet symbiotic ingredients to show how *premise, internal logic,* and *character* all work together to help create the best possible plot for your story.

What's the Big Idea?

For our purposes, let's say your latest story idea comes from a "what-if" scenario that's grabbed your fancy and refuses to let go. *You go down to your basement and see a puddle of mud on the dirt floor. The next day it's a little bigger. Obviously, there's a leak somewhere, so you call a plumber to check it out.*

But this situation has started itching at your "writer's nerve:" What if it's *not* just a leak? What if the puddle is growing *on purpose*? What if it's not mud at all—but something *alive* that's coming up through the floor? What does it want?

Of course, a horror writer's mind tends to jump toward the extreme when looking for motivation: Its natural feeding grounds deep within the earth have been destroyed by subway construction, so it's angry, it's hungry, and it's looking for something—anything—to eat. (In fact, you've already chosen its first victim: the plumber who just told you it'll be three weeks before the parts arrive to fix your leak and, by the way, he needs an exorbitant, non-refundable deposit right now ....)

There you have your story concept.

You've developed the basic premise, but you still must shape it into a coherent and satisfying narrative. You're also working in the short form, not a novel, and that comes with its own certain restrictions and necessities. Novels give you thousands and thousands of words to tell a story to its fullest, including long character arcs and interwoven subplots. Short stories give you a lot less space/time/word count to work with, and these limitations will inform every plotting decision you make.

Such as where to start.

Raising the Curtain

If this were a novel, you could open by providing a chapter or two leading up to the crucial scene of the discovery in the basement in order to acclimate your readers to the world you've created. You could show your protagonist working out at the gym, going out on a date, staying away from her office window because she's afraid of heights—whatever aspects and experiences of her daily life that would help readers get to know her better. In a short story, such scenes are sacrificed if not directly related to the central premise. If you open with a critical scene, such as our heroine finding a mysterious pool of mud in the cellar, there's a much greater likelihood that your readers will be pulled into the story than if you start with something insignificant that may drive them away before turning to page two.

That's not to say you have to open with an action scene or punchy dialogue. But you'd do well to begin as close to the main conflict as possible.

Though not *too* close. A buildup of suspense is one of the most important elements in horror fiction. While you cannot drag your feet with needless scenes or chit-chat dialogue, neither do you want to rush things.

You might launch your story with the mud having already filled up the entire basement and swallowed the plumber, but it's far creepier to show the mud growing mysteriously over time *before* the plumber kicks the bucket. You want to find a starting place *close* enough to the action to be compelling but *distant* enough to allow for suspense; that's a delicate (and difficult) balance to strive for in every story.

This principle applies to the rest of your story, too: Each scene needs to be directly linked to your premise. There would be no point to our heroine taking a break from running from the mud monster in order to phone for Chinese takeout, right? Consider any scene that you know is not vital to the story (no matter how brilliantly rendered you consider it to be) as a "phoning for take-out" scene—and then cut it.

The Big, Scary "Now What?"

You've already got your knock-'em-dead idea and can't-put-it-down opening, so … gulp … now what? Your story needs to have a coherent beginning, middle, and end. The events that bridge the space between set-up and resolution can often be the trickiest.

The best way to figure out the middle is two-fold. First, what would your protagonist *logically* do? Even if she's a nutcase, there must still be internal and consistent logic to her actions. Will she get out of the house the minute the plumber disappears, or will she stick around and try to learn what happened to him?

Second, what *needs* to happen next in order to advance the story? You don't want your protagonist immediately figuring out what's going on and scramming to safety, because then you don't have much of a tale to tell. At the same time, you don't want her to be such a foolish plot-puppet that your readers give up in disgust. Your protagonist's sensible, rational next steps should mesh perfectly with what needs to occur to advance the story toward its climax. For that to happen, you need to give serious thought to whom you're writing about.

Using Your Characters to Plot Your Story

Let's face it, when you boil a horror story down to its basic elements, it can sound ridiculous: "Woman vs. deadly mud monster—who will survive?" That's because we don't know anything about the woman in question. If our mud monster simply appears in Jane Everywoman's house, it won't be nearly as compelling as if it comes calling at the home of someone whose life will be the most affected by its invasion—even if she manages to escape.

You may want to choose a character who has the most to lose. Maybe our heroine is a rare art collector, and the idea of abandoning her priceless *objets d'art* to the rising mud ("The Mud munched my Monet!") is as much an abomination to her as the mud itself. Or maybe there's something of sentimental value she refuses to leave behind, say, the ring given her by her husband on his deathbed.

There! You've given her motivation *not* to flee the house immediately. She *must* retrieve that priceless/irreplaceable/precious item, but the mud—it's a comin'! It's rising from the cellar and up to the main floor. Will she make it back in time from where she keeps the ring in the second floor study or will she find the human-gobbling mud already pooling (hungrily) at the foot of the staircase?

Because your character's life now stands to be irrevocably changed by that conflict, you've not only given yourself a logical path for the sequence of events to follow, but a nice chunk of narrative tension to play with, too.

You might instead take the opposite approach and choose a character who has the most to *gain* from the events unfolding around her. Maybe our protagonist is no heroine at all. Maybe she's borderline bonkers, driven to wits' end by the insufferably bossy, wheelchair-bound mother-in-law who recently moved in with her.

The mud now becomes something more than a threat—it becomes a tool. If the protagonist does nothing to stop it, why, maybe it just might devour Mama-in-law, just like it did the plumber. No one would know her complicity, everyone would think her mother-in-law was just another victim, and she'd get off scot-free.

Again, this character choice maps out a lot of what will happen between set-up and resolution. Will she have time to position her mother-in-law's wheelchair in front of the oncoming wave of mud and still escape without being devoured herself? This adds narrative tension as well, though in a manner quite different from our previous example. Whether your readers root for her or not, whether they hope she escapes or pays muddily for her injustice, they'll definitely want to know what happens.

"Such Horrible People," Tina Jens's chapter in this book, offers many suggestions for creating complex, full-grown horror story characters. To emphasize (not repeat!) her point: If your characters are ciphers, uninteresting people who exist only so plot can happen *to* them, you'll find yourself getting stuck a lot more in plotting the story than if you create compelling characters who have something to lose or gain from their predicaments.

Plot Overload

When you're uncertain about "what happens next" in the tricky middle section of a story, there's often a temptation to overload the plot with too many events or conflicts in order to maintain a feeling of momentum. There's a Mean Mr. Mud in the basement—but uh-oh, there's also a nasty ghost in the attic! Well, unless that ghost is not only tied *directly* into the mud's arrival but also the resolution, it has no place in the attic, the basement, or even the story, for that matter.

Short stories usually focus on a single main conflict told over a necessarily short time span: The mud is rising, she has to get out of the house and not get eaten in the process. Though Raymond Chandler famously advised, "… if the plot flags, bring in a man with a gun," anything outside the scope of your premise—ghosts, meteors, rabid dogs, demon dust balls from outer space—will only serve to unravel the tightness of the plot, play havoc with internal logic, and shatter the reader's suspension of disbelief. They are distractions, the equivalent of the "phoning-for-takeout" scenes mentioned earlier.

Wrapping It Up

The ending you choose is up to you—she survives, she dies, she lures all her enemies to mud monster doom—but in order for it to be satisfying, the end absolutely *must* grow out of the main conflict.

Here's an example of an ending that doesn't: Our heroine hides upstairs as the mud level rises. There's not much time and ... the phone rings. Turns out her husband isn't dead after all; he faked it *because he's a spy*. The End! I think an ending like that would leave readers scratching their heads, don't you? Not that they'd get the chance to read it, since no one would probably publish such a story.

Another bad example: Our heroine upstairs and the mud ... you know. Then the sun goes down. At last she can turn into a bat and safely fly out of the house. See, she's a vampire! Get it? The End!

An ending that defies expectation and adds a new twist can make for a memorable story, but please remember, I said *twist*, not *gimmick*. The gimmick, that which is utterly unexpected because there has not been even a telepathic hint of its possibility, risks totally blowing the suspension of disbelief and ruining all your previous hard work.

Or, any ending that smacks of "it was all a dream" is even *worse* than our oft-cited "phoning for takeout."

Because your ending needs to wrap up all loose plot threads, keeping the plot tight makes doing so a lot easier. The end of your story should provide the climax and denouement so as not to leave behind any dangling threads.

In our example, the climax would probably be a final do-or-die confrontation between Heroine and Mud Monster. Seems Big Muddy is afraid of fire (the mud will bake and turn into an abstarct scuplture from Intro to Pottery 101) and, so, our heroine must sacrifice her home and everything in it. The denouement is what happens *after* the climax. Does she survive? What will her life be like now?

In short stories, the denouement is by necessity very short—if it's even there at all. We don't have the time (or the desire, really) to see our heroine talking with real estate agents and shopping for new digs after her life-changing encounter. We need only see her walking away from the wreckage of her house to know that real estate adventures await her down the road.

Although, maybe next time she'll rent a twentieth-floor apartment—instead of a house with a basement ....

Reality and the Waking Nightmare: Setting and Character in Horror Fiction
—Mort Castle

Lose Your Imagination

Undoubtedly, you have had the experience of picking up a novel at the end of the day, promising yourself you'll read a chapter before going to sleep, and then …

A surprised glance at the clock. It's five in the morning! Huh? What happened? You had taken no notice of time passing, not here in the real world—RealityLand. Instead, your time became the time of your novel, with perhaps a day depicted in thirteen pages or eleven months, flashing by in just three tightly constructed paragraphs. Nor while time passed on Earth were you thinking about such here-and-now concerns like the cluster of mosquito bites on your forearm, that difficult choice between paying the car repair bill or the pediatrician's child-repair bill, or your chances of winning the lottery.

As you read, your body occupied space in RealityLand—but you, the thinking, feeling, imagining, real you, were literally somewhere else. You were walking the suburban streets or city alleys, the forest paths or sandy beaches of a fictional world as you shared the adventures and thoughts and emotions of that world's people, people you had come to know and to care about. The late John Gardner, a fine writer and teacher of writing, called fiction a "waking dream." When you sleep and dream, you experience the dream as real. And when you enter the waking dream of a well-written short story or novel, it is just as real.

Of course, you're reading this because you are interested in creating not waking dreams, but waking nightmares. ("Daymares" is the term commonly used by some horror fans and a few writers, but I don't care for it—too cute!) You want to set spines a-shivering and souls a-shaking—and sometimes stomachs a-spasming.

How do you do that?

Perhaps you expect me to answer my own rhetorical question by saying something like, "Use your imagination. Dredge up the dreads in the dusty corners and subbasements of the brain. Set free the imagination to go on a scythe-swinging, chainsaw-slashing, Roto-Rootering rampage—and you've got a horror story." Sorry. Imagination will give you an idea for a horror story, but you're a long way from having the waking nightmare that will envelop and encompass readers.

The Reality Base

It's reality's "what is," not the imagination's "what if?" that can transform horror premise into horror story. It takes reality, heaps of it, to create and populate a story realm that gives readers the frights royale. It takes settings that have the reality of Lincoln, Nebraska; Tucson, Arizona; or Grenada, Mississippi. It takes breathing, thinking, feeling, story folks who are as real as your Uncle Albert, who always gets drunk and sentimental at family reunions; as real as Mr. Schlechter, your high school English teacher, who nearly flunked you for not handing in your term paper on "Washington Irving's Use of the Comma in *Rip Van Winkle*;" as real as your first puppy-love paramour or your last meaningful-relationship partner.

Good fiction, by definition, is credible. It is a lie that can be believed. Readers should be able to say of a contemporary or mainstream work of fiction, "Yes, given these circumstances, this could actually happen." Readers should be able to say that of a Western, romance, mystery, suspense, or you-name-it work of fiction.

And readers must be able to say of a story of the supernatural, the paranormal, the occult, the horrific, the weird, the wild, and the off-the-wall, "Given these circumstances, this could actually happen"—if they are to enter into and be held by a waking nightmare. The key to credibility in fright-fantasy fiction is *setting* and *character*. Your readers, after all, are already meeting you more than halfway, as they implicitly agree, "I want to be scared—and so I choose to willingly suspend disbelief in order to accept your imaginative premise. A manacle-rattling, saber-waving, or ice cream cone-licking ghost, a *were*wolf, *were*panther, *were*bear, *were*whatever, a two-hundred-year-old transvestite vampire who needs root canal work on his fangs ... okay, I'll go with that. I'll stretch my credulity that far ..."

But that's it! With one such leap of imagination/acceptance of the incredible, readers have given you all you have any right to expect. That means everything else in your waking nightmare must be true enough to life so that readers never say, "Uh-uh, I'm being lied to."

What's "everything else"?

Everything else = *setting* and *characters*. (Okay, fiction has setting, characters, and plot! Correct. But if your principal characters respond to their problem/conflict situations in credible ways, plot happens almost automatically. Besides, other people have chapters on plotting!)

Write What You Know

How do you make settings real? Bring out the old chestnut: Write about what you know.

It's hardly a surprise that Robert McCammon's evocative and frightening-as-hell novel *Mystery Walk* is set in Dixie. A graduate of the University of Alabama, living in Birmingham, Alabama, McCammon knows the territory.

J.N. Williamson often chooses Indianapolis, Indiana, as the setting for his fictive frights. Indy born, Hoosier-dwelling, sure to get all worked up over the Indy 500, Williamson knows Indianapolis and depicts it so you feel as if you know it, too.

A Maine native, Stephen King has lived in Castle Rock and Salem's Lot—even if those towns have other names on the auto club map.

I've lived in Crete, Illinois, one of Chicago's south suburbs, for nearly twenty years. I slide behind the wheel of my Ford Escort, and within twenty minutes, I'm strolling through Lincoln Mall, an under-one-roof shopping center that always smells of caramel corn; or Prairie State College, which in two years can provide you an associate's degree in English or air-conditioning repair; or Suburban Heights Medical Center, a modern facility with a large staff who are rightly termed professional health care workers. I can drive through Park Forest, a long-established, middle-class, planned community; or Ford Heights, as poverty-stricken and dangerous a ghetto as you shouldn't be able to find in our proverbial land of plenty; or Swiss Valley, where my poor compact car's ego sputters and dies as we pass driveways in which are parked Cadillacs, Mercedes-Benzes, and Jaguars.

You can understand, then, how I came up with a suburb called Park Estates for the setting of my horror novel, *The Strangers*. You know why my protagonist's wife signed up for a psychology class at Lincoln State College. You now have the inside info on the protagonist's daughter, struck by a car, winding up in the emergency room of the South Suburban Medical Center. Here's a brief passage from *The Strangers*:

> Two Park Estates Police Department officers and the paramedics arrived without sirens, their whirling lights fragmenting the neighborhood into coldly iridescent expressionist objects and angles: a birdbath, jumping shadows cast by the limb of a tree, an advertising circular blowing across a lawn, the eyes of a prowling cat ....

To write that, I employed *zero* imagination. Instead, I relied on memory and knowledge, and found words to convey to my readers what I see every day.

I hear a protest: "But I live in North Nowhere, Kansas, three churches, four taverns, and a trailer park. Our big cultural event is the annual VFW show when the guys dress up as women. How's a fictionalized North Nowhere to grab and keep a reader's interest?"

Sorry, I still maintain that North Nowhere is interesting—if you set out to discover the interest, that is. Maybe I'm not exactly a wild-and-crazy guy, but

I note all sorts of "local color" events in Crete that grab me (and, when fiction-alized a bit, often wind up in my writing): The eclectic Old Town Restaurant adds something new to a menu that already offers Mexican burritos, Chinese egg rolls, Italian ravioli, and Greek dolmaches; Crete Hardware has a sign, "Thanks for your patronage for the past 30 years," not because the store is going out of business or anything, but just to say thanks; the high school's cheerleaders slow traffic at the Main-and-Exchange intersection (the town's only stoplight), by holding a "Sucker Day" to raise money for new uniforms.

Granted, reality-based settings are prosaic and commonplace. The very ordi-nariness of such settings work for you in two ways.

First, readers are familiar with the ordinary; they live there. Readers relate to the ordinary without your having to work at establishing that relationship. And thus, readers will find your settings credible, as they must.

Then, if you have an ominous, thickly atmospheric setting—the phosphorescent-fog-shrouded swamp, the torture chamber of a crumbling castle, the burial ground of a satanic church—you will be hard pressed to spring a surprise on your readers, who anticipate an awful or nasty occurrence in such foreboding places.

But ...

Summer. A few minutes past sunrise. Birchwood Lane, a quiet suburban street. Mailbox on the corner. A parkway torn up to repair a broken sewer file. A squirrel zips up a tree, fleeing a gray tomcat ...

Ho-hum, humdrum ... until something sinuous, gleaming with slime, slith-ers from the mailbox's "in" slot ...

Or ...

The squirrel, safe on a limb, chatters defiance at the cat below .... and then, from the thick leaves behind the squirrel, a furry arm shoots out and a knobby-knuckled, four-fingered hand encircles the squirrel's neck ...

When the ordinary is invaded by the terrifyingly extraordinary, horror happens.

And thus, it is the intrusion of the extraordinary—the appalling unusual into the lives of ordinary, credible, for-real characters—that makes for compel-ling shock fiction.

People Like Us

A good horror story character is a fictional someone who is every bit as alive and as much a unique individual as anyone we really know really well out here in RealityLand. He must be for readers to care about him. If readers don't care, they will not give a rap about what the character does or what happens to him.

Your readers can like or dislike, love or hate a character—but you can never allow readers to feel only indifference toward him.

To illustrate this idea: Like you, I read the newspaper obituaries. I note the passing of eighty-two-year-old Lorinda Strudel, for four decades the third-chair viola with the Peoria Semi-Symphonic, or the demise of Andre Shutdehans, inventor of the pocket fruit juicer (no batteries needed)—and then I turn to the horoscopes or sports section.

I don't know these dead people.

They mean nothing to me.

But I can still remember, remember so well, how I felt when I learned Jack Benny had died. Jack Benny, the fictional comic persona, whose money vault inspired Scrooge McDuck, who drove that sputtering Maxwell, who could turn "Well!" into a bust-your-gut laugh line, who was immortally thirty-nine forever. Jack Benny, the man, the philanthropist, the concert violinist. Jack Benny, who visited my living room once a week on CBS, channel two, when the TV world was still in black and white and owned by only a very few networks.

And so, Jack Benny died, and there was that scraped-out feeling within me, that gone-forever, hurting emptiness that is personal loss. Jack Benny. I knew him better than I knew a number of my relatives: He was a nice man and a good man, and he made me laugh.

The real world of your waking nightmare must be inhabited by characters your readers know.

And that means you had better know those characters. How well?

You've not only fathered and mothered these characters, you've been their closest confidant as well as their psychiatrist. There is nothing they've kept hidden from you, including things they might have been able to keep hidden from themselves.

That's how well you know them.

That's how well I know my important characters, anyway. My readers might never need to know if my protagonist prefers real mayo to Miracle Whip, if his first car was a cherry-red '67 Ford Mustang, if he likes Willie Nelson's songs but can't stand looking at him, if he had a pet collie named Lizzie when he was five, etc., but I have to know if I am to present this character as a three-dimensional, well-rounded human being, as I must.

In "And of Gideon," my novelette in the John Maclay-edited collection *Nukes: Four Horror Writers on the Ultimate Horror*, my protagonist, Gideon, is a murderous psychopath. I wanted my readers to fear Gideon, to realize anew that such human aberrations do exist. I wanted my readers to pity him as well—this loser who'd been "programmed for pathology."

But more than that, I wanted readers to see Gideon as a credible human be-ing, one who would elicit the widest range of emotional response that only real people can evoke.

Here is some of what I knew about Gideon and what I wanted readers to know:

> … my father a drunk, had no love for my mother, another drunk, she none for
> him, and neither for me. [From] my early years, I cannot recall a single hug …
> My father would beat me, not with the flat of his hand or a belt but with his
> fists. In kindergarten, I could not color within the lines, could not catch a basket-

ball thrown to me from a distance of two feet, nor hang by my knees from the monkey bars …. I was always in trouble: for not coming to school on time; for not even trying on tests; for not doing this, for not doing that; always in trouble with the teachers, those despairing head-shakers, "Gideon, don't you want to learn? Don't you want to amount to anything? Don't you want to grow up and be somebody?"

Because your characters must have their own distinct personalities—just as you are the "One and Only You and Nobody Else," you cannot people your story with stereotypes. Your credible fiction is based on reality, and if you've ever been friends with a truck driver in RealityLand, you realize there's so much more to him than can be described by "Truck-Driver Type," more to the wife-beating drunk than "Wife-Beating Drunk Type," and way more to you than simply "Serious-Writer Type." Stereotypes aren't permitted to have unique personalities as do real people; they are limited in thought, emotion, and action by the terribly confining mold which created them.

In an earlier era, we had such stereotypes, offensive generalizations thinly disguised as human beings, as the Irish cop with the whiskey nose and the "Faith and Begorra" accent, and the shuffling African-American who, eyes-rolling, yelled, "Feets, do yo' stuff!" when confronted by "them haints." You can think of many others, I'm sure. I'm afraid horror fiction these days has its own stereotypes: The Ugly Duckling with the Paranormal Wild Talent; The Dedicated Psychic Researcher, so icily intellectual that he continues to take copious notes as Satan's personal imps disembowel him; The Catholic Priest Suffering Doubt; The Twins, One Good—the Other, Evil; The Yokel Preacher, who speaks in tongues and would quote more frequently from the Bible if it didn't have so many multi-syllabic words; The Helpless Female, who, although she is the vice-president of a New York advertising agency, nonetheless is totally incapable of dealing with a supernatural menace.

Don't use any of them! (Not that I'm being dogmatic …) Instead, apply that previously mentioned writing rule: Write about what you know. You know people. You have been a "practicing people" ever since you were born. That makes you a people expert!

You know what you think/how you feel when someone you counted on lets you down, so you know what your story character thinks/feels when someone he's counted on does the same. You have experienced disappointment, joy, hate, love, and so you can create credible characters who grapple with those same emotions. You've been embarrassed, you've felt pride, you have felt everything a human being can feel.

Your characters, animated by your knowledge of self, others, and the world, given your breath of reality as vital force, and placed in authenticity-imbued settings, will spring to life on the page.

They will hold out a welcoming hand … and yank readers into your waking nightmare—and keep them there!

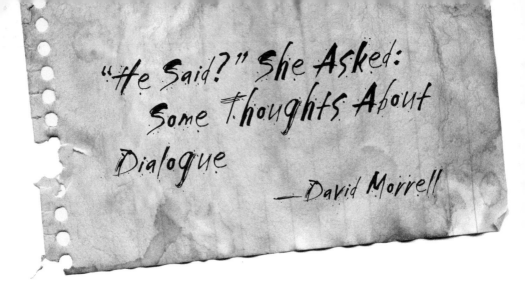

"He Said?" She Asked: Some Thoughts About Dialogue

—David Morrell

The principles of writing effective dialogue in horror fiction are basically the same as those for writing dialogue in any other type of fiction, with the exception that some horror writers need to make a more rigorous effort to avoid tilting their dialogue into melodrama. How to create first-rate dialogue is not something that can be taught, but the reverse applies when it comes to showing someone how to avoid the common mistakes that lead to dialogue that isn't acceptable.

So many errors come to mind that I'm going to choose one arbitrarily: the use of names in dialogue.

> "Jane, I'm going downtown to the library," Dick said.
> "Okay, Dick, I'll see you later," Jane said.

The needlessness of the repetition should be obvious, and yet I see writers repeating names all the time. Because the speech tags indicate which character is speaking, it isn't necessary, within the dialogue, to include the name of the person being addressed. Perhaps someone might object that names need to be included in dialogue for the sake of verisimilitude, to imitate the way we speak in life. The problem is that, for the most part, we do not in fact speak this way. Try an experiment. Listen to conversations with no other purpose than that of noting how often people say each other's names. It seldom happens.

Good Dialogue Imitates Life

As near as I can guess, many writers throw names into dialogue whenever they can because they're not imitating dialogue in life; they're imitating dialogue in the movies. On the screen, names have to be said often—at least a couple of times in each sequence—in order to identify the characters. But fiction writing isn't movie writing. As a discipline, to unlearn the unfortunate habits the movies have taught us, I recommend eliminating names from dialogue completely. When this avoidance becomes second nature, slowly introduce names in dialogue, but only when absolutely necessary. You'll find that it feels right to use names in dialogue when those names are included for unavoidable reasons—when people are being introduced to each other, when people are identifying themselves at the start of a telephone conversation, or during a dark scene in a cellar—in short, when there is no other way for a character to find out the identity of the person to whom that character is speaking. Or when there is no other way for the reader to find out a name.

Let's go back to the initial example. This time, the dialogue (and the use of names within it) are more acceptable.

> "Jane, I'm going downtown to the library."
> "Okay, Dick, I'll see you later."

This exchange isn't exactly true to life. I'm still not sure that Dick and Jane would go to the trouble of addressing each other. They know who they are, after all. Better to eliminate the names completely and use another identifying device. But because the clumsiness and wordiness of the initial example have been eliminated, the dialogue at least doesn't draw attention to itself.

Real Men (and Women) Don't Rumble

What has made the difference in the above example, of course, is that the speech tags have been cut out. Not a bad idea, it seems to me, for speech tags are an especially troublesome device, as you'll see in the following example.

> "I'll track you down and kill you!" Jane hissed.

Apparently, Dick failed to return from the library. Big mistake. So is the one in the dialogue, which should be obvious. You can't hiss if you don't use sibilants, and there aren't any in this speech. How about "Jane growled"? It won't work. In this speech, only "down" has the lower register sound that we associate with a growl. "Jane spat"? Have you ever seen anyone spit while they speak? And anyway, "spat" doesn't really communicate the sense of what the writer is trying to say. Similarly, characters shouldn't bark, rasp, or rumble their dialogue. At best, these expressions are inaccurate. At worst, they are clichés. In either case, they draw attention to themselves, and as was the case when names were used within dialogue, drawing unwanted attention is exactly what you don't want to do.

To eliminate the problem, restrict the verbs used in speech tags to "said" and "asked." In extreme cases, "demanded" or "insisted" may be used, and "shouted" or "screamed"—although, isn't that why exclamation marks were invented, to indicate that someone is shouting or screaming? But let's include the latter two anyhow. And maybe "whispered" or "murmured." Not many.

Dialogue Without Tags

If you limit your speech tags accordingly, you'll discover some interesting consequences. One is that your tone will be less likely to be melodramatic. Another is that any weakness in your dialogue will become more obvious once the crutch of an overwritten speech tag has been eliminated. Yet another benefit is that you will start to question the need for any speech tags at all.

Let's look at speech tags even more closely.

"I'll track you down and kill you!" Jane said.

After the exclamation mark, "said" seems an understatement.

"I'll track you down and kill you!" Jane shouted.

"Shouted" is redundant. So what is the proper verb? Do we surrender and say that speech tags are inherently problematic, but a necessary evil? Or do we look for a better way? After all, what is the purpose of a speech tag? Only one—to identify the speaker. But suppose what comes after Jane isn't a verb of speech. Why can't it be one of action or description?

"I'll track you down and kill you." Jane's cheeks were as scarlet as her hair.

Now that added sentence isn't going to win anyone a Nobel rize, but on the basis of economy, of getting bang for the buck, it does a good job. First, it provides a dramatization of Jane's anger (without the triteness of actually using the word "anger"). Second, it adds a physical detail that makes Jane more vivid to us.

That last point deserves elaboration. Unfortunately, description is almost always used in uneventful moments when someone strolls into a room, for example. We feel description coming on, and we go to sleep. Why not include description a little at a time—where there would normally be fill-in-the-blank speech tags?

"I'll stab you in your sleep." Jane's eyes meant every word.

The "Jane said" has been eliminated, but we don't miss it. We know who the speaker is. We intuit how the dialogue was said. There aren't any empty words. Of course, you can change the dialogue and decide that you want another detail besides Jane's eyes. But as the passage now stands, on its own terms, it has reached a perfect reduction. I especially like the notion that Jane's eyes aren't described—the reader does the work for the writer.

I don't want to give the impression that I'm against speech tags entirely. When carefully placed, their fill-in-the-blank quality can create interesting effects—subtle pauses, for example.

"I know he doesn't believe I'll come after him," Jane said. "His mistake."

Take out "Jane said," and the progression of the dialogue isn't as dramatic. Sometimes "Jane said" can be a version of "Jane hesitated" or "Jane thought about it." Conversely, "Jane hesitated" is sometimes more effective than "Jane said." Every speech tag is a challenge. Sometimes, for variety, writers invert a speech tag: "said Jane." I do not recommend this approach. It is not idiomatic and distracts the reader from what is being said.

Adverbs

While we consider speech tags, the topic of adverbs can't be ignored.

"I gave that jerk the best three days of my life," Jane said bitterly.

It shouldn't come as a surprise that "bitterly" is redundant, and yet we often come across redundancy of this sort. Does the speech tag look so lonely with its meager function of identification that some writers can't resist giving the verb a companion? The temptation needs to be resisted. If the dialogue communicates what it is supposed to, the adverb in the speech tag isn't necessary, and if the dialogue fails to communicate what it is supposed to, the adverb merely points out that the dialogue hasn't been successful.

One of the few cases in which a speech tag's adverb would be acceptable involves dialogue that is meant to be spoken in contradiction to its apparent sense.

"I gave that jerk the best three days of my life," Jane said proudly.

Here the adverb contributes something. The better way, though, would have been to cut "Jane said proudly" and add a narrative sentence in which Jane does something in a proud manner—but without the use of the word "proud."

"I gave that jerk the best three days of my life." Jane stood straighter.

When Gertrude Stein and Ezra Pound were teaching Hemingway, they told him to eliminate adverbs entirely until he learned to use them judiciously. If that advice was good enough for Hemingway ...

Punctuation

And then there are the problems associated with punctuation in dialogue, specifically the exclamation mark. Horror writers are especially inclined to overuse it. Page for page, are there more exclamation marks in horror-fiction dialogue than in any other class of narrative? Do some horror writers believe that by adding a lot of exclamation marks when characters verbally react to terrifying situations, the situation is going to be even more terrifying than it would be with a plain old simple period? If so, they are wrong. By its nature, the exclamation mark is an attention-getting device. It upstages. It draws attention to itself. When overused, it can even push the reader away, distancing rather than engaging.

To get in the habit of not overusing the exclamation mark ... well, by now, you probably have anticipated my recommendation: Don't use exclamation marks at all. After several hundred pages of purity, you can then slowly reintroduce them, one at a time, in special situations, after soul-searching justification. Some of you might object that it's impossible to avoid exclamation marks. I disagree.

Note the following:

"You son of a bitch, I hate your guts!" Jane shouted.

Poor Jane has finally found Dick, but she still has her problems, and so does her dialogue. The speech tag is redundant. So is the exclamation mark, which is implied by "You son of a bitch." The whole business feels stagy, hysterical, and off-putting. But let's try it this way.

"You son of a bitch, I hate your guts." Jane's gaze never left his.

The intensity has been retained, but the staginess has been eliminated. By cutting the speech tag and exclamation mark, the writer has been forced to find a better way to present the dialogue.

No one is going to complain that "Look out, she's got a knife!" involves an unnecessary use of the exclamation mark, but suppose "My God" is substituted for "Look out." "My God, she's got a knife!" is a much stronger statement, perhaps too strong, if you've got exclamation marks on the same page. "My God" *implies* an exclamation. It probably doesn't need enhancement. "My God, she's got a knife." I don't miss the exclamation mark.

This sort of bartering should become a deliberate exercise. Add and subtract to avoid stabbing the reader in the eye with too many !!!!.

Another punctuation problem that intrigues me is how to add emphasis to a question.

"What am I going to do?" Jane exclaimed.

Well, for starters, Jane, you should stop exclaiming. But "shouted" doesn't do the job, nor does "shrieked." "Wailed"? Maybe, but it's still melodramatic. Using an exclamation mark after a question mark, as in "What am I going to do?!" is an abomination. Let's try this:

Jane could barely get the words out. "What am I going to do?"

Again, finding a substitute for a speech tag has led to a solution.

> *"What am I going to do?"* Jane stared at every face in the library.

Here, the italics serve the same function as an exclamation mark. When used in moderation, they are an acceptable way to enliven questions and sometimes to improve the drab look of a page. But remember—if the question has some form of cursing, the italics become redundant, just as an exclamation mark is redundant after a statement that contains cursing.

One further category: colloquialisms. A certain amount of "well," "yeah," "you know," "okay," and the like are necessary to create the illusions of verisimilitude, but unless Jane is a Valley Girl and vapid expressions are a method of characterizing her, this sort of filler should be used in extreme moderation. The words don't say anything, after all. They are blank spots on the page and impede the flow of the story. Slang, too, is a form of colloquialism. It's necessary to enliven dialogue, but unfortunately, current slang quickly becomes dated.

> "That's cool. Give me a high five."

Unless your character is a parody, there's no reason to inflict these trite expressions on both your character and your reader. To avoid the problem invent your own slang.

What about spelling words the way someone sloppy with diction would pronounce them?

> "Dinja know he wuz gonna gitcha?"

I've never been fond of the technique because it upstages the dialogue. My immediate reaction is to note the unusual spelling. I slow my reading to try to understand what the character is actually saying. By then, the impetus of the narrative has been stalled. Sometimes, of course, a character is so illiterate that unusual spelling has to be employed. But must there be so much of it?

> "Didn't you know he was gonna get you?"

For my taste, the single misspelling adequately dramatizes the character's illiteracy—without the expense of obstructing the narrative.

The techniques of writing dialogue are too numerous to exhaust here. I'll close by emphasizing: Don't let yourself be contaminated by dialogue from the movies, the radio, or the stage, i.e., dialogue that is spoken out loud. Years ago, when I was a literature professor at the University of Iowa, I had a student who had been a news announcer. He was assigned to read a report to the class and did so brilliantly, his voice getting every nuance out of every word. But my suspicions were aroused, and when I asked to see the text of the report, I wasn't surprised to find that on the page the text was flat and clichéd. The student had been relying on a tone that he imposed. Someone once told me "I've discovered how to write dialogue. I talk into a tape recorder and pretend I'm various characters speaking to one another. Then I transcribe the results." A variation is to read dialogue out loud after it's written—to see how natural it sounds. All are bad ideas—they tempt a writer to add inflection, to supply a tone and a drive that are perhaps not in fact on the page. In fiction, dialogue is an act of silent communication. You can't rely on a reader to imagine that your characters speak with the inflection you intend. Rather, you have to invent visual cues that will force the reader to imagine the tone you require.

Which writers impress me with their dialogue? Elmore Leonard comes immediately to mind—because he invents his own vivid slang and uses sprung rhythm to make his dialogue appear colloquial. Even more, I'm impressed by Hemingway's lean approach in "A Clean, Well-Lighted Place" and James M. Cain's in *The Postman Always Rings Twice*. For each of these writers, every word of dialogue is carefully considered and never wasted. The more I read them, the more I learn from them. If you adopt their discipline and build on it, you'll have an advantage. But having learned from them, forget them. Don't try to imitate them. Your task is to be as fresh as they are—in your own way. Ultimately, no matter how much you avoid the technical problems I've discussed, there is only one method of creating brilliant dialogue, and that is by concentrating on the essence of dialogue, by giving characters something interesting to say.

Keep It Moving, Maniacs: Writing Action Scenes in Horror Fiction
—Jay R. Bonansinga

The action scene is a rabid animal, the pit bull in horror's backyard. It's the mongrel tearing at the cyclone fence, straining the envelope of taste and time-tested technique. It is the hyperbolic amphetamine rush of Rex Miller's *Slob*, the jagged word-jazz in the final chapters of Thomas Harris's *The Silence of the Lambs*, or the psychedelic dream-chase of Clive Barker's brilliantly demented novelette "The Body Politic."

The bottom line: Action is the engine inside much of our finest postmodern horror.

Literary action arises from a strange intersection of events, the moment where terror coalesces into movement. Action beats (moments of pure kinetic suspense) keep the pages turning, and often, as is the case in a book like Stephen King's *The Shining* with its psychic battlefronts and ghostly archetypes, they complicate and deepen both the text and the subtext.

But what's the secret to writing a killer action scene?

What's it like to be inside the skin of the horror writer as they commit their feverish fantasies to parchment? Well ...

Sometimes the "act" imitates the "art."

For instance ...

Chapter One

Something ominous was brewing. The horror writer had been sensing it for weeks. An imminent change in the weather. A dark, foreboding cold front rolling across the lonely spaces of his daily routine.

Then, late one night, alone in his cluttered little garret, he decided to let it happen.

He felt a weird certainty deep down in his marrow as he poured the first few fingers of the evening's espresso and lit his first Camel straight. He welcomed the feeling as he settled into his leather swivel and switched on his IBM Selectric. He knew what the feeling meant.

It meant great things were in store for his horror story.

He began typing.

At first, the synapses sputtered weakly. The ideas came slowly. The characters seemed stuck in their prosaic world, their behavior mired in a kind of cut-and-paste progression of events. The plot points were there, certainly, but the action seemed dull and listless.

The story was frightening, sure, but it wasn't gripping. It wasn't riveting. It seemed to plod lifelessly along, merely following the prepared outline.

Then the music started.

At first, it was nothing more than a subtle, metronomic beat in his head, a rhythmic ticking that began to build as he wrote the next suspense sequence. He began to hear a sort of internal percussion, complete with cymbal crashes, tempo changes, drum solos, and a constant beat underscoring it all that became the literary glue holding the sequence together, and soon there were characters fleeing monsters, and floors collapsing, and fireworks erupting, and the action began to flow like furious river-rapids flowing, FLOWING, furiously carrying the reader away in its currents, and the storm raged in the writer's mind, and the thunder rumbled, lightning strikes searing the sky at odd intervals, floorboards beginning to QUAKE-QUAKE-QUAKE, seams in the wallpaper separating, plaster crumbling, dust and debris beginning to sift down from the ceiling—

The typewriter erupted.

Flames leapt up from the keyboard, singeing his eyebrows, flash-burning his face, tossing him backward, his swivel chair sliding out from under him. He went down hard on his posterior, the breath knocked out of him, and he gasped for a moment, completely dazed, flailing at the air. His fingertips were still smoldering, tiny, thin tendrils of smoke coming off them where they had contacted the molten hot typewriter keys. He finally managed to catch his breath.

He stood up and looked down at the page still crimped in the typewriter carriage.

The perfect action sequence.

Not bad.

Let's look at the layers. On one level, this sequence exaggerates the perfect *modus operandi* of an action writer, the way the writer gets inside the sequence and almost channels it on a visceral level. But on a deeper level, the actual style in which this sequence is written illustrates some of the basic tricks of the action trade, which are as follows.

Establishing a Rhythm

Great suspense literally sings off the page. If you don't believe me, check out the basement sequence toward the end of Harris's *The Silence of the*

Lambs. Clarice Starling is plunged into darkness, alone with a mad killer and a six-shot service revolver, and the prose turns into a literary version of Charlie Parker wailing a sax solo ("He cocked the Python as he brought it up snick snick and the figure blurred, bloomed bloomed green in his vision ..."). The key is to find the rhythm of the drama itself, the internal "beat" of the scene, and then let it drive the prose as a percussionist would drive a band.

Consider our little barn burner with the mythical horror writer as an example. Notice the way in which the rhythm develops dynamically from the terse, tick-tock sentences of the early moments—

> Something ominous was brewing. The horror writer had been sensing it for weeks. An imminent change in the weather.

—to the increasingly free-form, rocket-sled, run-on sentences of the latter paragraphs, moving rhythmically in a manner emulating the actual thought patterns of the character:

> ... the action began to flow like furious river-rapids, flowing, FLOWING, furiously, carrying the reader away in its currents, and the storm raged in the writer's mind, and the thunder rumbled ...

There are a myriad of other devices—technical tricks—you might choose to employ within the action scene in order to juice up the "psychological edge." Both Rex Miller and Stephen King are masters of this particular technique. You might abruptly insert a word in all-caps ("flowing, FLOWING") to suggest a sort of frenzied chaos, a rush of activity or thought, or you might utilize alliteration at the right rhythmic point ("flow like furious river-rapids, flowing") in order to drive home the unstoppable aspect of your juggernaut. You might even adopt an intermittent sing-song style ("floorboards beginning to QUAKE-QUAKE-QUAKE") in order to further drive home the inexorable rhythm.

Finally, like the crash of a cymbal, the rhythm of a scene is broken by cutting (via our old friend the dash) to a new, single-phrase paragraph:

> ... QUAKE-QUAKE, seams in the wallpaper separating, plaster crumbling, dust and debris beginning to sift down from the ceiling—
> The typewriter erupted.

When you abruptly cut to this new paragraph, it works best when it represents a single snippet of action (or a single thought), which punctuates the sequence ... preferably something pivotal that happens within the context of the overall flow.

Like a typewriter erupting.

Getting Inside the
Point-of-View Character

Clive Barker writes action scenes like a mind-vampire, assimilating the point of view of the protagonist, literally getting inside the character's sensory perceptions of what's happening. Look at the second act of his incredible story "Dread," when the hero falls to the floor-grating of a sinister prison and then passes out. ("*When he woke up he was unaware of his consciousness. There was darkness everywhere, on all sides.*") It's a *tour de force* of subjective action, and it illustrates the axiom that suspense looks boring from a distance, much like ants in an ant farm. But when viewed up close, seen through the living lens of the human being caught up in the suspense, things really start to get dramatic.

Let's turn again to our mythical writer.

As he starts to cook, really cook, the idea is to get inside his head. Get the reader to feel his energy. Taste the coffee, smell the cigarette smoke, hear the rising clackety-clack of the typewriter, and ultimately experience the action just as the protagonist experiences it. In this particular scene, we hear what's in his head:

> At first, it was nothing more than a subtle, metronomic beat in his head, a rhythmic ticking that began to build as he wrote the next suspense sequence. He began to hear a sort of internal percussion, complete with cymbal crashes, tempo changes, drum solos, and a constant beat underscoring it all ....

When the real action kicks in, the scene should always be perceived—whenever possible—from the inside character. When gunshots are fired, don't merely describe how they sound to the characters; describe how they *feel*. When someone is hurt, don't merely describe the blood and guts; describe the mind, what the pain and the fear feel like, the colors and the textures. When the characters are in motion, the landscape rushes past them. With sincerest apologies to Galileo, in action scenes, the universe revolves around the central characters.

In fact, true action can only be generated through character. Period. We must know his quirks; we must know he's got an adjustable-rate mortgage going through the roof and his kid just got back from the orthodontist with a mouth full of metal. And then, and only then, do we care about the outcome. In other words, only then do we feel as our character feels.

And remember, action is a virus. It's radioactive, and it spreads from the main character's mind to the minds of others. A shift from one point of view to another is like a ratchet tightening suspense, intensifying the action, pumping up the energy about a million foot-pounds per square inch.

Engaging the Environment

There's a thin membrane between horror and pure slapstick comedy—especially within the body of an action sequence.

One of the great tenets of slapstick is to engage the surrounding environment. The Keystone Kops. The block-long fire engine comes screaming around a curve, the cops hanging off the ladder, holding on for dear life—what happens? The ladder slams into a stack of melons, and melons go flying. The cops go catapulting off into various pie shops, pies erupting everywhere, hitting faces, cops scurrying every which way.

It's a recipe for laughs—and screams as well.

The Keystone Kops routine underlies all great action sequences.

Let's return to the basement in *The Silence of the Lambs*. In Jonathan Demme's brilliant film adaptation, we find the hero—FBI Agent Clarice Starling (played by Jodie Foster)—alone in the serial killer's cellar. Starling has just discovered the grisly remains of several victims, and she now knows that the killer is hiding somewhere in the basement, waiting for her. Suddenly, the lights go out, and now we see Starling stumbling around in the dark, banging into things, touching hot furnace pipes, and tripping over her own feet. Add a laugh track and you've got a sparkling, little screwball comedy. But watch the poor woman through the infrared green of a killer's gaze, and the comedy curdles into a nightmare that's twice as frightening.

The key is to find artifacts in the environment—the hot furnace pipes, the pie shops—and integrate them into the action. Just as our old friend the mythical horror writer sees "the wallpaper separating, plaster crumbling, dust and debris beginning to sift down from the ceiling," you can build your scene by logically asking yourself what parts of landscape would be impacted by this chase or fight, or gunplay, or attack. Not only does it reinforce the authenticity of an action scene (this kind of stuff would naturally occur in the real world), but it also intensifies the experience for a reader.

Which is the object of all literary technique, right? Which brings us to …

Seasoning Your Scenes With Detail

Horror fiction (perhaps more than any other genre) depends on a suspension of disbelief. Harlan Ellison knows this perhaps better than anybody in the game. Ellison's flights of fancy are driven by copious detail—animal, vegetable, mineral, and *emotional*—which gives them incredible verisimilitude. This allows Mister "E" to take us any damned place he wants to take us; and believe me, it's always worth the price of admission.

In his strangely poignant, Lovecraftian short story "On the Slab," for example, Ellison gives us a classic case of details motoring an action scene. Late in the story, the protagonist, Frank Kneller, has accepted the Herculean task of protecting a modern-day Prometheus who happens to be locked up in a museum; it seems a giant carrion bird has arrived from the netherworld, has crashed through the skylight, and is now bearing down on the ancient man. The hero, Frank Kneller, immediately springs into action, ripping a fire extinguisher from its brackets on the wall and

> ... the virulent Halon 1301 mixture sprayed in a white stream over the bird's head. The mixture of fluorine, bromine, iodine, and chlorine washed the vulture, spurted into its eyes, filled its mouth.

Amid the feverish action, Ellison projects this weird litany of chemical minutiae. Why? Because Ellison has one of the best "eyes" in the business; he draws us in through detail, through seeing and smelling and tasting the terror, through dreamlike reportage. In real life, during violent events, we do indeed fixate on such minute details; we see these little odd textures. Ellison is merely translating the raw experience onto the page.

And this, gentle writers, is the foundation of good, visceral action.

Funneling Time

Ultimately, good literary action should feel like (if not look like) an inverted funnel.

In other words, as a scene progresses, time should compress in—on itself.

Take our old friend the mythical writer, for example. Early on, in the initial few paragraphs, we are covering large stretches of elapsed time. First, weeks. Then, days. Then, hours:

> The horror writer had been sensing it for weeks. An imminent change in the weather ....
>
> Then, late one night, alone in his cluttered little garret, he decided to let it happen ....
>
> He felt a weird certainty deep down in his marrow as he poured the first few fingers of the evening's espresso and lit his first Camel straight ....

As he prepares to write his scene, the passing of time becomes more and more compressed. The tension mounts. Then, as the words start flowing, the passage of time is tightened down to a moment-by-moment roller coaster:

> At first, it was nothing more than a subtle, metronomic beat in his head ... He began to hear a sort of internal percussion ....

Then as the action progresses, the passage of time is compressed so tightly that each moment seems to stretch into a surrealistic tableau.

... and the action began to flow like furious river-rapids, flowing, FLOWING, furiously, carrying the reader away in its currents ....

Finally, the ultimate time compression flattens the event down to a series of vivid, gut-wrenching images.

The Final Blow

Think of literary action as a car accident. You, the writer, are in the driver's seat. You are feeling everything; you are sensing that time is slowing down and all you can do is watch the horrifying movie in your mind. Think of that feeling—the way movement seems to blur and get all bogged down like a taffy pull. That's the moment just before impact. Find the literary equivalent and you'll be holding your reader rapt.

More than anything else, however, the key to writing excellent action is perception. The rhythm, the point of view, the environment, the detail—it's all filtered through the human perspective.

That's what action is.

A human being in peril—forced to *perceive*.

The Dark Enchantment
of Style
—Bruce Holland Rogers

Read, Analyze, Practice

When I was a much younger writer, talk of style frustrated me. I understood that style was important and knew that the right narrative voice, like quicksand, could gently pull me into a good story up to my chin. But I didn't know how to cultivate that effect of language. Where did style come from?

"Read," said my teachers and mentors. "Read, read, read, and read some more." I did.

"Analyze," they said, "and figure out why effective passages of writing are just that—effective." Okay. I did my best to read like a writer.

"Practice." So I wrote and wrote and wrote some more.

All of that was good advice, and it kept me busy doing things that a beginner ought to do. It wasn't enough, though. The most helpful key to learning about style was something that I discovered on my own, by accident. It's *my* secret—and I'm going to let you in on it.

But first, I have a fight to pick.

Finding a Voice and Finding Voices

I'm a nice guy. Really. It's not like me to begin an essay looking for trouble or calling anyone out, but here goes: To all those English teachers and creative writing professors who tell developing writers that they must "find their voice," that they can't write successfully until they discover their own personal style: You're wrong. Let's take it outside. You are confusing and messing up a lot of writers, both beginners and a few well-established writers, and I'm here to put a stop to it. Since we're talking horror writing, let's take it outside with a vengeance; outside—with meat cleavers.

It is true that many accomplished writers come to write in a voice that is recognizably their own and unlike anyone else's. Their word choice, sentence rhythms, and syntax become distinctive. It is true that a stray paragraph of Hemingway or Lovecraft or Rice can be identified by its characteristics, almost as if it were listed in a field guide by the color of its tail feathers and the curve of its beak. But being able to match the prose to the author is *not* the purpose of style.

The purpose of style is enchantment. That's all that matters.

An effective voice pulls the reader into the story. An effective voice is one that suits the story so well that the reader can't help but come along for the ride. Style in storytelling also helps to evoke emotion, like a musical score that shapes the feelings of moviegoers.

As a result of the "find your voice" advice, some beginning writers waste time trying to invent unique verbal mannerisms or invent a uniquely personal vocabulary. A few misguided beginners avoid reading what other writers have written so as not to be "contaminated" by voices other than their own. The cult of the unique voice even lures some established writers onto the rocks with the false belief that once they have found a voice, they must stick with it. "If I changed my style, my readers wouldn't know it was me." When good writers begin to produce bad writing, it is sometimes because they are trying to tell new and different stories using the same old voice. That's how some writers, late in their careers, end up writing parodies of their own best work. They have come to think that "their voice" is an unchangeable part of who they are. Nonsense. The effectiveness of style is that it weaves just the right spell to draw the reader into this particular story.

In fact, the writer's ideal should not be to *find a voice,* but a facility with *voices.* And to be perfectly clear, I'm not talking here primarily about the need to develop an actor's sensitivity to the way that different characters sound, although that's also a great skill to have, and useful for writing dialogue. Indeed, that sensitivity to how different characters sound in speech can be a step toward learning to be a flexible stylist. There are even cases in which the voice of the character is the voice of the story because a particular character is narrating. Most of "Heart of Darkness"—a horror novella of the first rank—is narrated by the character Marlow: "It was upward of thirty days before I saw the mouth of the big river. We anchored off the seat of the government." Marlow's choice of words—that is, his voice—determines our experience of his story. In most cases, though, the narrative voice, the style, doesn't belong to a particular character. The voice, rather, is one that is just right for telling a particular kind of tale.

Here, by way of example, are two different passages recounting the same events at the beginning of a story:

The unusual cut and color of the blue satin jacket—it looked Chinese with its banded collar and elaborate frog closures—was the first thing that drew York's attention to the man, but then there was the matter of the package wrapped in newspapers tucked under his arm, the way that the man looked straight ahead as he walked from the glow of one streetlight to another, and the interesting datum that two other men were trailing him by half a block without any effort toward subtlety or art.

The man wore a Chinese-looking jacket. Banded collar. Elaborate frog closures. Unusual. That was the first thing York noticed. Under the man's arm, a package. A package wrapped in newspapers. The man walked from the glow of one streetlight to another—straight ahead. Eyes straight ahead, too. Two men followed him—they certainly weren't making any secret of it—obvious as hounds at a fox hunt, almost as if they wanted it that way.

Each passage conveys nearly the same information. The point of view is the same, as are the details and even, to a great extent, the vocabulary. But depending on the story that follows this opening, one passage or the other is a better fit for the material. Is the story more urbane or is it hard-boiled? Is the ending going to turn more on thought or action? Are the horror elements to be in soft focus or conveyed in glaring detail? The author of a tough, blood-splattered action story would be wise to avoid the first version of this opening. If the story is shadowy, spooky, and subtle, though, the first opening may be just the thing.

Not one style. Not one voice. Styles. Voices. A good writer suits the telling to the tale.

Read, Read, Read

All right. I've set down the meat cleaver that I waved at English teachers and writing professors and I'm calming down. I think I have made the point that style exists to serve the story, not to individuate the author.

Armistice established, I'm going to sit down next to those profs and instructors and offer some advice that sounds a lot like what they often say: *The best way to develop style is to read.* Read the long-ago masters of horror. Read your contemporaries. Read writers of other kinds of fiction, particularly the work of writers who are good at making you feel. As a horror writer, you want to pay particular attention to the ways that writing shapes emotion.

Read, read, read. When you find an interesting emotional effect, stop and ask yourself how the writing worked its magic on you. Try imitating the various styles of other writers. Read for technique, and try to absorb technique.

Practice. Take what works for you. Discard what doesn't. You'll find that you are using the techniques of the writers you study, but in *new* combinations. Your style will become more and more original.

If that sounds exactly like the advice of the English teachers and creative writing professors, here is the difference: I'm advising you to not only notice the *techniques,* but also the ways in which they *suit the stories* in which you encounter them. Aim not to develop "a voice," but a variety of voices that you can call upon for all the different tales you will tell.

Here are some things to think about as you consider aspects of style.

1. How does the language identify the subgenre? What words immediately tell you that you are reading a dark fairy tale, a supernatural thriller, or realistic suspense? How is the story's vocabulary used to keep reminding you what kind of story you have entered?

2. Does the story give you minimal detail? Maximal detail? How does a spare or lush style serve the story's needs?

3. Style is a window. At one extreme it can be a pane so transparent and clean that you totally forget it's there, or, at the other extreme, it can be stained glass that is so elaborate and interesting for its own sake that you can barely see the story through it. On this continuum, what sort of window are you looking through in this story? What makes it the right window in this case?

Read. Read, read, and read some more. Read, analyze, and practice.

The Secret Revealed

Yeah, yeah, yeah, you may be thinking. What about your promised *secret* to learning about style?

Thanks for your patience. Here it is. It sounds simple, but don't let that fool you. The secret is … *S-l-o-w d-o-w-n.*

Slow down when you read.

And when you write, slow down then, too.

When I was about twenty, I wrote stories at a furious pace. My pen could barely keep up with my streaking imagination. Zoom!

At about the same time, I tried my hand at literary translation. Even for translations I did from Spanish, my strongest language, I had to consult the dictionary often. When it came to translating a short story from German, the task was just short of absurd. I had taken four weeks of "German for Reading," and I understood the basics of grammar, but my vocabulary was minimal. It took me a week to translate a story of words. For every other word, I had to consult an enormous two-volume *Langenscheidt* dictionary, not only looking up the German words, but often double-checking to see how their English equivalents were explained in German.

It was long, tedious work. I might spend a quarter of an hour on a difficult sentence. Especially compared to the pace of my story writing, translating from a language I didn't know well was agonizingly slow.

Except that it wasn't agonizing. It was interesting. By spending fifteen minutes to discover, check, and reconsider the first sentence of a story, I found myself thinking a lot about what the first sentence of a story does for the reader. The same for the second sentence, and the third. I couldn't hurry through the story I was translating. I had to plod. And in my plodding, I absorbed lessons about narrative pacing, guiding the reader's emotions, and style.

The experience changed how I read stories in English. I found myself reading the same sentence over and over again, noticing things that I might not be able to explain, but could certainly feel about how or why the sentence worked.

Does this mean that if you want to use my secret technique for learning style, you need to study another language? No! (Although it wouldn't hurt. It's useful for writers to have at least a smattering of other languages.) You can get much the same effect as translation by trying to imitate an interesting style one sentence at a time, slowly, word by word. "High up, crowning the grassy summit of a swelling mount whose sides are wooded near the base with gnarled trees of the primeval forest stands the old chateau of my ancestors." That's Lovecraft. You might write, "Far downstream, crowding the crumbling banks of a muddy river whose flow is choked in winter by dense mats of rotting cattails stands the plantation mansion of my ancestors." That is, you write a sentence that tries to capture the structure, vocabulary, and feel of the model. You probably can't do this fast. Lovecraft's vocabulary and rhythms are not your own. But this kind of slow imitation can help you to think about the effects of a sentence that is built this way. It helps you to experience another writer's style in your bones.

Read slowly. Take time to analyze. Imitate slowly, with care. When you compose, slow down.

That's my secret. It's that simple. Write as if you had to look up each word.

In the end, you may still be a writer who writes first drafts fast, barely able to keep up with the pictures racing across the screen of your imagination. That's fine. Anything you do to get the story down is good. But eventually, if style matters to you, you'll want to write a slow version, translating your fast notes into a carefully constructed enchantment that pulls the reader in with deceptive ease ... up to his or her chin in the quicksand of your making.

Part Five

Horror, Art, Innovation, Excellence

5:00

Innovation in Horror
—Jeanne Cavelos

When I teach creative writing and ask my students what they believe their strengths and weaknesses to be, almost all of them include creativity as a strength; virtually none list it as a weakness.

As a result, few developing writers spend a lot of time and energy making their work creative. They feel, by the very act of typing words, they are already being "creative." After all, they are creating something new.

But that's the rub: *Just how new is it?*

Horror is a genre with certain identifiable characteristics. When people who enjoy horror read your story, they are not reading it in a vacuum. They are reading it as part of a genre, constantly comparing your story to other horror stories they've read. If I had never read Edgar Allan Poe's "The Tell-Tale Heart" and then wrote a story very much like "The Tell-Tale Heart," readers who know Poe's story may not be quite as thrilled with my Big! Surprise! Ending! as I had hoped. To them, it's no surprise. They've read it before, only a better version (you can't beat Poe).

To be a creative, innovative horror writer, you must read a lot of everything— and a lot of that everything must be horror. You may be thinking: *How can I be creative and original with all these other authors' ideas floating around in my head?* This is critical: The sheer amount of material floating around in your head will actually prevent your copying from any *one* author in particular.

Instead, you will find a tiny piece of character from this book, a tiny piece of plot from that book, a certain stylistic technique from that other—to combine into something totally new. It is the writer who reads only Stephen King who will turn out stories that sound like Stephen King—on a very, very bad day.

If you can accept the need to know the horror writing that has gone before, you might still have difficulty with the idea of extensive reading outside the field. Simply by the law of averages, more great writing has been done outside the field of horror than within it. Another law of averages: The more great writing you read, the more that is likely to rub off on you. Read works from different periods of history, from different cultures. Read fiction and nonfiction. Many innovations arise from taking ideas outside the genre and bringing them in. Some of our favorite stories even mix genres.

When a story is innovative, it brings fresh ideas and techniques to the genre. It helps enlarge the genre and renew it. It helps keep the genre exciting and alive for future generations of readers. And it creates one hell of a great story.

Innovate or Imitate?

Why do so many people think John Carpenter's *Halloween* is a great movie? (I'm using a movie rather than a novel as an example because I think more of you will be familiar with a particular movie than a particular novel. But my point holds equally true for novels and stories.) If you watch it now, it may seem a rather tame and predictable slasher movie. But when it came out, nothing quite like it had ever been done before.

It was intense, tightly plotted (the whole story takes place in one night), concerned itself very little with explanation (we have no idea why the killer goes after Jamie Lee Curtis with such determination), and had an incredible amount of suspense (every scene either had the killer in it or had evidence of something the killer had done—evidence like a dead body). It didn't spend half its length building up to killings, as so many movies of the day did. A murder occurs in the first five minutes. Each of these elements was not new, but this combination of them was, and it was very powerful, touching off a whole series of sequels and imitators. *Halloween* expanded and renewed the genre.

Stephen King has had a similar effect. He combined elements in a totally new way. Never before had classic horror archetypes, like the vampire (*Salem's Lot*) or the haunted house (*The Shining*), seemed so possible in our mundane, middle-class world. He brought these horrors down to earth, making them not the province of unstable minds and rarefied atmospheres, but of Anytown, U.S.A., in the plumber's house, the son's room, right under the bed. In the early 1980s, King had a huge impact on the genre, expanding and renewing it and spawning hordes of imitators. Even today, his influence is strong on many developing horror writers; there are more than a few who believe that to write horror is to write "Stephen King horror"—since they've never read anything else they've liked.

The question is, do you want to be an innovator or an imitator?

It's normal for young writers to be inspired by books or movies and to begin writing by emulating those sources. But horror that simply reflects the source that inspired it is not going to be rich and powerful; it's going to be a pale reflection of its source. A writer must take various sources of inspiration and filter them through his own unique sensibilities.

There are, of course, an infinite number of ways you can make your story in-novative. Writing is a layered and complex process, and each story combines mul-tiple elements. In creating new combinations and new patterns, you are innovating.

Innovative Plotting

What will the plot of your story be? What fear will it focus on? Many writ-ers choose a plot by choosing a horror archetype to write about. Maybe you decide to write a vampire story, or a ghost story, or a serial killer story, or a zombie story. That's okay. These archetypes have developed and persisted over the years because they tap into our fears and have a strong, resonant ef-fect on us. But they also present a serious challenge to today's writer: What is your vampire story going to do that no other vampire story has done before? (This is quite a question, considering how much material has been written about vampires.) What unique sensibility do you bring to a vampire story? If you don't have a powerful, significant difference to offer in your story, then you probably shouldn't write it.

Maybe you decide to center your plot around a specific fear—one of your specific fears. This can be a wonderful technique, because if you are afraid of "it," chances are you can also make the reader afraid of it. But when I ask writers what they are afraid of, they usually come back with answers like "cockroaches." That's a perfectly valid answer, and if you are truly afraid of cockroaches, per-haps that can play a part in a story sometime.

But that's not a very deep-rooted fear. What I want to know is what fright-ens you at all levels, not only at the surface but at the deepest levels. That way, perhaps cockroaches cannot only be scary and gross, but can symbolize a deeper fear, the fear, perhaps, of chaos, of forces beyond your control. Most of us fear this a lot more than we fear cockroaches. Don't just throw a ton of cockroaches in a story and assume your reader will be horrified (how many cockroaches are in a ton, anyway?). The cockroaches need to tie into a deeper fear: Why do they scare you so much? Becoming aware of the unique way that you see things and writing a story that reflects your unique sensibility is the key to writing innovative horror.

Once you have a basic concept for your story, you need to develop it into a plot. Now, the great thing about the horror genre is that, unlike other genres, it allows infinite possibilities. The horror genre has one requirement for member-ship: The story must make the reader feel ... *horrified*. Many writers don't real-ize how revolutionary this is. In other genres, a fairly strict plot is imposed. In a mystery, a crime must occur—usually a murder—which must then be solved by the end of the story. In a romance, two people must meet and fall in love. But the plot of a horror story can be anything, as long as it makes the reader feel horror. So why is it that the plot of so many horror novels can be summarized like this:

Prologue: Evil creature is awakened and kills one or more victims in spectacularly gruesome fashion.

Chapter 1: Introduction of thirty-something family man (often a writer) who's carrying around a problem from his past.

Chapters 2-15: Evil creature creeps into life of family man, killing numerous other victims on its way (in spectacularly gruesome fashion) while threatening members of the family man's family. The family's pet usually gets it at this point. Family man continues to suffer over problem from his past.

Chapters 16-19: Family man recognizes the threat of the evil creature, fights evil creature, figures out the secret to killing it, and triumphs, killing the creature in spectacularly gruesome fashion and simultaneously resolving his problem from the past.

Chapter 20: Family man and his family (minus pet) live happily ever after. Creature is dead (or is it ...?).

If horror, as I said, puts no constraints on plot, why does this darned thing sound so familiar? As an editor, I have read this plot more times than I can count, and many more than I want to remember. These days, any horror manuscript with a prologue makes an editor sigh in despair. Reading a lot in the field will help these old, tired patterns become more apparent to you. Then, as a writer, you can decide to avoid them, or you can play off them, beginning your novel in a way that makes us think we know exactly what is going to happen and then surprising us by taking the plot in a totally different direction.

Innovative Style

So one important method of innovating comes from choosing and developing your plot, in deciding what you are going to say. The other method arises from deciding how you are going to say it. Your writing style, or your voice, reflects your personality, your beliefs, your concerns. In writing, you are commenting on life, the human condition. What do you believe? What do you want to say?

Just as each person has a distinctive speaking voice, a distinctive tone and timbre, a distinctive way of putting words together, and certain preferred words, so do we each have a distinctive writing voice. This is often more difficult to develop. Beginning writers tend to write like the authors they have read. One of my students told me she would write like Stephen King when she was reading King, like Harlan Ellison when she was reading Ellison, and on and on. She had no style or voice of her own. And truth to tell, she wasn't really writing in King's style one week and Ellison's style the next (a writer could have worse problems); she was writing in a style that was a pale, inferior reflection of King's style or Ellison's style. She could never write King's style as well as King, because King's style reflects who he is, how he thinks, and how he expresses himself. Your style, if it is to be truly yours, must do the same for you.

How you say something is just as important as what you say. Critics today bemoan the elevation of style over substance, but style is critically important in powerful and innovative writing. In fact, much of the innovation in horror in recent years has come in the area of style. While Stephen King introduced a style that was immediate, concrete, accessible, and down-to-earth, post-King authors are introducing literary, postmodern, experimental styles.

To get a better idea of the possibilities for innovation in horror, read these genre-stretching works: Patrick McCabe's *The Butcher Boy,* Jennifer Lynch's *The Secret Diary of Laura Palmer*, Ian McEwan's *The Comfort of Strangers*, or Tim Lucas's *Throat Sprockets.*

Innovation is a critical component in any strong work of horror, and it does not come easily or automatically to us "creative" souls who write. Strive for innovation in your writing and never give up. If you can express what concerns you in a way that reflects your own unique sensibility, then you are being truly innovative, and the horror you create will be truly special.

Depth of Field: Horror and Literary Fiction
—Nick Mamatas

There are two mutually exclusive claims found amongst many beginning horror writers, and more than a few veterans as well. The first is essentially a complaint: Horror is not respected as a literary form unto itself. Advances are low, publicity nearly nonexistent, bookstore horror sections minuscule, and the reading public—Mrs. Grundys and beret-wearing aesthetes, the lot of them—confuse today's written horror with the cheesy, awful slasher films of the 1980s. The second claim made by these same writers is that they are entertainers peddling good ol'-fashioned scares and the occasional bucket o' grue. To attempt to do anything else with horror would be "pretentious," if not a downright betrayal of the genre.

The commitment to fun fiction—the one our friends proudly declare may actually lead to the dispiriting state of affairs they decry—never seems to occur to these writers, and that's a shame, because a significant amount of the horror published every year can be found within other genres. Two romance subgenres, romantic suspense and paranormal romance, invoke horror tropes. The bloodier police procedurals, particularly those dealing with serial killers, take a page or two from horror as well. Plenty of science fiction and fantasy slides over into horror as well: future dystopias, contemporary settings featuring secret or occultic histories or monsters—you name it, you can find it.

Less attention is paid to horror in the "literary fiction" category, despite the fact that some of the best horror written today *is* literary fiction, and there is plenty for a writer who just wants to entertain to learn from novels and collections on the *general fiction* shelf.

Literary Fiction: The Three Genres

A bit of taxonomy. Literary fiction is itself made up of three genres. The first genre is *literature*, which is work that has stood the test of time sufficiently to be considered classic. Shakespeare, Dante, Poe—there's plenty of horror in literature.

The second genre is *realism*. Realism refers both to a set of techniques that simply render reality accurately, and to a genre of fiction that examines the psychology of characters existing in everyday life. Plot, the way it is conceived of in genre fiction (rising action, excitement, an attempt to keep the audience guessing), gives way to intense, even minute, descriptions of "how we live now." Events are plausible and personal: the miscarriage, the bitter marriage, the coming of age. The social world around the characters is vitally important to understanding why the characters act and respond the way they do. Henry James, Mark Twain, and William Dean Howells are classic realists.

The third literary genre is *postmodernist fiction*. Postmodernism is fiction that seeks to undermine its own form through linguistic games. Metafiction—the use of techniques including footnotes, reportage, list-making, columnated texts, the intrusion of "paraliterary" texts, and virtually anything else that can be done to words and sentences—is done to make the point that all narratives are contingent, and reality itself cannot be trusted. Thomas Pynchon, Kathy Acker, and David Foster Wallace are among our leading postmodernists.

At first blush, there doesn't seem like there would be much to learn from the genres of literary fiction, especially the latter two (engaged in an aesthetic war of their own), but both styles have much to offer a horror writer looking to add something different to her own work. And writers are already doing it.

Realism

David Searcy's *Ordinary Horror* is an excellent example of a novel that combines the real, the horrific, and the postmodern. It begins "Here's a horror story for you," and then we get an ordinary life of an old man, with only hints of menace and discomfiture. "Where's the payoff?" you can hear the horror fan crying out, and the answer is that there isn't one, and that is what leads to the horror of the novel. Category horror is in the business of cathartic climaxes; whether our heroes triumph or not, we close the book satisfied. *Ordinary Horror*, on the other hand, does its work in a way that doesn't ever let go. The smallest everyday occurrence is fraught with foreboding, thanks to Searcy's linguistic gymnastics. From the beginning of the book's seventh chapter:

> Faint dreams all night, inaccessible even as he sleeps; thin, rudimentary dreams like an infant might have, a screen of static with something behind it coming and going and waking him periodically like sand in his bed, the grainy anxiety of it, over and over until morning and even then for a while the feeling stays with him till he's showered and dressed and moving about, removing cold Salisbury steak from the microwave, dropping it in the trash and rinsing his hands and looking out the window at the flowers.

Quite a sentence, no? As dreamy and frustrating as a half-sleepless night, to be sure. Here's the next sentence:

> They're still black.

And no, Searcy does not use the cheap trick of putting "They're still black" in a new, single-sentence paragraph of its own. It's wedged in the middle of the paragraph, with three sentences (that do not refer to the flowers) coming after it. The black flowers, the flowers that are still black, sneak up on the reader. I turned the pages back more than once to see if I had actually read what I thought I had when I first sat down with *Ordinary Horror*. And that's a feature, not a bug. Realism seeks to replicate objective reportage with a minimum of authorial intrusion. We see what the main character sees, as *he* sees it. If his view of the black flowers is incidental to his feeling of near-somnambulant dislocation, then that's all we get from the author.

If the horror of category horror depends on taking a ride with characters who don't know what's happening to them until it's too late, the horror of realism is literally seeing no more than those characters do. The latter is less safe for a reader, and thus potentially far more frightening. One needn't have buckets of gore to use realistic techniques (though they're not forbidden either; see *American Psycho* by Bret Easton Ellis); one only needs a certain amount of facility with language. And the realists have a century and a half of practice in perfecting the use of language to achieve psychological veracity and produce psychological effects in the reader. There's plenty to learn from.

Postmodernism

If realist fiction depends on the *use of language* to inspire dread and fear, postmodern fiction depends on the *misuse and abuse of language*. One of the most powerful horror novels of recent years was also one of the most intriguing postmodern novels: *House of Leaves* by Mark Z. Danielewski. *House of Leaves* is essentially a haunted house story, with annotations and so many degrees of separation from "reality" that the house may well not exist. Johnny Truant discovers a monograph written about a blind man about an apocryphal documentary about a photojournalist who stumbled upon the haunted house. The seventh degree of separation is yours. As Truant guarantees the reader:

> For some reason, you will no longer be the person you believed you once were. You'll detect slow and subtle shifts going on all around you—more importantly, shifts in you. Or worse, you'll realize it's always been shifting, like a shimmer of sorts, a vast shimmer, only dark like a room. But you won't understand why or how.

Thousands of readers had exactly that experience. *House of Leaves* is a triumph of not only postmodern narrative, but of typography: There are footnotes with footnotes, columns, text in different colors that are subliminally and hypertextually connected to other parts of the book. You have to turn the novel upside down to read some sections; during others, you'll find yourself in front of your bathroom sink, holding the pages up to the mirror to read writing that is both upside down and reversed. Not only are the halls of the house haunted, so are the columns of the book. It consumes you.

Did you think you were the sort of person who'd march into a bathroom and stare into a mirror because "a novel" told you to? Well, you are now. Truant was right. That's the power of the literary tricks and tropes that make up postmodern fiction. Instead of escaping into a story, the way genre fiction works, the postmodern stuff hopes to escape into you. Dread and unease are the horror writer's forte, but too many ignore a whole new toolbox of literary tricks that build a sense of dislocation into sentences themselves.

Literary Horror

Of course, literary horror can be a bit heady, and not all of it works, but that's certainly true of normal, safe, category horror as well. However, there are advantages to writing literary horror, even if one has to bone up on both the classics and the bleeding edge to do it.

1. *Literary fiction sells.* As of this writing, none of the Big Five publishers has a dedicated horror line. Some publish occasional titles, and then mostly as mass market paperback originals, but that's it. Dorchester, an independent specializing in mass-market paperbacks, has a horror line, and Kensington puts out a significant number of category horror titles, but horror makes up a small fraction of its output. On the other hand, every one of the Big Five publishes what they call "quality fiction"—and quality fiction has few limits as far as plot or theme go. It can be domestic or transgressive, cooked or raw, everyday or horrific.

2. *Literary fiction gets reviewed.* The work that gets reviewed in the major newspapers and magazines in the United States is often simply those books hyped by publicity departments. However, reviewers will also go out of their way to pick up and review novels that intrigue them. Few are intrigued by the same old white-people-in-danger and lusty vampire novels of category horror, but reviewers love a breath of fresh air. My first novel, *Move Under Ground*, which brought the voice of the Beat Generation, Jack Kerouac, into a Lovecraftian world of cosmic horror, was reviewed in *The Believer*, *The Village Voice*, and the *American Book Review*, in addition to fantasy/horror venues like *Locus*, *Fangoria*, and *Rue Morgue*. *Move Under Ground* was published in hardcover by a small press, Night Shade Books. There was no hundred-thousand-dollar publicity blitz; what we

had was nothing but an intriguing book, and that interested reviewers enough to help sell both copies and foreign rights to the book.

3. *Literary fiction is significant.* All novelists want to entertain, and all novels that actually get read must be entertaining—at least on some level. If they weren't, the reader would just put the book down. But literary fiction, tangling as it does with how we live now and the language in which we express it, has the potential to go beyond entertainment and actually mean something.

One of the frequent criticisms of literary fiction, especially amongst the horror cognoscenti, is that it is "pretentious." All that means is that many people don't know what the word pretentious means. Literary fiction, horrific or otherwise, is pretending *to be what,* exactly? Literary fiction is fiction that concentrates on the writing and how language can be used to express (and undermine) narratives. There's no pretense there; skillful writing is a prerequisite to being published at all. Writing that goes beyond the skillful is just something that many writers excel at and many readers enjoy reading. In horror, this is an underdeveloped market niche.

Part of why it is so underdeveloped is due to a false metaphor propagated by too many writers and readers. These people see a piece of writing as an engine. To succeed, a story or novel has to hit on all cylinders: plot, characters, atmosphere, writing, pacing. And indeed, many books do hit on all cylinders. Everything in it is good, but no part of it is great. A perfect story, one that is genius, is of course as impossible as a perfectly efficient engine. But the metaphor itself warns writers against concentrating on anything too much, leading to many mediocre novels where all cylinders are hitting at the same speed: slow.

So, allow me to close by suggesting another metaphor. A story isn't like a smoothly running engine, but is rather like a photograph. Photos can never be a perfect representation of what an eye looking at the same subject will see, partially due to the limitations of lenses and emulsions, but largely due to the conscious choice of the photographer. Photographers manipulate the focus of their work to highlight certain elements and occult others. Depth of field is a subjective quality; a photo that shows the petal of a single flower in perfect focus while defusing the other petals, the stem, and the leaves around the flower is as beautiful and worthy as a photo of the whole garden, where every flower is a sharp, but minor, part of the landscape.

As writers, we all choose to focus on some elements of our work. Many horror writers opt for the "rollercoaster ride" of plot, and many readers enjoy the experience of reading such books. I know I do. But nobody wants to live on a rollercoaster, week after week. Horror writers should consider changing their focus occasionally. Characterization, artful language, and grammatical fancy-dancing, socially relevant themes—the stuff of literary fiction—are just as worthy of horror's attention as blood and brand names.

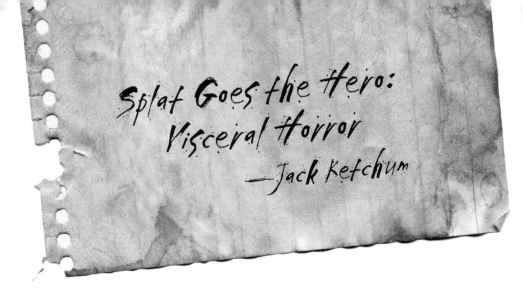

Splat Goes the Hero: Visceral Horror
—Jack Ketchum

I wrote a book awhile back called *The Girl Next Door,* which opened with the line, "You think you know about pain?"

Personally, I'm no expert (so far, knock on wood), although as a kid I certainly had my share of broken bones and various other less-than-delightful body surprises: a cortisone shot into an inflamed tendon; my upper jaw peeled and scraped—did you know that pain can be a *sound?*; and a fall, stark naked, through the branches of a tree that left me looking like something out of *100 Days of Sodom.*

(Curious about that one? Too bad. You'll have to wait for the story.)

But the point is that if you're writing about violence, you're writing about pain. Somebody's pain. Maybe not yours, but somebody's. And my preference is to face it squarely as honestly as possible, and very much up close and personal.

I've noted this elsewhere but it bears repeating here: The great director Akira Kurosawa once said that "the role of the artist is to not look away."

That pretty much defines what I try to do.

There are plenty of ways to look away, and bad writers, at some point, have found every last one of them. We'll get to some of the more disastrous ways later, but right now let's just stick to violence.

Remember those old Hays Office-era cowboy movies where everything is completely bloodless—where people get shot, with a rifle that would stop a bear for God's sake, and fall down and die as neatly as Baryshnikov executes a *tour jeté?* Then along came *Bonnie and Clyde* and *The Wild Bunch* and blew all that away forever. A little later, horror movies kicked some dirt over the grave.

The first tentative steps in that direction had come earlier from Hitchcock, with black-and-white blood swirling down the drain in *Psycho*'s shower scene, and with Tippi Hedren pecked nearly to death and the bloody, empty eye-socket in *The Birds,* from Hammer Studios in England; and from that master of gore and total boredom, Herschell Gordon Lewis. Then suddenly things exploded with items like *Night of the Living Dead, The Last House on the Left, The Texas Chainsaw Massacre* and the early Cronenberg films.

I just couldn't believe 'em.

I *expected* none of them.

They each dropped me like a steer and collectively changed the way I looked at death-as-popular-entertainment forever. People didn't just die in these movies, they got gnawed on right in front of you, before and after death, and by God—you saw it! They wanted you to see it: people hung out to die on meat hooks that were raped and murdered and hacked and chewed in detail so graphic you almost wanted to look away.

Almost. But not quite.

Not Looking Away

I remember seeing each of these movies while sprawled in my seat, feet spread across a popcorn-crusted, Coke-and-let's-not-think-about-what-else-sticky floor, smoking Winstons with complete impunity, at all those old, 42nd Street grind-houses in Manhattan. And, at some point, I realized I wanted to carry this new sensibility I was seeing into writing, drag it—popcorn, Winstons, graphic-sex-and-violence and all—screaming into a novel.

Then along came this idea. I went to work, using freelance jobs writing for magazines to support time on the book. A year later I had it. There were instances when what I was imagining made me cringe from my keyboard, but I had it.

Texas Chainsaw and *Night of the Living Dead* were my main models. They have obvious things in common. For one thing, both exist in a universe of simulated real time. They begin in the afternoon, run howling and screeching through the night, and end at dawn. Both have intimate violence. They seemed to shrink from nothing—no atrocity, not even from the very bleakest of endings. That was the innovation I had in mind. I'd never seen it done before, even with all my reading in the genre. Stephen King got pretty gruesome—but there were things Steve would not show you; He'd use a cutaway. I loved what he and others were doing in the field, but it wasn't what I was after.

I wanted to show you everything. I wanted to make you feel everything—every last nasty detail. The knife sinking into your very own flesh while you watched and listened and struggled not to die.

Off Season was an updating of the Sawney Beane story, a true story, set along the rugged cliffs of Scotland, about a family (a rather big one from kids to ancient crones) of seventeenth-century highwaymen-turned-cannibals. I was transplanting the notion into modern times and posited an equally repulsive *familia ferox* hidden for years off the coast of Maine, forced suddenly onto the mainland to wreak bloody havoc upon a group of vacationing Manhattanites on one gruesome rollercoaster of a night.

The rollercoaster being the third thing *Chainsaw* and *Night* had in common.

I researched and researched and researched; a non-negotiable necessity in providing emotion-invoking detail. If you're going in for the really tight close-up, you've got to get it right. I talked to doctors, asking basically the same questions all the time: *If I do this and this and this to him, can he still survive? And then what if I do this, is that one going to kill him? How much will he bleed? Are we talking drops of blood here or gouts of blood or what?*

I studied recipes. I went to the library and read everything I could find about cannibalism. Some of the early shipwreck accounts like *Mrs. Frazier on the Fatal Shore* included delightful hints on humans-as-cuisine. Others details I extrapolated from books like *How to Survive in the Wilderness* and Vardis Fisher's *Mountain Man* (made into the movie *Jeremiah Johnson*). I figured that, except for the fat-to-muscle quotient, there's not much difference between jerking deer meat and jerking Newt Gingrich.

Make It Real

It should go without saying that realism's the key here, just as it is with a lot of other aspects of fiction. You don't want to jar a reader who may just know about a certain subject—top to bottom, inside out—while you haven't quite done all your homework. You'll block his flow; kill his suspension of disbelief. Every writer makes mistakes, but it's important to catch as many as possible.

An example: At the end of *Off Season*, I have a character riding in an ambulance. She's been through 108 forms of hell by now, and she's practically delirious. She looks up at the figure riding with her and wonders briefly if he's a paramedic or a doctor and hopes that he's a doctor because she knows she's hurt bad. After the book was published, I got a letter from a guy who said he loved it—though he had one wee bitty problem with the end: Because he was a paramedic and he knew that, in a situation like this one, a paramedic's much better trained to save her butt than a doctor is. I'd gotten it wrong. I blew it for the guy.

I wrote back and apologized and promised that if I ever had a chance to correct the thing in reprint, I would; when the book came out in England, I did.

You also have to know your setting—inside out. If an attack is coming through a window, you'd better not have said previously that in this space we have a large oak door. And you must also know your instruments of mayhem: What sort of entrance wound is made by this kind of gun? What sort of exit wound? In what part of the body would I most likely have to shoot somebody (and how many times?) in order to stop him? That sort of thing. If you've got a character shooting a .357 magnum without ear protection, especially if he's shooting indoors, he'd better be deaf for a few pages. Maybe even a few chapters. A .22 rifle? No problem.

These are mechanical things, but they count. Anything short is just laziness and merely a form of *looking away.*

It's also important—and this goes for realism, too—to engage all the senses. Not just sight and sound—those are the easy ones—but smell, taste, touch. Remember, we're dealing with somebody's pain here; we're engaging the reader in someone's *experience* of pain. And you can't "do pain" properly without touch. The reader has to feel what the character feels when the blade touches the body, presses into the body, invades the body, and then finally roots around in there. In this kind of writing, it's every inch of the way or nothing at all.

Rehearsing for Death

The question, of course, is: Why the hell do this stuff in the first place?

I have to go back to my first question.

You think you know about pain?

There is nothing I can think of that is ennobling about pain, be it emotional or physical. Suffering breaks us down in both body and spirit, isolates us in our misery, cuts us off from one another. It's also something we'll all experience someday in one form or another, whether in a hospital bed or on a dark city street in the wrong part of town. Pain partakes of something primal in us, something all sentient creatures know, not just humans. And we'd sure better have a look at it—at what it does to us, how it changes us, at why and how it grows.

Someone once theorized that horror films and horror writing allow us to rehearse for death. I don't know about that, but I do know they rehearse us for worlds of grief and agony. They reflect those worlds, our worlds, through someone else's: the characters in a novel.

There are few things I find hard to watch in movies, but inevitably, they're the most familiar, the least removed from my experience. There's a scene in *Marathon Man* which roars instantly to mind. You know the one. Larry Olivier going at Dustin Hoffman's teeth with his power drill. The thing makes me cringe. And, as far as I'm concerned, the hardest thing to watch in *Chainsaw* is Granddaddy trying over and over again to coldcock Marilyn Burns with his hammer. Ever go to a sloppy dentist? Ever miss that nail and plant one on your finger?

You feel those scenes because you know them.

As Doug Winter says, horror's not a genre; it's an emotion. Likewise, *pain is us:* We've all had it, we'll all have it again. To shrink from pain in any form of art is to shrink from something fundamental about life—from part of the human, animal condition. Not that everybody has to tackle it, but that's not to say we should walk away from it either. It's dishonest.

There's a fine line, though, between honesty and exploitation; I've walked it many times. Because pain is also fundamentally grotesque. You don't go to that sloppy dentist every day, thank God. You don't whack yourself with a hammer on a daily basis either, or get beaten in an alley or hit by a truck or a roller-blader or suffer bone cancer or lose a loved one or, dare I say, get munched by cannibals. The major part of most people's lives is lived without pain. Most days, there's fair weather. Pain happens when the normal day breaks down, when something fails in the system, when things go haywire.

It's unusual, and like anything else unusual (as Madison Avenue would say), it's sexy.

Make Us Care

Have a look at your basic daytime talk show. One day they're interviewing teenagers with pierced tongues or women whose husbands have cheated on them with their own mothers, and the next day they're doing a satellite broadcast from prison and we're listening to Diane Downs try to convince us that she didn't really murder her kid because her boyfriend preferred her to be childless.

We are curious about anything unusual—including agony, including bloody murder.

We want to know what it feels like and I believe that we *should* know what it feels like. That's one thing writing's good for—getting us into dangerous waters while keeping us safe and dry at home. But there's only one way to do that, folks—to get to the actual feeling—and a lot of the writing in the area doesn't even try ... still another form of looking away.

You've got to make us give a damn—about all this grief, about all this suffering. You've got to exercise the compassion muscle.

If we don't care, it's just teenagers with pierced tongues again. The keys to making it more than that involve character, intent, and meaning—intertwined:

1. *Your characters—real people.* Take the time and care to make them real, to submit to the truth of your characters, their histories, their hopes and fears, with as much truth as you can muster. They'll reflect us only if you let them have their way as people. People can be zany and unpredictable sometimes, but for the most part, they pretty much go by the book. So you don't just waltz your second female lead into a darkened room in a spooky, old house with a candle and no weapon saying "Larry? Larry?" because you figure it's time to *off* her. You arm her to the teeth and she turns on every damn light in the joint.

2. *Your intent.* You must want us to care for these people, one way or another, even if it's only to despise them. Often, I contrast one evil with another and let you take your pick. Who's worse? Cannibal or scofflaw dad? Moral choices.

3. *The meaning of their suffering.* I'm not talking philosophy here. I suppose some would say suffering doesn't necessarily have any meaning at all, but I

don't agree—it sure as hell has meaning for the sufferer, even if he can only arrive at the question *Why me?* But it seems to me that pain always involves the loss of something—not necessarily the loss of life and limb, but sometimes of capability, innocence, personality, the capacity for joy. Loss eddies outward into other lives and it always has meaning for the loser. And the writer's job is to find it, know it—then share it with the rest of us.

Here's an example from my own stuff:

At the beginning of my book *Red,* I've got an old man fishing by a stream, his tackle box and his old dog Red—a long-ago birthday present from his now-dead wife—lying beside him. Along come three boys, one with a shotgun. They ask for money. The old man doesn't have any, so the kid shoots his dog, and not for any particular reason. Just out of meanness and because he can.

The line is, I think, appropriately nasty:

> And there wasn't even a yelp or a cry because the top of the dog's head wasn't there anymore nor the quick brown eyes nor the cat-scarred nose, all of them blasted into the brush behind the dog like a sudden rain of familiar flesh, the very look of the dog a sudden memory.

So the dog goes splat. The boys just laugh and walk away. Leaving the old man to deal with it.

> He got up and closed and locked his tackle box and set his rig, picked them up along with the cooler and walked back to where the dog lay. He tied the arms of his shirt around the dog's neck against the seep of blood and picked him up and tucked him under one arm with the rig and the cooler and tackle box all gripped in his other hand and then he started up the path.
>
> The dog grew very heavy.
>
> He had to stop twice to rest but he would not let go of the dog, only sat by the side of the path and put down the cooler and fishing gear and shifted the weight of the dog so that it rested in his lap across his knees, holding him in his arms until he was rested, smelling the familiar scent of his fur and the new smell of his blood.
>
> The second time he stopped he cried at last for the loss of him and for their long fine past together and pounded with his fist at the hardscrabble earth that had brought them here.
>
> And then he went on.

Could be I'm just tooting my own horn, but I think I got it right that time. No goofs like the one with the ambulance.

At least I'm happy with it.

I didn't look away.

Darkness Absolute: The Standards of Excellence in Horror Fiction
—Douglas E. Winter

What makes great horror fiction?

As a critic, I am called upon regularly to pass judgment on the writing of horror fiction's leading talents. I've probed the phenomenal success of Stephen King in a book-length study, and I've also written a history of modern horror, *Faces of Fear: Encounters With the Creators of Modern Horror*, as told through the lives of seventeen of its brightest and best-selling talents. As a compulsive reader and filmgoer, I've experienced nearly everything the field of horror has to offer, and my own fiction returns with regularity to themes of violence and fear.

This book offers a wealth of practical advice to the fledgling writer and certain insights into the business of writing that most of us learn only from experience. But recipes for success? There are no such things when we talk about quality fiction. Indeed, the best horror fiction is often that which breaks the perceived rules.

What follows, then, is a series of principles intended to offer general guidelines to the developing writer. As generalizations, they are subject to inevitable exceptions, and they must not, under any circumstances, be considered hard-and-fast rules. They deserve your attention, but not slavish devotion. These principles also have little, if anything, to do with best-sellerdom, a phenomenon that may (as in the case of Stephen King) concern talent, but that is more often the result of extrinsic factors. If your sole ambition is commercial success, look elsewhere for guidance; you probably lack the courage to write great horror fiction.

Originality

Perhaps the most difficult lesson for would-be horror writers to learn is that their stories rarely offer anything new. Few plots in this field are fresh and exciting; indeed, most editors lament how easily horror stories can be pigeon-holed into recognizable types.

The problem, simply stated, is that most horror writers are, first and foremost, horror fans. Their stories naturally tend to emulate, in style and subject, the film or fiction that they like best. There are, then, hundreds of published and unpublished books that read like rote imitations of best-selling novels or popular films, replete with such well-worn icons as Indian burial grounds, small towns besieged by evil, and ghastly presences that are revealed as the spearhead of an alien invasion.

Familiarity has its benefits. Imitation is a time-honored method of learning the fundamentals of writing. Moreover, to judge by the book racks, an audience exists for the paperback equivalent of leftovers. But, as the saying goes, familiarity also breeds contempt, and it certainly does not make for memorable horror fiction.

If you would excel in this field, remember that a fundamental mistake is to strive to emulate the commercial horror novel or story. The bulk of this fiction is poorly written and itself imitative; you will risk learning your craft at the feet of mediocrity. And even if you choose the field's most original voices to guide your efforts, the dangers of pastiche should be obvious.

If you admire Stephen King or Peter Straub or Dennis Etchison, fine, but save that admiration for party conversation. When it comes to committing words to paper, you are the writer, and it must be your ambition to better those you admire. If not, you are condemning yourself to be second-rate before you even get started.

Originality cannot be taught. But the task of finding your own voice will be eased if you stop reading what the marketplace calls horror fiction and join me in an important bit of heresy:

Horror is not a genre. It is an emotion.

It can be found in all of great literature. Read Conrad. Read Faulkner. Read Kosinski. Read Ballard, Cormier, Fuentes, McGuane, Stone, Whittemore. Read and read and read of the ways in which writers relate horrors without the strictures of genre.

Then return to your writing with a new perspective. Recognize that the fiction we hold dearest, the fiction you seek to write, is not a kind of fiction, meant to be confined to the ghetto of a special bookstore shelf like science fiction or the Western.

It is any and all kinds of fiction.

Characterization

A common mistake of beginning writers is to assume that horror alone is sufficient; but horror, as an emotion, is measured by its context—its time, its place, its characters. Anyone who has sat through a body-count film, like those of the *Friday the 13th* series, will understand that we care about the outcome of a story only if we have some emotional stake in its context.

For this reason, an essential element of great horror fiction is character. "You have got to love the people," says Stephen King. "There has got to be love involved, because the more you love—kids like Tad Trenton in *Cujo* or Danny Torrance in *The Shining*—then that allows horror to be possible."

One clue to developing effective characterizations is to recognize that stories do not proceed from events, but from the *perception* of events. Your story will be colored in its telling by your personality; similarly, the acts and words of its characters should, in turn, be colored by *their* personalities.

Unfortunately, most beginning writers tend to focus on character types (tough-guy cops, dizzy blondes, gays, misunderstood Vietnam veterans) rather than per-sonalities. If the reader can identify with the hopes, fears, flaws, and foibles of your characters, then love—and thus horror—is possible.

Reality

The emotion that is horror contrasts violently with our understanding of all things good and normal. There is thus no effective horror without a context of normality. Indeed, the best horror fiction effectively counterfeits reality, plac-ing the reader firmly within the worldly, even as it invokes the otherworldly.

For this reason, Richard Matheson is the most influential horror writer of this generation. In novels like *I Am Legend* (1954) and *The Shrinking Man* (1956), as well as his teleplays for *The Twilight Zone*, he helped wrest the fic-tion of fear from such traditional locales as mist-laden moors and gothic cas-tles, and invited it into our shopping malls and peaceful neighborhoods—into the house next door.

Embrace the ordinary so that the extraordinary events depicted will be heightened when played out against its context. Eschew exotic locales and the lifestyles of the rich and famous—rock stars, best-selling novelists, world trav-elers—in favor of all that is mundane in your world.

Mystery

The workaday world is indeed mundane when compared with the prospect of vampires, ghouls, and demonic possession. But it is a world whose ultimate meaning is shrouded by unanswered and unanswerable questions.

Where did we come from? Where are we going when we die? Does evil exist beyond the mind of man?

It is not the purpose of horror fiction to answer such questions. Indeed, nothing could be less frightening than most stories of so-called black magic, which suggest that the chaos of our world is nothing but a form of science, capable of invocation by formulaic chants.

When the printed tale of terror was young—in those days of "penny dreadfuls" and Gothic novels—a rigid dichotomy was observed between supernatural fiction and fiction based in rational explanation. The latter form, exemplified by Ann Radcliffe's *The Mysteries of Udolpho* (1794) and reprised briefly in the "Baby Jane" maniac films of the 1960s, proposed apparently supernatural events that were explained away at the story's end, usually as the nefarious deeds of another.

But today, explanation, whether supernatural or rational, is simply not the business of horror fiction. One source of horror's popularity is that its questions are unanswerable. At its heart is a single certainty—that, in Hamlet's words, "all that live must die"—and a single question: What then?

We're not looking for answers to that mystery—we know, if only instinctively, that these are matters of faith. What we are looking for is a way to confess our doubts, our disbeliefs, our fears. The effective horror writer cultivates our existential dilemma rather than arrogating the power to resolve it.

Bad Taste

Horror fiction is rarely in good taste. Indeed, most conventional horror stories proceed from the archetype of Pandora's box: the tense conflict between pleasure and fear that is latent when we face the forbidden and the unknown. In horror's pages, we open "the box," exposing what is taboo in our ordinary lives and witnessing both its dangers and its possibilities.

Not surprisingly, the best horror fiction tests the boundaries of acceptable behavior—consider, for example, the undercurrent of lesbianism in Shirley Jackson's *The Haunting of Hill House* (1959); the cruel violence of Iain Bank's *The Wasp Factory* (1983); the obsessive sexuality of Thomas Tessier's *Finishing Touches* (1986). A horror writer should be prepared not only to indulge in bad taste, but also to grapple with the taboo, dragging our terrors from the shadows and forcing readers to look upon them and despair—or laugh with relief.

The risks of bad taste are obvious; but in the words of James Herbert, "You can forgive virtually anything—any perversion, any nastiness—if it's really done with style." Most great horror fiction is informed with a keen aesthetic sense. The writer must know when the boundary has been reached, and when he is stepping over the line into the no-man's land of taboo. Those without this sense are doomed to purvey cheap thrills, confirming the worst doubts of the Meese Commission.

Suggestion

Although bad taste is intrinsic to great horror fiction, a "show-and-tell" mentality is not your key to success. While a current trend in horror fiction is toward explicit imagery of sex and violence, few writers seem to recognize that such explicitness is often anathema to horror.

How many times have you been disappointed by a motion-picture adaptation of a favorite horror novel? The reason is usually simple: The pictures were those of the director's choosing, not those you had seen with your mind's eye while reading the book.

Reading is an intimate act, a sharing of imagination by writer and reader. Its power is undoubtedly heightened when the subject involves our deepest and darkest fears. When a writer chooses explicit images, spelling out his horrors, he (like a film director) provides the picture, depriving the reader of the opportunity to share in the act of creation. Reading explicit fiction is thus a passive act, a take-it-or-leave-it proposition that may soon cause the reader to lose interest in you and your story.

But there is a more fundamental objection to explicitness. Too many purveyors of the "gross-out" are working from the proposition that the purpose of horror fiction is to shock the reader into submission. They indulge in the cheap tactic that motion-picture directors call "pop ups:" the hand thrusting into view, the sudden close-up of a ravaged corpse. But shock is a visceral experience, a sensory overload from which most of us recover quickly, with a laugh or with a scream.

Great horror fiction is rarely about shock, but rather more lasting emotions. It digs beneath our skin and stays with us. It is proof that an image is only as powerful as its context. Stylists such as Ramsey Campbell and Charles Grant can invoke more terror through a lingering shadow, a fugitive stain, than most "splatter" films can produce with gallons of spilled blood. That power—not only to scare, but also to disturb a reader, to invoke a memory that will linger long after the pages of the book are closed—is the true goal of every writer of horror fiction.

This should not suggest that the gross-out lacks effectiveness as a tool of the horror writer. There are moments when a vivid image is the only means by which the heights (or depths) of horror may be expressed. Special effects are also useful to open the readers' minds to possibilities; indeed, the outlandish violence of Clive Barker's *Books of Blood* (1984-85) or Lucio Fulci's zombie films can be seen as acts of liberation, freeing the viewer's mind to resonances of mythic proportions.

Subtext

D. H. Lawrence wrote of Edgar Allan Poe's horror fiction: "It is lurid and melodramatic, but it is true." Great horror fiction provides the shocks, the scares, all the entertainments of the carnival funhouse; but it also offers something more: a lasting impression, one both disturbing and oddly uplifting.

The best horror stories move beyond entertainment to serve, consciously or not, as imperfect mirrors of the real fears of their time. The masterpieces of "yellow

Gothic," such as Oscar Wilde's *The Picture of Dorian Gray* (1891) and H.G. Wells's *The Island of Dr. Moreau* (1896), echoed the fears of an age of imperial decline. The big-bug horrors of the 1950s were analogs of the Cold War mentality and the sudden shadow of the atomic bomb. More recent examples are discussed below.

Subtext is not simply the source of much cognitive power in horror fiction; it is also the means by which the traditional imagery of horror may be reenacted, updated, elevated. *Dracula's Children* (1974) by Richard Lortz and *Salem's Lot* (1975) by Stephen King are ready examples, infusing fresh blood into vampire mythology by imprinting it with sociopolitical themes.

Subversion

The best horror fiction is intrinsically subversive, striking against the pasteboard masks of fantasy to seek the true face of reality. Indeed, the great horror fiction being written today runs consistently against the grain of conventional horror, as if intent on forging something that might well be called the *antihorror* story.

American horror, particularly in film, has always been rich with puritan subtext: If there is a single certainty, it is that teenagers who have sex in cars or in the woods will die. Most books and films of the '80s offer a message as conservative as their morality: conform. The bogeymen of the *Halloween* and *Friday the 13th* films are the hitmen of homogeneity. Don't do it, they tell us, or *you* will pay an awful price. Don't talk to strangers. Don't party. Don't make love. Don't dare to be different.

Their victims, lost in the peccadilloes of the "me generation," waltz again and again into their waiting arms. Their sole nemesis is usually a monogamous (if not virginal) heroine—a middle-class madonna who has listened to her parents, and thus behaves. And it is proper behavior, not crucifixes or silver bullets, that tends to ward off the monsters of our times.

But the antihorror story tells us that conformity is the ultimate horror—and that monsters are, perhaps, passé.

Monsters

The monster is the paramount image of horror fiction and film, a trademark as enduring as the spaceship of science fiction, the hard-boiled detective of mystery fiction—and, no doubt, as inescapable. But those monsters have changed; indeed, the great horror fiction being written today is rarely about monsters.

The vampire is an anachronism in the wake of the sexual revolution. The bite of Bram Stoker's *Dracula* (1897), sharpened in the repression of Victorian times, has been blunted by the likes of Dr. Ruth Westheimer. The bloodthirsty count and his kin survive today because of sentiment rather than sensuality—

and as a fantasy of upper-class decadence, the commoner's forbidden dream of languorous chic (replayed by Catherine Deneuve and David Bowie in the film adaptation of Whitley Strieber's *The Hunger*).

The werewolf, too, has grown long in the tooth; its archetypal story, Robert Louis Stevenson's *The Strange Case of Dr. Jekyll and Mr. Hyde* (1886), also hinged on the Victorian mentality, with its marked duality of civilized gentleman and low-brow brute. As class distinctions wane in our populist times, the duality blurs. The werewolf will live so long as we struggle with the beast within, but its modern incarnations, from Whitley Strieber's *The Wolfen* (1979) and Thomas Tessier's *The Nightwalker* (1979), suggest that the savage has already won and is loose on the streets of the urban jungle.

Gone, too, are the survivals of past cultures—the mummies, the golems, the creatures from black lagoons; they cannot survive in a no-deposit/no-return society whose concept of ancient history is, more often than not, the 1950s.

The monsters of our time are less exotic and more symptomatic than their predecessors. A soulless insanity sparks the finest horror novel of the '80s, Thomas Harris's *Red Dragon* (1981). Child abuse is the relentless theme of the best-selling novels of V.C. Andrews, while the dissolution of family and mar-riage haunts the fiction of Charles L. Grant. The curse of socialization—notably venereal disease—infects the films of David Cronenberg as well as the fiction of Clive Barker. Urban decay is the relentless background of Ramsey Campbell's short stories. Stephen King glories in the malfunction of the mundane, giving life to the petty tyrannies of our consumer culture—our household goods, our cars and trucks, even our neighbor's dog.

And the true monsters of the '80s, still with us today and still relevant, look even more familiar. We may call them zombies, but as a character in George A. Romero's *Day of the Dead* announces, "They're us."

Endgame

Whether your story involves traditional monsters or more progressive forms of horror, there must come a time when it draws to a close. Ending a hor-ror story, particularly one of novel length, is probably the writer's greatest challenge. Its success often distinguishes the best horror fiction from the merely competent.

In the final trumps, the quality of horror is proportionate to its cost. Most horror fiction is about payback: the restoration of order, normally by destruc-tion of the agent of chaos. In the archetypal horror story, some malevolent phe-nomenon is loosed upon an unsuspecting world, claiming stock victims from central casting as appetizers for the main course, a virginal heroine or an in-nocent child. At the last moment, the phenomenon is understood and destroyed, order is restored, and all is well with the world ... until next time.

This hackneyed formula—which nevertheless serves as the basis for most horror novels published today—works passably until its ending. But when a writer imagines a horror of overwhelming proportion, the reader will normally feel cheated by the last-minute intervention of God or nature or man-made solutions. This strategy may have worked for H.G. Wells's *The War of the Worlds* (1897-98), which saw its invincible Martian invaders felled at the last moment by microbes, but today's readers are wiser—and *perhaps* more cynical.

After all, we know that horror exists in our world; indeed, we need look no further than the daily newspaper. We know, if only implicitly, that consummate evil cannot be overcome, cast out of our world completely.

We also know that the good in this world is not free—that there must be *payout* as well as *payback*.

The conclusion of a novel is not merely the stopping point of your plot; it is the vehicle by which the reader is awakened from your nightmare and returned to his workaday world. Writers who recognize the importance of this reintegration to the reader will tend to craft the most satisfying conclusions. Those who do not are doomed to such devices as the infamous "It was all just a dream," or the false ending, exercised brilliantly by Brian De Palma in his film adaptation of *Carrie* and trivialized by ham-fisted writers and directors ever since.

A Final Note

The standards of excellence in horror fiction are constantly growing, shifting, expanding—certain evidence of a thriving art form. Despite its rich traditions, horror fiction should not look back. Its best writers constantly push at its limits, redefining its limits even as they are established.

In the end, it is writers, not principles, that make great horror fiction. Writers with persistence. Writers with a vision that extends beyond marketing categories.

Writers who care.

On Horror: A Conversation With Harlan Ellison
—by Richard Gilliam

Editor's Note: Harlan Ellison has, for more than a few years, been openly critical of some of the commercial and artistic aspects of the horror genre. Yet during this period, he has received four Bram Stoker awards plus the Horror Writers Association Lifetime Achievement Award. The following interview was conducted in December 1996, but in considering it for publication in *On Writing Horror* (OWH), Ellison decided to change nothing and thought that events in the "horror genre" (sic) have added validation to his opinions.

OWH: You were toastmaster at the 1996 Horror Writers Association Banquet and delivered a surprisingly well-received speech that attacked the amateurism of a large segment of horror writers. It's been called a "ferocious" speech … What prompts this passionate assault?

Harlan Ellison: My feeling about contemporary horror writing is that it suffers from the same malaise that is suffocating most art forms in our time: widespread and deep-seated illiteracy on the part of the body politic and a lack of historical memory. People apply for editorial positions at fantasy magazines and book publishers, and when asked for their credentials as evaluators of the genre, they declare themselves well-versed, call themselves "big fans" of the field, and then they list having watched *The X-Files* as a qualification.

This wouldn't matter so much if they said they watched *The X-Files* and read books, but watching idiot television is what passes nowadays for an education in the genre. Ill-informed and semi-literate amateurs pollute the market and downgrade the literature. They make it impossible to reach, or create, a smarter audience.

OWH: But it isn't just *The X-Files* influence. You've been aggressively critical of the horror genre for the past seven or eight years.

Harlan Ellison: In my view, the horror story has always been a constrained form, even though the definition of "horror" has been expanded to include straight suspense or mystery fiction featuring serial killers. For years, I've been cautioning writers not to cling to a sinking ship; and even after one disastrous season atop the last, validating my observations, I'm witness to the ongoing uproar from people who don't want to hear that the engine room is filled with water. "How dare Ellison piss on the parade yet again!" they bleat. I don't much like being the specter at the banquet, but I do keep my eyes open, and I do listen. And as a consequence, I do think that, in many instances, writing horror became an activity for people who were better suited to be in other occupations. Check it out: all the pointless vampire novels that get published. The whole vampire *idea* is one of the dumbest that's ever come down the pike. Once you've read *Dracula* and Suzy McKee Charnas's *The Vampire Tapestry* and seen George Hamilton in *Love at First Bite*, what further is there to say about vampirism? It always boils down to "may-I-suck-your-neck?" No wonder—employing such creaky, familiar, dopey materials—that there's a record number of good writers in bankruptcy, and less-good ones who have had to take jobs at fast-food joints to survive in a time of desperation. The bad writers have driven away the readers. There's just too much imitative, semi-literate, in-joke crap out there. Excuse me if I display almost no compassion for people who are simply under-talented, jumped-up amateurs!

OWH: A few writers continue to have success. Stephen King, obviously.

Harlan Ellison: Stephen King single-handedly resurrected the horror novel. He's an unprecedented force in literature, *sui generis,* and there just isn't anyone in the history of American letters who has had that sort of success.

That didn't stop people from trying to jump on the King ship, though. When Stephen became a publishing phenomenon, through dint of hard work and by demonstrating a singular, universally accessible talent, a great many parvenus of limited ability, who were doing other things, fled across, slavering with greed—with not much else to recommend them—into horror. Fantasy writers came; science fiction writers came; romance writers came; mystery writers and suspense writers and true crime writers … and most of them not much of a writer to begin with, purveyors of derivative *crap.*

In only a very few cases were any of them successful. Dean Koontz, as a diametrically opposed exception, is a fine example of a real writer, because Dean is an accomplished storyteller who has a fecundity of imagination. And he's paid his dues. He has spent years learning to write well. But I could also list dozens of others, of less talent, who failed to fear the iceberg even after their personal *Titanic* hit it. The smart ones knew the ship was sinking and took to the life-boats, most often into suspense and mystery. The others got drawn down into the whirlpool and didn't get away from the genre quickly enough before it sank. The people who insist on calling themselves "horror writers" exclusively have stifled themselves; they're like those tunnel-visioned, superannuated "fanboys" who write "science fiction" exclusively or write "westerns" exclusively. It's an ama-teurish way for someone who thinks he or she is a writer to run a career. If you're a *writer*, you should be able to write more than just one type of fiction … which is also smart from a commercial perspective, since it opens additional markets—it opens the world—for the writer!

Those who have been earning a living for many years as professionals already know these truths in their blood and bones. Amateurs who stumble about and get published occasionally … and think they're writers … do not. They just ain't got a clue.

OWH: You also dislike the term "horror fiction."

Harlan Ellison: Jeezus, yes! What an off-putting appellation. I would much rather use the phrase "fiction of the macabre." Consider: Most people, what we like to call "normal people," spend most of their lives trying to *avoid* horror. The six-car pile-up on the freeway with beheaded corpses is horror. The mother who straps her children in a car and drowns them … that's horror. Bosnia, O.J. Simpson, church bombings by skinheads, all of that. It's horror. Sickening, paralyzing, horror, worse than splatterpunk shockstuff.

What I write is "fiction of the macabre," not horror.

OWH: And yet, you've continued to maintain connections to the genre, men-toring new writers who want to write horror.

Harlan Ellison: Correction: I support writers of talent who fight the odds in order to create *Art*. My connections are with writers, not with some bullshit category designation. Just because I visit a whorehouse to deliver succor and medicine don't make me no whore. I look at the horror field with a jaundiced eye, and I say this having read much of the recent work published in the field, including a great many of the anthologies and the semiprofessional maga-zines. Most of what gets published these days as horror writing is just *bad* writing. Sincere, maybe, but bad. Amateur. But the good news is that it isn't much worse than what's being published in other fields, and there are occasionally writers who deliver something good enough to make wading through the crap worthwhile.

When working with new writers, a mentor who means well *must* be selective and not profligate with his aid. Compassionate but tough … and pragmatic. You have to be able to differentiate between the ones who aren't threatened by constructive criticism, who are not in the game for self-aggrandizement and that fantasy lure—success—but are in the game to write what no one else has written, and those who are simply looking for undiscriminatory praise or validation. As long as the latter continue to seek that useless pseudo-confirmation, they're going to have a tough time getting any better. Get this: Writers always control their destiny. It's one of the few professions where a person can program him- or herself into being at the right place at the right time. There's no such thing as luck. It's how well you run your life—this cottage industry you call your writing career. It's the one great secret of writing that I've learned over the years, and the secret is not how to become a writer. If you look at the crap Judith Krantz writes, you'll know that ants or aphids can do it; paramecia can become writers. The secret is *staying* a writer. And staying a writer is hard. To stay a writer you have to keep growing, have to be flexible, have to be able to recognize when the world has gone on and changed without asking your opinion. Do that, and you can not only *become* a writer, you can *stay* a writer.

Part Six
Tradition and Modern Times

No More Silver Mirrors: The Monster in Our Times
—Karen E. Taylor

Everything old is new again. Or so it certainly seems these days. There is a pro-liferation of the classic stories; everyone seems to be taking Bram Stoker's *this* or Mary Wollstonecraft Shelley's *that* and putting a different, (usually) mod-ern spin on the story, twisting the original details and events to fit individual perspectives. From novels to anthologies to movies, we are being regaled with portraits of traditional and familiar monsters from new points of view.

Some may see this as a bastardization; others, as a natural evolution of the genre.

The purpose of this chapter, though, is not to pass judgment on current hor-ror trends, but to attempt to show you (at least from this author's viewpoint) how oft-told legends and venerable (okay, *old*) monsters can be brought into contemporary times.

A basic truth: People love monsters. Whether these monsters are vampires, ghosts, werewolves, demons, or shapeless blobs that devour everything in their paths makes little or no difference.

Today's readers, like yesterday's, pick up a horror novel to be purposely scared, to be entertained, to be drawn away from the conflicts of their own life and into the conflicts of the supernatural. They want larger-than-life struggles, heroic efforts facing almost insurmountable odds.

But modern readers are more sophisticated than their parents and grandpar-ents. Today's readers also require credible premises and explanations; they want things to be scientifically possible. They want reality in their non-reality. Very few people truly believe in the old monsters, and in order to produce an effective novel or story, the writer must foster a belief strong enough to carry the reader through-out. Talk about insurmountable odds!

But there are ways around the nonbelievers; ways to drag those old-fashioned monsters kicking and screaming, and dump them full-grown and growling into the "here and now," right where readers live. "I am here," you want your monster to say, "and I exist in your world. Deal with me, if you can!"

Know the Rules

So where do you start? First, approach your monster scientifically. Sedate him if necessary, lay him out on the examination table, and take him apart piece by piece. What is it that makes him what he is? What are the rules of his existence? Exactly what makes a vampire a vampire?

These rules are extremely important to your monster's believability. The writer must know them intimately—because the readers do. They know emphatically that a vampire feeds on the blood of humans, that he must shun the daylight, that he sleeps in a coffin, and is repelled by holy water and crucifixes. They know this not from firsthand experience, but because other writers have told them so.

Before beginning your project, research as much as you can, read as much as you can, and catalog the rules for your particular monster from the most basic to the most trivial and ridiculous. Gain an understanding of the perspective from which these rules have come.

There must always be inner rules for each monster that are "true" if he is to be recognizable to the reader. Decide within the context of your story which rules are basic to your creature, and stick with them throughout. Consistency might be "the hobgoblin of little minds," but it is the backbone of an "old monster made new" story.

If your vampire feeds on souls instead of blood, you can't have him vary his diet halfway through. If your werewolf must see the full moon to effect his transformation, you can't have him growing hairy in a windowless room. The readers will cry "foul," and rightly so.

Once you have delineated the essentials of your monster, you can (and *should*, in my opinion) break some of the other rules. Stretch the limits ...

But be prepared to defend your actions. Your vampire has a reflection in the mirror? Perhaps it's because mirrors today are made with mercury and not a holy/mystical metal like silver. He doesn't sleep in a coffin? Well, maybe he never knew he was supposed to, and therefore adapted to other methods of slumber. Or maybe your particular vampire is just plain claustrophobic and would rather chance facing the sun than being trapped inside close, wooden walls. Don't be afraid to play with the rules, to twist them to your purposes—to update ancient myths to reflect modern sensibilities.

This is *your* story. This is *your* monster.

Characterizing Your Monster

After rules have been made, and a few have been broken, you must deal with the character of the monster. He has to have a strong enough presence to balance out microwaves, satellite dishes, and neon lights, to stand up to a society that says "There's no such thing as you!" Remember that he should remain larger-than-life in today's world, while still seeming real. Give him a purpose in life (*unlife*, in the case of Mr. Vampire)—a goal for his actions.

Is he interested in world domination, creating and unleashing legions of his own kind on an unsuspecting human population? Or is he hungry for revenge, searching for a lost love, or just struggling to survive in a world that has left his kind behind? Give him a job, glamorous or mundane.

Just as in mainstream fiction, or the bleakest, most minimally plotted "slice-of-life" story, the monster character must have human traits with which readers can identify: lust, love, anger, hate, pain. And, like all of us, he has weaknesses as well as powers; there is nothing more dissatisfying in fright fiction than an invincible creature—who must be "defeated in the end" by totally implausible means.

Now take your monster by the claw and help him, even force him if necessary, to face modern-day situations. Regardless of the type of being he is, he needs to learn to deal with ordinary, day-to-day events. So have him ride the subway, take a cab, order a meal from a hot dog vendor, meet a mugger in a dark alley. How he reacts to "outside stimuli" goes a long way to bringing this creature to life. If he can strike a familiar chord, if he can evoke a response of "I would have done that, too," then you have succeeded in making him a viable character.

Believability of characters is integral in any story, horror or not. Creating human characters that seem real is an important and difficult job; the task is doubly difficult when you are working with a creature readers know does not exist. There are no chemical formulas for giving your creation life in fiction, no special laboratory equipment, no convenient lightning storms. Instead, you must rely on your skills as a writer.

Point of view is essential in making your unreal characters real. Get inside the creature's head as much as possible; show the reader what he is thinking, what motivates him, the senses driving his instinctual behaviors. Is your vampire's hunger nothing more than a pang, akin to something as trivial as a human missing a meal? Or is it a soul-devouring, conscience-overcoming rage? Is the transformation of your werewolf a painful process? When the hair grows in, does it tickle? Hurt? Itch? Give your reader the benefit of the monster's experience; guide the reader on a trip deep inside the monster's psyche. It is not necessarily important or even always desirable to garner sympathy for the creature (some monsters are evil and meant to stay that way), but try to provide an understanding of the internal as well as the external processes that make this particular being possible.

Know the Reader

Finally, you should attempt to understand the audience you are trying to reach. Horror fiction contains many subgenres, and readers who are voracious for one type (vampire fiction, for example) may not read another. So it is important to realize that your readers may hold certain expectations about what a "traditional" monster should be.

Vampires are portrayed today as sexual and ultraseductive creatures, deadly but ultimately attractive (as well as closely related) to humankind. From our human perspective, they appear sophisticated and desirable; often, they are pictured as misunderstood heroes. Yet this does not mean that they cannot also be the repulsive, ugly, and blood-thirsty creatures of the original legends. Hold true to *your* image, *your* view of your monster.

Yes, writers have an audience, and therefore an obligation to fulfill some audience (reader) expectations. If you meet the audience halfway, then you are safe in grafting your new vision onto the established one that is in the reader's mind. The guideline: Your monster is indeed yours, grown out of legend, yet belonging to your world and your times.

Make rules, break rules, and provide your character with traits and skills enabling him to make his way in our modern era, while still remaining true to that which makes him what he is.

The Prime Rule of Modern Monster-Making: Know Your Monster!

He is your creation, your responsibility, and your child—misbegotten or not, loved or hated, hero or villain.

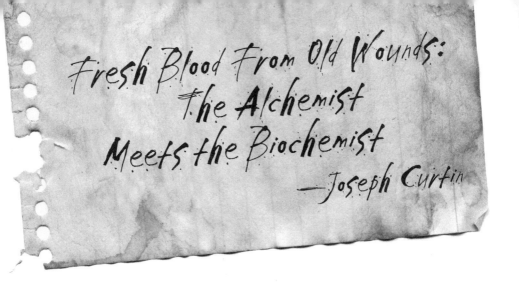

Fresh Blood From Old Wounds: The Alchemist Meets the Biochemist
—Joseph Curtin

I'm a sucker for the classics. Growing up reading *Famous Monsters of Film-land* and watching *Creature Features* and *Screaming Yellow Theatre*, I developed a soft spot in my black heart for the archetypical man-as-beast monster.

But horror stories have been around at least as long as the first campfire, so let's face it, being original in presenting classic tropes or even stylistic variants thereof is, let's say, a challenge.

My first novel, *Daughters of the Moon*, dealt with vampires—not a terribly original concept, but I did my best to keep it fresh and contemporary. I placed my protagonist, Erszébet Báthory, the Blood Countess of sixteenth-century Europe, in 1980s America and hooked her up with a rock 'n' roll garage band. I say (with no small amount of pride) that she was the first vampire to meet her doom on the spiky end of a splintered Fender Stratocaster guitar neck.

Science and Alchemy

With my obligatory tribute to bloodsuckers under my belt, I moved onto another tried-and-true: the werewolf. I was well into researching the material when I was struck by the similarities between the groundbreaking Human Genome Project, which had been dominating the news at the time, and the transmutational aspirations of the alchemist.

While outlining *Monsterman*, I had blessed the hero (a young-adult werewolf-to-be) with a brilliant father; a genetic biochemist and alchemist who sought to parlay his groundbreaking genetic research into a cure for the corrupted bloodline of his centuries-old, inbred werewolf clan.

Alchemy, I had learned, holds, at its core, three basic goals: (1) the transmutation of the baser metals into gold and silver, (2) the discovery of an elixir by which life may be prolonged indefinitely, and (3) the manufacturing of an artificial process of human life. The keystone for this three-fold quest was the discovery and fabrication of a powder or liquid universally referred to as the philosopher's stone. With the philosopher's stone, a seasoned alchemist could conceivably not only transform lead into gold, but also distill the elixir of life, the spiritual fluid which is the wellspring of human existence.

Aside from the metallurgical aspects of the first objective, the goals of the biochemist and the genetic engineer vary little from their medieval predecessor. By deciphering the chemical letters of the genetic code, the Human Genome Project has provided us with an essential blueprint, a map, of what makes us human. Upon identifying the twenty-five thousand genes and sequencing the approximately three billion base chemical pairs that make up human DNA, the information was put into a database and the resultant technology was made available to the private sector.

Crossing Boundaries

Almost overnight, limitless applications were crossing boundaries: from medicine to food to energy to environmental resources and beyond. Walls came tumbling down in hard-medicine research as the new biotechnology enabled overnight advances that were unfathomable only a decade ago. Life sciences has now grown into one of the largest sectors of the U.S. economy. The completion of the Human Genome Project has been called the greatest achievement in medical science since Dr. Salk's polio vaccine and the discovery of penicillin. Cancer-fighting DNA enzymes are on the verge of FDA approval, and many predict human life spans can be increased geometrically. Cellular regeneration—indeed, complete cellular reconstruction—is now a feasible application. Need a new liver? The next generation will be able to manufacture a fresh, compatible organ from the stem cells harvested from the subject's placenta at birth. Designer babies (you will be able to pick and choose your child's sex, hair color, and basic physical make-up) are right around the corner. A new dawn for mankind is breaking just over the horizon.

The Glow-in-the-Dark Bunny

Oh, and they also made green, glow-in-the-dark bunnies—just to see if such a thing could be done.

Eduardo Kac, a self-proclaimed "bio-artist," persuaded a French laboratory to splice fluorescent genes from a jellyfish into a rabbit embryo. The altered embryo was planted in a female rabbit, which gave birth to a bunny that glows neon green when placed under ultraviolet light (you just knew the pocket-protector crowd was going to have a field day with this one).

The ability to cut DNA from one organism and splice it into another is the foundation of biotechnology. It is also the process that allowed the French scientists to create the glowing bunny and is nowadays considered routine. In theory, they could have used the same technique to create a glowing human baby.

So great is the potential for abuse that the U.S. Department of Energy and the National Institutes of Health devoted 3 percent to 5 percent of the annual Human Genome Project budget to studying the ethical, legal, and social issues (ELSI) surrounding the availability of genetic information. Now that's probably a nice chunk of change, and I'm sure ELSI will provide high moral ground, but policing and enforcing any guidelines they provide will prove next to impossible. If the private sector can generate glow-in-the-dark bunnies just for grins, I shudder to think of what our own government is doing behind vaulted doors with this transgenic philosopher's stone.

Biotechnology, gene splicing, genetic mapping, cloning, stem cell research— the prospects for the horror writer are boundless.

But here's the best part: DNA is interchangeable between species.

Our Island of Dr. Moreau

See where I'm going with this?

H.G. Wells's mad Dr. Moreau is alive and well and his island is rising up out of the ocean and swallowing entire continents.

What's to stop a government from engineering a genetically crossbred man-beast in its quest for the perfect soldier? Let's take your basic infantryman, combine the savagery of the wolverine with the tenacity and speed of the mongoose, and create the ultimate killing machine. A new amphibious threat? The Creature from the Black Lagoon is not as far-fetched (funny-looking, sure) as it was in 1954. We share so many chromosomes with our ocean-dwelling brethren that the development of gills within a human mainframe would seem perfectly feasible. Lest you think I'm going a bit off the deep end here, check out this headline from the *New York Times*, November 27, 2002:

STEM CELL MIXING MAY FORM A HUMAN-MOUSE HYBRID

By Nicholas Wade

Space allows me to include but a snippet of the entire article, but it speaks volumes:

Dr. Irving L. Weissman, an expert on stem cells at Stanford University, said that making mice with human cells could be "an enormously important experiment," but if conducted carelessly, could lead to outcomes that are "too horrible to contemplate."

"... outcomes that are 'too horrible to contemplate.' I love that line and, as a horror writer, I choose to ignore Dr. Weissman's advice and contemplate the experiment's outcome with great forethought and—I must admit—a touch of glee.

Finding horror in the laboratory is nothing new. Shelley's *Frankenstein* is, of course, the most famous, and a fine example of how a twenty-first-century scribe may benefit from mining the same stratum. Dr. F's dream of creating human life from existing tissue is a hell of a lot more feasible today than when Shelley penned it in 1831—and that makes it all the more frightening. Frankenstein has been adapted and reworked ad nauseam, but it is fair to say no one has applied a biotechnical upgrade to the story more successfully than Dean Koontz in his brilliant four-book series dealing with the re-animated giant and his mad creator. No one can accuse Koontz, along with Kevin J. Andersen and Ed Gorman, his collaborators on the first two of the planned four-part series, of grave-robbing (sorry) for revisiting this timeless classic.

In 1990, the father of the techno-thriller, Michael Crichton, reached back to 1912, dusted off Sir Arthur Conan Doyle's *The Lost World* and created a mega-franchise with *Jurassic Park*. What makes *Jurassic Park* such a compelling read is Crichton's ability to convince us that creating genetically engineered dinosaurs from amphibiously enhanced scraps of their DNA is entirely possible. Crichton, armed with a medical degree from Harvard, incorporates just enough scientific jargon (for the layman) to back it up, and it's that sliver of believability that swept the novel off the sci-fi shelves and propelled it into the heart of mainstream America.

The science at our fingertips is no longer science fiction, and the gleam of the new technology belies the abhorrent potential lying dormant just beneath the shiny surface.

Robin Cook, another doctor-turned-novelist, saw the bio-storm coming years ago and invented the subgenre known as the medical thriller. Cook appreciated the potential for terror visible only through a microscope. Bioterrorism and bacterial poisoning are frightening realities that most of us don't like to think about—much less discuss. Verbalization makes it all the more real, you see. A quick scan of some of some recently published essays from biomed graduate students at San Francisco State University's medical school casts an eerily prophetic tone on some of Cook's earlier work:

"The Bio-Tech Century: Playing Ecological Roulette with Mother Nature's Designs."

"*GM Microbes Invade North America (*genetically manufactured)"

"Killer Virus: An engineered mouse virus leaves us one step away from the ultimate bio-weapon."

"Biohazards: The Next Generation?"

Bio-Tech Terror

Scary stuff, by any standard, but there again, it is the very plausibility of the threat combined with our inherent fear of the unknown that makes it doubly frightening.

This generation's fear of the altered chromosome is no different than the fear of the split atom our parents and grandparents felt back in the early 1950s. Nuclear power and its fallout spawned a new subgenre in horror films: the *atomic monster*. Mutant amphibians, enormous insects, and half-human/half-fishlike carnivores poured out of upstart studios almost quicker than the film could be developed. Sure, most of the stuff was drive-in movie filler and more comedy than horror, but there were a few rare and thoughtful exceptions. Chief among these was *Godzilla*; unmistakably Japanese and clearly representing the nuclear dread entrenched in the national psyche of the island after Hiroshima and Nagasaki. The footage of Tokyo smoldering in radioactive ruin beneath the monster's fiery breath remains a powerful metaphor and most humbling experience, even when viewed today.

Cold War paranoia was not just limited to Japan; in 1953, Warner Brothers released the giant, mutated ant saga *Them* amidst the continued nuclear testing taking place right on our own desert soil. Oppenheimer's terrible gift lent an all-too-real face to fear and changed the world forever.

Biotechnology will also change the world—you can bank on it.

The most tragic horror starts in the laboratory wrought from the minds of brilliant men with only the best intentions—just like Dr. Frankenstein's monster.

Nuclear power and radioactive fallout. Biotechnology and gene-splicing. Different fruit from the same Tree of Creation. As long as man continues to uproot the foliage of Eden and slog deeper into the primordial soup from which we crawled millions of years ago, we will carry with us the potential for our own destruction.

As a parent, it makes me shudder.

As a horror writer, it makes me tingle.

More Simply Human
—Tracy Knight

Horror fiction deals in aberrations—aberrations of nature and circumstance, of fate and destiny, of the cosmic and the exquisitely human. Of these facets, the most memorable and compelling are the human beings who populate the writer's fictional world. Through their eyes, the reader is able to behold existence from a unique and unexpected perspective. The reader is able to live another human's endeavor in order to understand, avoid, or defeat an unimaginable reality, a loathsome monster, or a mind-bending situation.

Creating believable characters who invite a reader's identification and investment is the hallmark of effective writing of every genre. In horror fiction, this can be particularly challenging since, in so many ways, the writer is asking us to accept and embrace the unreal. For this reason, characterization in horror writing is central to a story's success.

Characters who embody the struggles, tragedies, and terrors of mental disorders—from eccentricities of personality to psychoses—are widespread in horror fiction, no matter whether they are the protagonist or, as is the case all too often, the malevolent horror itself. When they are effectively developed, nurtured into completeness, these characters become the centerpieces of unforgettable short stories or novels. Consider Norman Bates in Robert Bloch's *Psycho*; Hannibal Lecter in Thomas Harris's *The Silence of the Lambs*; the characters' interlocking pathologies in Ed Gorman's political thriller *The Marilyn Tapes*; the stark, chilling, and sometimes comedic psychopaths in J.N. Williamson's *The Book of Webster's*; and the alien derangement of George Smith in Theodore Sturgeon's *Some of Your Blood*.

As a clinical psychologist, I am interested in how writers portray personality types and mental disorders. However, with alarming frequency, authors make basic errors that interfere with the enjoyment of their fiction. Perhaps because we all possess our own personal psychologies, we tend to assume that we know how human difficulties and insanity manifest themselves, and how they are expressed in thought, perception, and behavior. Couple this with the strange and inaccurate portrayals of psychological difficulties in media of all ilk and you have a recipe for a myriad of fictional missteps.

Yet, in order to create compelling characters who accurately portray human personality types and mental disorders, a writer need not pursue an advanced degree. The necessary tools with which to build such characters are literally at one's fingertips. Adding these psych resources to your existing ability to create characters will sharpen your proficiency to integrate human aberrations into your horror fiction, thus fashioning characters who not only are beyond the norm of most readers' experiences, but believable as well.

I hasten to add that I am not sounding a call to create characters with mental disorders to merely add color and strangeness to your stories. Rather, these characters are used so frequently, I'm only interested in it being done more accurately—and, ultimately, more humanely.

In past months, I've read works of horror fiction in which: (1) a schizophrenic switches personalities helplessly, from priest to murderer to three-year-old child; (2) a severely depressed law enforcement officer engages in car chases, leaps from building rooftops in frenzied pursuit of suspects, all with incredible energy; (3) a "psychotic killer" methodically plans a series of murders with clarity and an extraordinary lack of emotion; and (4) a psychologist laments the fact that she cannot treat mental illness, since psychologists are only trained to work with family relationships, then later injects a patient with medication as part of his treatment.

What do all of these examples have in common? They are *wrong*. They rest on foundations of inaccurate information, thus splintering the seamless dream the writer is attempting to create.

To quickly address each of the above-mentioned errors:

1. Schizophrenia and Multiple Personality Disorder (now termed Dissociative Identity Disorder) are distinct clinical entities. Please write this down in large block letters. If I accomplish nothing else in this chapter other than to reduce the grotesque number of times this error is made, I will consider my existence on this planet well spent.

Schizophrenia is a devastating mental illness that may manifest itself as hallucinations, delusions, disorganized speech and behavior, social withdrawal, and dulling of emotional responses. While the term "schizophrenia" is derived from Greek words meaning "split mind" (which may be where the confusion originally arose), a more accurate definition is "shattered mind." The split is not between personalities; it is between *self* and *world*. The boundaries blur, or even vanish. Thus, an internal image becomes an external phenomenon; an idea becomes a worldly truth.

What has been known as Multiple Personality Disorder is marked by the presence of two or more distinct (albeit interestingly incomplete) personalities that repeatedly take control of an individual's behavior, often with the activities of one personality remaining virtually unknown to another. Even more interesting is the debate in psychology and psychiatry regarding the existence of this syndrome as a pure disorder; an increasing number of professionals believe that this disorder is often created or encouraged in psychotherapy.

2. A severely depressed man would not likely have the physical energy to engage in James Bondian adventures. Cardinal signs of a major depression include loss of interest and motivation, difficulty concentrating, diminished energy, and feelings of worthlessness, none of which is particularly conducive to the spirited pursuit of a quarry.

3. A *psychotic* killer and a *psychopathic* killer are not synonymous. A psychotic person has experienced a break with reality, likely including delusions and hallucinations (and on the whole is *less* likely to be dangerous than the rest of us, by the way), while the common use of the term "psychopathic" refers to an irredeemably antisocial individual who is impulsive, deceitful, aggressive, and has little to no conscience or empathy.

4. A psychologist treats mental illness, but is not a *medical* doctor, per se. Although most psychologists have doctorate degrees (e.g., Ph.D., Psy.D., or Ed.D.), they generally do not prescribe or administer medication. However, their central function in a clinical setting is the diagnosis and treatment of mental disorders through assessment and psychotherapy. There is perhaps no stronger or odder commentary on the portrayal of mental health professionals in the media than the observation that Bob Newhart's sitcom character was among the most accurate—which says much about the media's accuracy.

A psychiatrist is someone who has earned an MD degree, then goes on to specialize in the medical treatment of mental illness. It is the psychiatrist who prescribes and monitors the use of psychotropic medications.

Getting It Right

These inaccuracies represent common errors writers make when including psychological terms in their fiction. However, as is the case in the whole of life, it is much easier to point out errors and mistakes than it is to chart a positive course. As I have often told my clients, "If blame cured anyone, we'd all be perfect by now." In the remainder of this chapter, therefore, I will offer horror writers a few suggestions on how to more successfully integrate human aberrations into their fiction.

Invest in a copy of the American Psychiatric Association's *Diagnostic and Statistical Manual of Mental Disorders* (currently in its fourth edition and often referred to as the *DSM* or *DSM-IV*). It is the standard diagnostic reference for psychiatry and psychology. Used by researchers, clinicians, and insurance companies to approach some consensus about the definitions and signs of everything from childhood disorders to organic brain syndromes, from psychotic disorders to anxiety disorders, from sexual disorders to personality disorders. This book is a treasure for the writer seeking to portray human psychological difficulties accurately. It contains not only basic descriptions of currently recognized mental disorders, but also enhances these descriptions with information on the prevalence, course, and associated features of those difficulties.

It is important to recognize that psychiatric diagnoses undergo constant change as new evidence emerges to help shape our understanding of human difficulties. Did you know, for example, that "homosexuality" is no longer a psychiatric diagnosis or that "neurosis" as a concept has all but disappeared from current diagnostic formulations? Because of the changes in diagnoses that occur over time, if you are writing a story set in a time other than the present, it will prove valuable to research the psychiatric diagnoses which existed *at the time* of the story.

For example, in Ed Gorman's *The Marilyn Tapes*, Marilyn Monroe's psychiatrist diagnoses her as evidencing Cyclothymic Personality, a diagnosis that no longer exists today—but did when the story took place.

After using the *DSM* for basic research, a writer can then bolster understanding of a disorder by using the countless books and journal articles available on each disorder, or even by perusing a standard college textbook on abnormal psychology.

Recognize that most modern psychotherapy is not Freudian psychoanalysis. Writers have a tendency, when including psychotherapy in their stories, to include a couch, free association, dream analysis, endless discussions of childhood, and the ubiquitous Rorschach inkblots. These are all facets of classic psychoanalysis, which, while it still exists, is not currently practiced by many psychotherapists. There are over 350 distinct and definable systems of psychotherapy. I recommend that you avail yourself of Raymond Corsini's excellent series, *Current Psychotherapies*. Each edition of this work includes succinct and clear coverage of a number of psychotherapeutic approaches, including a brief statement of the underlying theory, the basic concepts of the system, its history, its current status, its applications, and even a case example.

Resources such as these will not only strengthen the factual foundation of your fiction, but can also spark a legion of creative ideas.

Caveat. The *DSM* poses the same danger as any other research resource: It can inadvertently encourage a writer to create a caricature rather than a living, breathing human character. Therefore, I offer here some further insights on human functioning, in hopes that these simple ideas will help you to create characters in your horror fiction who not only display all the color and uniqueness you hope to invoke, but also the internal consistency that a reader expects from any fictional character.

Personality

What is personality? Human personality is the characteristic and enduring way that each of us perceives and interprets the world; the beliefs and assumptions we make about ourselves, the world, and other people; and the patterns of behavior we are likely to show regularly. These patterns range from the smallest (the way a man plays with his mustache) to the most general (reacting with rage whenever one's judgment is questioned). In short, personality is the map we use to navigate our lives.

It is as if each of us wears a pair of colored eyeglasses with its unique hue. Everything we experience is filtered through those glasses, and thus each of us has a uniquely individual take on the life we're living and the world in which we're living it.

When someone has a personality disorder (distinct from a clinical syndrome or illness), he or she has a rigid, predictable, and inflexible way of perceiving, interpreting, and acting on the world. Thus, a paranoid personality will interpret a comment, no matter how benign, as demeaning or threatening; an avoidant personality will perceive remarks from others as indicating potential rejection or humiliation; a schizoid personality will show little interest in relationships with others and will be unaffected by comments, good or bad. Because the inflexibility is so much a part of a personality disorder—indeed, of most mental disorders—many clinicians, myself included, believe the word "disorder" to be somewhat of a misnomer. If anything, most of the clients we see are too ordered, too predictable, and limited in their perceptions and responses, and a goal of psychotherapy is to help them become less predictable.

Too often, unbalanced or psychotic characters in horror fiction deviate from this insight. Apparently the writer assumes that since he or she created a "crazy character," that character can do virtually *anything* in the story, and that the label of mental illness is a license to act totally unpredictably and irrationally. This is not true. Which leads me to my next point:

Setting Goals

Every behavior has a goal. When I was an intern psychologist, I was called in to see my first floridly psychotic patient. She was a pleasant and polite woman, but insisted that God was talking to her even as we conversed, and that she was afraid her husband would cause her to lose the child she was carrying— the result of God impregnating her. At first, being a wide-eyed intern, I made feeble attempts to somehow reel her in and encourage her to share the world that I was inhabiting. Suddenly an insight struck me: If I had God talking in one of my ears, and a young psychologist in the other, whom would I listen to? Having recognized that, I proceeded to immerse myself in her world and, to my surprise, found not that her behavior was horribly disorganized or random, but rather that every single behavior had a goal. *Of course she walked backward with her hands on her stomach because God had told her he would strike her dead if she didn't protect their child.* It all made sense.

In the same way, you must know not only what your character's "symptoms" are, but also how your character views the world from the inside. To truly captivate your reader, that world must be coherent and consistent, no matter how bizarre it may seem on its face.

The Best

Everyone is doing his or her best. Upon first glance, this may sound ludicrous, but it's true. With the world they perceive, the view they have of themselves, and the options they recognize, people, in general, make the best choices they can at any moment. Remember this.

More Than Symptoms

Everyone is more than a collection of symptoms. Although the *DSM* is a wonderful way to provide some structure to your aberrant characters, to give them a coherent and accurate form, it is crucial to understand that not one person is contained in any diagnostic description. The diagnostic system, like all systems, was created in order to simplify the world; therefore, the search was not for ultimate truth but for patterns—characteristics that tend to appear together. No one perfectly exemplifies any diagnostic pattern, and no diagnostic pattern captures a human being. Not even close.

There is a philosophical concept known as the "A/Not A Absurdity," which states that when one draws a line between any two constructs—whether those constructs are mentally ill/mentally healthy, diabetic/non-diabetic, even dead/ alive—and then one construct approaches that line from either direction, the line disappears. There is relatively little difference between people who are considered mentally ill and those who are not. Psychiatrist Harry Stack Sullivan said it best: "We are all much more simply human than otherwise."

Perhaps that is the secret of creating believable characters who portray any type of human aberration. It's not that they are radically different than the rest of us; it's that we share so much with them. We share their irrational fears, their unacceptable desires. We have our moments when we feel out of control or when our ruthlessness rushes to the fore.

That is why the most effective characters in horror fiction who display some mental or personality disorder prove so chilling. After all, even cold-blooded killer Hannibal Lecter gave voice to the romantic notion that he and Clarice were looking up at the same stars. Even Norman Bates quietly mourned his mother.

We are all more simply human than otherwise.

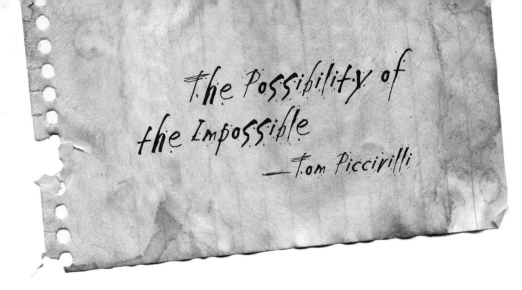

The Possibility of the Impossible
—Tom Piccirilli

Postmodernism, absurdism, slipstream, nihilism, magic realism—call the surreal by whatever name you like. But we still all know what it is, even though, at last look, nobody's come up with an adequate definition to describe exactly what it does or, more specifically, how it's used as a literary device.

Like everything you find in the subjective, shadowy corners of what we call *style;* you feel it more with your gut than see it with your eyes. That's all right, though. Horror writers are accustomed to working in the dark.

For the sake of this piece, let's just say that it's the kind of narrative voice that breaks from the normally plotted, linear story rooted in reality. Instead of a natural, logical progression from point *A* to point *B* or *C* or even *Z*, you go from point *A* to Point 89.134 Alpha Magenta. Things get weird fast, but they get there with an emotional impact. You wind up with Kafka's "The Metamorphosis," where poor Gregor wakes up one day as a giant cockroach for no reason whatsoever and discovers that his family accepts that fact without question.

So why do it? Why go to all the trouble to break with a realistic, practical approach when you're already dealing with plenty of horrific images, monsters, mayhem, and bucket loads of trauma?

Surreality = Originality + Freedom

The short answer to the "why do it?" question: so that you can *shatter* the mold and break new ground through originality and unpredictability.

To make the unnatural *seem* natural gives a writer the chance to explore new layers of allegory, irony, and even satire, within the complex arena of dark fantasy. The essence of our genre is not solely to tell a scary tale, but also to deeply unsettle and disturb the reader.

It might be done by taking the reader on a bizarre journey during which the world either slowly shifts into nightmare by degrees or goes all to hell with an immediate left turn.

To dip into the surreal allows a writer to take wondrous risks, to press at the thresholds of thought and imagination, to twist the borders of what's considered normal, and employ the unknown. It allows you to cross genres at a whim and not be burdened by the precepts of one or another. Other adjectives you can apply include: quirky, nonconformist, aberrant, unpredictable, grotesque, unconventional, unexpected, eccentric, and atypical.

Metaphors can take on whole new meaning. In Barry Yourgrau's "By the Creek," a young man takes the head of his sleeping father and wears it as his own. Got daddy issues? Got something to say to or about your old man? Imagine the freedom to do so if you are completely unfettered by a realistic plot. To write a tale in which you are not hampered by a linear or realistic plot. *Hey, want to wear your dad's head? Put it on!*

You can set up that sort of complexity which affords you a better view of themes that have a wealth of significance. You can cast doubt on whether something fantastical is actually happening—or if all the cool, weird stuff is occurring in the psyche of an unreliable narrator. You keep the reader interested and you keep him guessing.

A Surreal How-To

Okay, so now *how* do you do it—keep the reader reading, that is?

One definition of humor is when two concepts, not normally put together, are fused into one. To me that's as good as any explanation of how to approach the surreal. Donald Barthelme's "Some of Us Had Been Threatening Our Friend Colby" deals with a group of friends who decide to hang their buddy, Colby, because "he'd gone too far." His crime (if there even was one) is never explained. The group simply decides to throw a gala-like event complete with printed invitations, a full orchestra, wine and food, and a large guest list. Colby never really argues and "performs creditably" at his own hanging.

On one level, that's pretty damn funny; but on another, you can see the potential for pure horror: There's plenty of shock value in a world where your friends turn on you in a calm manner and righteously declare they're going to kill you.

In Dennis Etchison's "The Dog Park," we're introduced to a screenwriter out for a day in a dog park that's become a meeting ground for folks in the industry, where previously his own pet had been lost. He meets a colleague, who's also lost her dog, and the two go in search of it as the park nears its closing time. The high deck of a neighboring building seems to be filled with people watching in an excited manner, as if some evil will soon befall the writer and they're perched just waiting for it to happen. The world that had been relaxing, familiar, and comfortable—Etchison even pokes a few funnies at Hollywood—is soon completely upended even though, aside from the missing dogs, nothing horrific actually happened. Etchison relies completely upon the atmosphere he's created, subtly shifting it from humorous to hair-raising.

Again, we see that: the surreal is related to comedy; the absurd can be extremely funny; and something too absurd can easily make that not-so-broad leap into terror.

In my novel *A Choir of Ill Children*, my protagonist, Thomas, is caretaker to his three brothers, "Siamese triplets," conjoined at their frontal lobes. He must navigate his way through a mystery involving swamp witches, a preacher overcome with the power to speak in tongues, a decades-old murder, ghostly children, a mysterious figure who keeps kicking dogs in the county, a carnival geek, a teen seductress, and a monastery called the Holy Order of Flying Walendas.

Why in hell would anybody want to write something as screwy as all that?

Because, as Robert Frost said, "All of art is metaphor." That's right, we're back to metaphor: the capacity to illuminate one thing by telling the audience something else.

By using those bizarre images, characters, and subplots, I was able to relate the tale of several lonely, dysfunctional, lost people who come together to work out their troubles. By using such exaggerated circumstances, I could reflect on various concepts of family and faith at length. In the inhuman, I focused on the human.

In the impossible, we convey not only what is possible, but what's meaningful to us. My short story "The Misfit Child Grows Fat on Despair" starts off normally enough with a poor overweight schlub in line trying to cash his meager check at a bank. Suddenly, a robbery erupts around him. While everyone else is screaming and diving to the floor, the schlub shows no fear. He seems accustomed to this sort of situation. Is he a cop? A hero?

Originally, I intended to create a darkly humorous action tale about an unarmed fat guy named John, who takes on the three hardened, gun-toting criminals, even though he's untrained, out of shape, and huffing terribly. But no matter how much I twisted the action tale around, I couldn't squeeze any kind of real tension out of it. Lots of *comedy*—but no intensity or apprehension.

So I let it percolate awhile longer and, eventually, the story became something stranger and darker. The plot line shifted to where it only *seems* that John is going to leap into the fray and duke it out with the murderous robbers.

Instead, he swallows their souls. The dead go to live in a town called Gethsemane Hills, which exists inside the big guy's belly.

Do I give any kind of a reason or explanation? No. It's simply a grotesque fact of the tale. For the sake of the story and to make the impact I was trying for, this was the most powerful way for the piece to go. No need for a long expository justification. No haunted Indian burial grounds, alien-probe DNA mutations, nuclear fallout, demons from the sixth level of hell, or tentacled Elder Gods returning to destroy earth. It just has to work.

From that initial narrative change, I was able to go off in a completely new direction: Inside Gethsemane Hills, John is lord and master, who not only torments the bank robbers, but also one of the bank cashiers murdered during the stickup. He can force them to do whatever he likes, bending them to his almighty will. John effectively becomes the devil.

There's the duality. I started off with a humorous set-up that could've been a comedy of errors, but instead, chose to suddenly do a 180 which converts "misfit" into a perverse, offbeat, eerie tale in which the laughable figure is now a monster. I took what were, essentially, two distinct stories and welded them into something that took me to a place I'd never been before. From the oddity itself came the horror.

New Paths

Rearranging the normal can take you off the maps you're familiar with to chart entirely new courses. It can help you find a narrative voice or expression that not only plumbs new depths of originality, but also helps you to discover how to use a distortion of your own familiar world to ratchet up the fears and tension that exist in all of us.

Don't be afraid to investigate an unexpected turn in your tale. Remember that a key phrase in horror literature is "internal logic" — the rules of rationality that are applied by you to your story. You can make two contradictory, conflicting, or just plain weirdo concepts fit together — so long as it underscores whatever you're trying to say in the narrative. Bring a sense of realism to the dreamlike, and you'll be able to effectively create a mood, situation, or character that your reader can accept — no matter what kind of unusual or outlandish incidents you present.

In the end, not only style, voice, or marketability make a good horror writer, it is also his or her vision and how that vision is used that enhances the power of this fiction.

Now go on out there.

And get unreal.

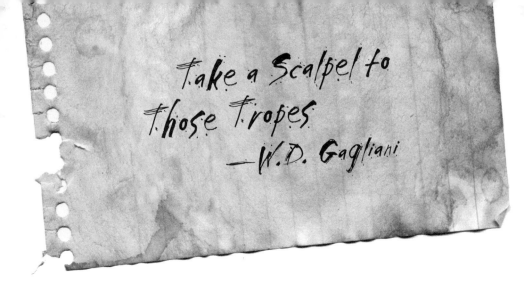

Take a Scalpel to
Those Tropes
—W.D. Gagliani

Trope: in literature, a familiar and/or often used (and perhaps overused) symbol, style, character, or element.

You're about to start writing your first horror novel. You have a story to tell, but will you employ a completely new, never-before-seen "monster" as antagonist? Or will you choose a classic monster: a vampire, zombie, or werewolf?

Hybrid Horror

Maybe it'll be a combination of both. You'll carefully examine the tropes; then genetically engineer a hybrid.

If so, you'll have taken a trope and updated it for today's readers, making something familiar into something new.

That's what I tried to do when I started *Wolf's Trap*, a novel that would take ten years to publish, but would earn a Bram Stoker Award nomination and lead to a mass-market deal. (Why ten years? That's another essay.) I can't tell *you* how to do it, but I can tell you how *I* did it—and why.

Growing up, I thrilled to WGN's *Creature Features* on Saturday nights. I loved the classic monsters, but always associated most with the Wolf Man. A tragic figure, Talbot was cursed by his monstrous appetite and tormented by his doomed place in the world.

What better metaphor for youth?

As I began writing *Wolf's Trap*, serial killers were all the rage (had even become an overused trope, some would say), but a serial-killer backlash was developing. I still liked their cold-blooded ways, however, so I decided a serial killer with revenge on his mind would be my antagonist, twisting the trope ever so slightly.

And a *werewolf*—that tragic symbol of youth, duality, and suppressed rage …
There's my hero.

Hero, you say?

Well, why not? Did the werewolf have to be the bad guy? Better yet, why
couldn't he be someone whose curse had cost him plenty, but it wasn't his fault.
I called him Dominic (Nick) Lupo (easy choice, since *lupo* is Italian for "wolf"),
thereby giving him a built-in destiny to fulfill.

Most people know that much of the werewolf's cultural trappings come
straight from Hollywood and Universal Studios. But a little research also
shows that werewolf sightings, tales, and legends (like those of vampires) are
found throughout Europe and other cultures, from the Dark Ages to the present. Interestingly, wolf tales also permeate Native American mythologies.

Since *Wolf's Trap* is set in Wisconsin's sprawling natural forests, wherein
dwell various Native American tribes, I decided to create another hybrid trope
and blend mythologies. It wasn't completely original, as others have trod similar ground, but I added the serial-killer trope and a subplot involving sex and
porn as well. By the time I was done blending, *Wolf's Trap* no longer relied
solely on the overused werewolf-as-monster trope.

But what of the Hollywood werewolf?

Much of what I'd loved as a wide-eyed kid, scaring myself half to death on
Saturday nights, was a part of me, too. I couldn't let go of all that, so I kept a
few selected elements, mostly as homage.

Traditional Trappings for the Trope

The moon's influence forced my protagonist to combat the beast within, a
motif I especially liked. But I altered that somewhat: The full moon forced a
change, but our hero could also learn to *control* his changes. His mastering of
the *change*, after a disastrous early attempt, becomes an important subplot
that also works as part of the extended metaphor—the young and rebellious
eventually learn to control their wilder impulses.

Another trope altered … and renewed.

The pure Hollywood artifact, silver, I kept. It allowed for some tinkering
with the serial killer's point of view and his inside knowledge. He commissions
a gunsmith to make silver bullets, then murders him to send my protagonist
a message. Silver is Lupo's Kryptonite, and it figures heavily in the climax,
which is styled on the classic encounter in the mist-shrouded forest.

More tropes met my scalpel and were reshaped to fit the story I was telling.
The result: a novel that borrows equally from erotic horror, noir crime, suspense, and the thriller to spin what I hope is a unique and surprising tale.

Yes, I'm aware that much of my trope-surgery and element-tweaking was
initially subconscious, as are the processes in writing, the only profession in

which we psychoanalyze ourselves every moment. We sprawl on the proverbial couch in order to let our inner monsters out or, at least, to project some bits of ourselves onto a cracked and peeling wall for others to see.

But with a conscious knowledge of what we're doing and a grasp of what techniques can "give us the new," we can refurbish and revamp the tropes every time we face our keyboards … and our fiction will be better for it.

That Spectred Isle: Tradition, Sensibility, and Delivery Or Ghosts? What Ghosts?

—Steven Savile

British Horror History

The mid-1970s saw an explosion in the world of horror, as a genre. Across the pond, Stephen King unleashed *Carrie*, the prom date from hell, but over in dear old Blighty, James Herbert took us on a descent into a post-holocaust world overrun by giant plague rats. These books paralleled each other, paving the way for the joint successes that followed, and together opened up Joe and Jane Public's eyes to the legitimacy of horror.

Of course, you and I, wise reader, know that horror was no new thing.

Britain has a strong tradition of dark literature, dating back to the melancholic graveyard poets and the Gothic romances of Anne Radcliffe's *Mysteries of Udolpho*; Horace Walpole's *The Castle of Otranto* (which initially tried to pass itself off as a translation of an ancient foreign manuscript, layering Gothic device upon gothic device); Matthew Lewis's extraordinary *The Monk;* and even Jane Austen with the haunting novel *Northanger Abbey*, a joke that, in turn, became perhaps the best of its type. By the mid-1700s, the British sensibility was attuned to the darker side of humanity with the menaces of familial horror, incest, and oppression prevalent. These were horrors presented in classically British *subtle* fashion, hints of what lurks beyond the veil or hides behind the statue in a dimly lit corridor, what evil prowls behind the closed door—although with exponents like Lewis's, the "extreme" possibilities of horror were not ignored.

Showing how science had caught up with the shadows of ghosts and vampires, Robert Louis Stevenson and Mary Shelley embody the fear of the modern age. There's an explosion of technology gone mad with Stevenson's Dr. Jekyll using science to unleash the monster within, and Shelley arguing passionately that there is no place left for religion in the modern world because the rigors of science had replaced God to the extent that man, himself, could master the last power of the Almighty: the creation of life.

British Sensibility

From these writers, we draw what I term the "British sensibility" in horror and supernatural literature. Modern exponents like Ramsey Campbell and Terry Lamsley owe more to Arthur Machen, M.R. James, Ambrose Bierce, and Algernon Blackwood than they do to Salem and the Witchfinder General (we save that honor for Dennis Wheatley).

The question is ... *why?* To that, there is no easy answer. Let's be honest: We all sound exactly the same, waking up in the middle of the night with the bejesus scared out of us, those ghosties and ghoulies on the prowl in our imagination, don't we?

So, back to ghosts. In Britain, we've even tied ghost stories into the tradition of Christmas, thanks to Charles Dickens's *A Christmas Carol*, so the holiday season isn't complete without Christmas pudding, the stocking hung at the bottom of the bed—and the late-night ghost story before midnight mass.

It is ironic, really, if you think about it, Spiritu Sanctu aside, ghosts being as far from Christian as the pagan celebration of Yule itself—but then, we have always been preoccupied with Robin Goodfellow, Hern the Horned God, the very embodiment of nature, and the restless dead. One reason, of course, for the enduring nature of ghost stories is the fact that we have "serious history" in Britain. Our castles, churches, and great manors date back hundreds of years. I went to school in a manor house built in the 1500s. Is it any surprise we entertained ourselves with ghost stories of Grey Ladies and tortured monks still treading our hallowed halls? Roundheads fought Cavaliers on the playing field, and Henry VIII imprisoned a wife just across the road (just before beheading her). This sense of dark, tortured history is all around us as we are growing up. It seeps into our consciousness and matures into an acute awareness of our personal place in the world.

Britain also has her proud heritage of withstanding atrocities with that stubborn stiff upper lip for which we're known worldwide. We don't back down to our foreign foes; we may have cities destroyed in war and underground stations bombed in peacetime, but it scarcely slows us down: Trains are running the very next day, and houses can always be rebuilt.

That is the British way.

We can *deal* with it because we can *see* it; it is concrete.

What Cannot Be Seen

What frightens us is when it isn't concrete ... when it can't be seen.

This, of course, resonates in the British reader as much as it does in the British writer: There is an expectancy by the British horror reader for more than thud and blunder and blood and guts. That isn't to say that with James Herbert, Shaun Hutson, and Guy N. Smith, we Brits aren't capable of killer slugs, giant crabs, and plague rat munch-out stories, only that these are *tempered* by the subtleties of our strong ties to tradition.

Even relatively new literary movements, like the Miserablists of the early 1990s and the New Weird of today, are firmly grounded in that British sensibility. Remember the harsh industrial nature of Britain in the 1950s and 1960s: coal-mining villages, steel towns, shipbuilding communities. These places bred a certain kind of writer. If you compile a geographic spread of British horror writers, you develop a strong sense of clusters forming: Clive Barker and Ramsey Campbell, Liverpool; Stephen Laws, Chaz Brenchley, Newcastle; Stephen Gallagher, Peter Crowther, Mark Morris, Leeds. There are, of course, plenty more examples, but here you have shipbuilding, mining, and steel towns responsible for some of the most refreshing British horror writing in years. A correlation? Probably, considering that in these heavily industrialized regions where writing and school work are often considered a "girl" thing, telling horror stories took on a credibility for these guys; it allowed them to express themselves and work out the horrors of Thatcherite Britain in pen and ink.

Horror, during this time in the UK, changed from the comfortable horrors that were traditionally conservative in nature. The threat from outside—the type that communities could band together against—gave way to a more modern, darker, socialist horror, where the enemy was *us inside us*. This is what distinguished *Clive Barker's Books of Blood*; Barker's fiction was not ghost stories or aliens or monsters risen from the deep or lurking out of space and time, it was up close and personal.

Ramsey Campbell, perhaps our greatest living exponent of subtle horrors, penned one of the most truly disturbing horror novels of all time, *The Face That Must Die*, which tackled social ills in Ramsey's home city of Liverpool (a failing welfare state and care in the community programme), and, more than any other novel of its time, climbed successfully into the head of a madman.

American Monsters and British Spectres

For me, that is probably the defining feature of modern horror in Britain: that British horror has tended to shy away from the monsters our American cousins love, the werewolves and vampires, and held fast to the human horrors of ghosts and society's ills. When Britain suffers depressions and turmoil, our writers are there sucking the marrow out of life, bringing the horrors home to us in styles and iconography that apply to *us,* but not just in terms of shambling undead roving across the countryside.

All of this isn't to say that American horror doesn't have its own traditions. Of course, it does—the cosmic threats of Lovecraft's Old Ones, the burgeoning madness of Poe—but these influences fed through in different ways to our writers today.

King and McCammon have obsessed over nuclear explosions and disease run rife in end-of-the-world novels, Koontz has perhaps become Mary Shelley's true progeny with his fusion of science and fear, and Bret Easton Ellis has served up the classic *American Psycho.*

Of all of these, it is Easton Ellis, I think, who comes closest to the British sensibility, getting into the head of the madman and reveling in it, drawing a beautifully rendered 1980s hip culture, much as the socialist brand of British horror demands that we do.

Are we that different then?

As Shakespeare has it:

> If you prick us do we not bleed?
> > If you tickle us do we not laugh?
> > If you poison us do we not die?
> > And if you wrong us shall we not revenge?

What he failed to mention was: If you scare the crap out of us, do we not scream?

We all know the answer to that: Yes, yes—a resounding thrice yes!

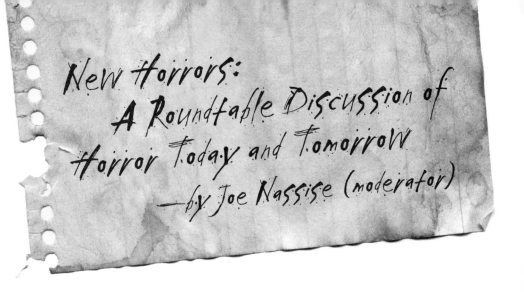

New Horrors:
A Roundtable Discussion of Horror Today and Tomorrow
—by Joe Nassise (moderator)

There's an old saying that it's hard to see the forest through the trees; that once you've been involved with something long enough, it's difficult to step back and get a new, and perhaps different, perspective. Horror writing and publishing has its ebbs and flows, just like anything else, and those who've been intimately involved with it for long periods can sometimes get caught up in its tides without being aware.

To be certain that *On Writing Horror* (OWH) provided both sides of the situation in its examination of the craft and art of writing horror, OWH, in the incarnation of yours truly, Joe Nassise, sat down with four writers who have just started making names for themselves in the horror industry. Their work is varied, from short stories to fiction collections to novels, and their viewpoints are as different as the mediums in which they currently operate.

OWH: What are the three most important skills a new writer should have and why?

Paul Tremblay: Know the difference between showing and telling. Be able to avoid tedious information dumps in the narrative and be willing to get that same information across via action or meaningful dialogue.

Know how to build real characters. Make the reader want to learn about your characters and care about how they cope with the circumstances into which you drop them—no matter how clever or original your concept or plotline, the story won't be as effective without flesh-and-blood characters.

Commit to your vision. If you have something you want to say, say it—no faking it, no going halfway. If you, yourself, don't believe in what the story is communicating to the readers, then why should the readers?

Gary Frank: Only three?

The ability to look at the world and wonder. It is much too easy to lose that sense of awe as we grow up. But as a writer, it is important to cling to that ability so that you can look at a situation and say, *What if ...?*

The ability to think differently. It has been said that there are no more original ideas. So, the ability to take an idea that's already been done and give it a fresh twist is a special gift ... one every good writer needs. Otherwise, we wind up with just more of the same old, recycled stories.

Having a grasp of story construction is also very important. Knowing where to start a story, how to end it, and what really needs to be in the middle is a skill that's learned by trial and error.

Melinda Thielbar: Patience is the number one, and I think a sense of humor should be right behind that. Writing good fiction is hard, and selling good fiction is harder. When we're sitting behind our desks polishing our masterpieces, we sometimes forget that we're competing with people who've been at this business for a long time. It's hard to remember that just because a story is the best thing *you've* written so far doesn't mean it's the best thing an editor has seen this week. But that certainly doesn't mean give up; it means be aware that everything is probably not going to happen as quickly as you'd like.

A sense of humor is a must because you are going to hear a lot of advice and criticism—some of which will be condescending, mean-spirited, or outright wrong. Your favorite friend/relative/writing group member may be trying to help with that explanation of "what your book is really about," and your mother probably *means* well when she asks "Why don't you write about something *nice* for a change?" But ...

I once heard Joe Lansdale talk about how a creative writing teacher told him she hoped he wasn't going to be a writer, and followed it up with "That sort of stuff never bothered me." I think being able to see the humor in situations like that will keep you away from the shotgun when those kinds of things happen.

Failing numbers one or two, a decently-trained liver and a well-stocked liquor cabinet are musts.

Nate Kenyon: New writers need to master the basics: Vocabulary and sentence structure should be second-nature for any successful writer—you shouldn't waste time thinking about how to construct sentences that make sense, keeping tense consistent, and staying away from passive voice. Writing fiction is like learning a second language. There is that moment when you begin to think in that language, when you dream in it. That's when you know you're ready for prime time.

I would put persistence at the top of this list as well—and yes, it is a skill with networking being its close cousin. In the current competitive market, writers must be willing to knock on the door and keep knocking. But there's a difference between knocking politely and pounding with both fists. You will receive ... rejections, and it is a delicate skill to keep submitting "your stuff" without burning bridges and appearing unprofessional. There's a great deal of frustration involved in learning your craft and making that first sale, but you have to be able to duck and roll, and then pop right back up again—smiling.

Accepting criticism and learning to edit your own work is another essential skill. There's a lot of advice out there, and no lack of people willing to comment on your writing. The trick is to figure out which advice is sound (and which isn't), and how to implement it.

OWH: There are pieces of advice given to new writers. Name three pieces of advice you do *not* agree with and explain why.

Paul Tremblay: "Write what you know" is bad advice. How else are you going to grow as a writer if you don't take chances, if you don't branch out into areas that don't fit into your particular sphere of experience? I would advise just the opposite: Don't be afraid of research and reading outside your chosen field, welcome any and all new ideas or experiences. It will only serve to improve your writing, and, really, make you a more well-rounded person.

Writing for exposure instead of payment is very bad advice. Writers get paid. Period. The cliché of "no such thing as bad press" does not apply to writing. Bad exposure or bad publication will not help your career.

I don't think writing to an audience (which is different than *knowing* your audience) is sound advice. The best writers set themselves apart by forcing an audience to come to them. Watering down your voice or vision to appease some nebulous and fickle audience usually yields forgettable fiction. I don't think any writer starts out with the goal of becoming mediocre or average or forgettable.

Gary Frank: "Same time every day." I write when I can without sticking to a particular schedule. It can be detrimental to a new writer if you can't make the same time every day and feel you're not doing what you should.

"Set a daily word count/time frame." If I'm writing and the words are flowing, I see no reason to stop because I've reached my word count or my time limit. Conversely, I don't think it's a great idea to get frustrated with writing because I can't fill a certain amount of time or reach a certain word count. This is something writers have to decide on their own.

Any rule that inhibits a writer's imagination. Any of the *should* advice that new writers take to heart. As one best-selling author said to me, "Break every rule of writing; just make sure you know what you're doing and do it well."

Melinda Thielbar: "Never rewrite until you're finished, is a popular piece of advice for young novelists. When I'm working on a book, I start each writing day by going back over what I did the day before. I find that a little editing boosts my confidence ("Wow, it's not as bad as I remember.") and gives me something concrete to do before I get on with the harder challenge of writing new words.

"Finish every story you start" is another piece of advice that I'm ambivalent about. When I first started writing, I wasted a lot of time chasing ideas that weren't all that good. Maybe I needed the practice in writing a complete story, but I was a lot happier once I gave myself permission to dump the ideas that weren't working as opposed to beating a dead horse.

"Don't start by writing novels. Start with short stories" seems like telling a distance runner that he won't know how to run a marathon until he learns how to sprint properly. Writing short stories is a different skill from writing novels. I started out trying to write novels, turned to writing short stories because I was told not to write a novel first, and then ended up trying to write novels again after discovering that the stories I wanted to tell were not short. I think I would have been better off sticking it out with the novel-length stories.

Nate Kenyon: "Join a writers group." I'm sure there are groups out there that are full of published authors and brilliantly talented up-and-comers just waiting for their first break. But for the most part, writers groups are made up of other new writers, and a lot of them don't have the first clue about providing effective criticism. If you were going to learn how to swim, would you jump in the lake with six other people who were just learning, too?

"Don't read in your own genre." I understand the reasoning behind this: You don't want your own style and voice to be influenced by others. But I think it's vitally important to read everything you can, to keep up with what's happening in your backyard, and to put yourself in a particular frame of mind or mood.

"Work through writer's block." I disagree with this, but only to a point. Again, I understand the reasoning behind the idea of forcing yourself through a tough spot, but I don't think it's particularly effective most of the time … at least not for me. The stuff that comes out is junk, and it doesn't get much better as I go.

What helps the most is a change of scenery, a walk outside, a movie, or some other way to shut off the brain and let the subconscious work through the particular problem. This shouldn't go on any longer than an hour or so, if it's your writing time, because you don't want to turn it into a real battle. But nine times out of ten, I'll get a sudden breakthrough on that walk or feel more refreshed after I give my mind a break—the words come faster, and I'm less frustrated.

OWH: What were the biggest surprises you encountered once you began writing for publication?

Paul Tremblay: The appalling number of people willing to give away their work for free, whether it be to short-fiction markets or to vanity presses.

Having previously assumed that most novelists were rich, rich, rich and then discovering how difficult it is to make a living from writing fiction was another. I also learned that writing is no different than any other career, complete with rewards but also with petty office-type politics.

I was pleasantly surprised to find the majority of professional writers I've met … truly want to help new writers become better at their craft. I've been the beneficiary of quite a few mentors, and I'm indebted to all of them.

Gary Frank: I was surprised by how many people are writing good horror that more people should know about but don't, the sense of community among *horror* writers that I didn't experience with mainstream fiction writers, and how few publishers and agents are willing to look at horror stories.

Melinda Thielbar: I think my biggest surprise was the general cattiness in the fiction community—horror and otherwise. When you're a professional in another field, the last thing you say is "So-and-So's product sucks," particularly within So-and-So's earshot. In the writing community, it's a badge of honor to have more friends than enemies. It seems to have been that way since the days of the Algonquin roundtable, but it's still odd to know that your fellow writers are going to be as critical of you as anyone else, if not more so.

Nate Kenyon: It's harder than you think. There aren't that many solid, paying markets out there, and most of them are already deluged with submissions, a lot of which are coming from writers who already have a name and many friends in the industry. You might read a lot of the stuff getting published and think, *I can do better than that.* But to succeed, you have to treat writing as a business. Put a plan together that includes a written schedule. Learn to market yourself and treat your work as a product you're selling. If you feel personally offended by rejections, or if you can't take criticism and use it to improve what you're doing, you're in trouble.

OWH: What is different about the publishing industry today than when you started out? What do you expect to happen over the next year or two?

Paul Tremblay: I don't think the publishing industry is all that different than it was when I made my first short-story sale in early 2000. Certainly, there has been an increase (both in numbers and in relevancy) in online short-fiction markets, which I would expect to continue. As far as novels are concerned, it's still a tough fiction market that will continue to become more and more marketing driven. I suppose it's a pessimistic view of the publishing industry, but based on my and other writers' experiences, it's becoming more difficult to sell something that doesn't fit neatly into a marketing niche. That said, writers like Chuck Palahniuk, Stewart O'Nan, Will Christopher Baer, and Mark Danielewski serve as examples of writers who are publishing daring horror or dark fiction.

Gary Frank: There are fewer *big* publishers than ever, making it harder for unknown writers. I think the *horror* genre may disappear completely and be labeled as *fiction* for bookstore convenience. With larger publishers turning away quality horror, more small presses are likely to come into being. There is no lack of readership, just a lack of publishers willing to publish these authors.

Melinda Thielbar: In 1920, H.P. Lovecraft bemoaned the state of genre fiction, citing how magazine and book publishers of his time were only interested in making money, when they used to be focused on publishing works of literary value. The complaints haven't changed much since H.P.'s time, and I don't see much progress ahead. Perspective only comes with time.

I think it's a mistake for young and old writers to pen too much commentary about current situations or far horizons.

Nate Kenyon: The Internet has changed everything. Connections can be made in moments, queries can be e-mailed, writers groups meet and critique online, and entire communities can be formed on message boards. The Web really has revolutionized writing and publishing, but, oddly, most of the large publishers themselves have no idea what to make of it.

Small presses *are* getting it, promoting in online communities, accepting electronic submissions, publishing online, selling directly through Web sites, offering e-books ... and they use the Internet effectively to promote their products as well. So many of the larger publishers are entrenched in the old process of acquiring and preparing manuscripts, and worried about copyright infringement, that they're frozen in place.

Many people are predicting that the e-book will never gain popular acceptance and that readers will continue to want a printed copy of a book. I think that's nonsense; any true revolution seems impossible at first. It's only when looking back that you can clearly see the path of history. But, if you look at blogging and the popularity of sites like MySpace and LiveJournal, you'll discover a whole new generation that is growing up reading online—and they don't seem to have a problem without a printed copy of anything ... because that's what they are accustomed to.

OWH: Why horror? What do you see as horror's value to the literary community?

Paul Tremblay: Great horror fiction, and this applies to great literature in general, makes you confront and/or question reality, or at least, *your place* in reality. It's horror's job to not be safe or tidy or clean, which, unfortunately, is not the case with much of mainstream horror in both fiction and film. And I don't mean "safe" in terms of a gore or violence factor, as slashers and demons and vampires and the other tropes tend to represent safe horror. Safe horror (or bad horror) has drawn a clearly marked good-and-evil line in the sand.

Real life doesn't work that way, and neither does the best horror fiction.

Gary Frank: Well-written horror reminds us how little we know about our world. Ghosts, demons, and such are found throughout history, so they're not just fabricated creatures. Some of the best horror makes us question how we view the world and what we hold as important. "He Who Increases Knowledge," a story by Wrath James White, made me think about how I view God. When a story can do that, it has certainly earned a place in literature.

Melinda Thielbar: Clarification: Value as it currently exists or its potential value? Never mind. I'll answer the question I want to answer.

Horror is about fear, and how we think about, write about, and deal with fear says a lot about us as people.

My greatest worry for horror, in general, is that we're losing relevance because we're focusing on ancient evils instead of turning our eyes to the frightening things that are happening right in front of us—today. I don't know how anyone can hear about what's happening in the world without being moved and horrified. Those are the places where horror fiction has a real opportunity to add literary value to the world, and yet we're strangely silent.

Nate Kenyon: … [H]orror gives a writer the opportunity to write with more emotion, more drama, more passion that a lot of other genres. Horror is really about conquering fears, facing that dark closet or that lump in the latest hospital X-ray and coming away whole. Good horror investigates those dark corners of the mind and leads to important discoveries about the human condition.

Four new writers—four new voices—devoted to the act of facing a blank page each and every day, and who have had the courage to fill those pages with words that flow from within. Four artisans who have obviously given their genre and their work more than just a passing thought. And, perhaps, four new voices with something to teach even the most experienced of us, as well.

Part Seven

Genre and Subgenre

Archetypes and Fearful Allure: Writing Erotic Horror
—Nancy Kilpatrick

Erotic horror—either alone or as a couple, these two words evoke a strong re-action in most people. The spectrum ranges from revulsion to titillation with a myriad of emotions caught in between.

Both separately or combined, these words have never been politically cor-rect, so if being that type of writer is your goal, you'd better not attempt writing erotica, horror, or erotic horror. Despite the fact that some cultures during some eras have been more liberal than others, those are the exceptions in human his-tory. Edgy genres always evoke a reaction and, in more conservative times, that reaction can be not only unpleasant, but could prove dangerous to the writer.

But, of course, if you weren't interested in writing erotic horror, you wouldn't be reading this, would you?

Because erotica and horror have always been outside the mainstream, they hold a strong appeal. Forbidden fruit is the tastiest, and readers are drawn to these genres, although often surreptitiously, which means there is and always will be a market for this type of writing.

At this point, it might feel much like a cold shower, but starting with a dictionary will help clarify just what I'm talking about when I use the words *erotic* and *horror*—and link them. *The Random House Dictionary of the Eng-lish Language* defines *horror* this way (emphasis mine):

> An overwhelming and painful feeling caused by something frightfully shock-ing, *terrifying, or revolting*, a shuddering fear ... Anything that causes such a feeling ... *A strong aversion; abhorrence.*

About the word *erotic*, the same dictionary says (emphasis mine):

> Arousing or satisfying sexual desire ... *Subject to or marked by strong sexual desire.*

These two words seem to create an oxymoron and should have little in com-mon. Horror we move away from, the erotic we move toward. Or do we?

The Complexity That Is (Wo)Man

Human beings are complicated creatures. For example, we have been responsible for more atrocities on this planet than all other life forms and natural forces combined. Yet, in fiction, there exists a popular category called "horror," which focuses on atrocities committed by humans, by natural forces, by supernatural forces, on humans who are the victims of these horrors, either individually or collectively.

In real life, people are drawn to the scene of an accident, and readers go out of their way to unearth horror books.

So the dictionary is right and wrong. Horror is an emotion, extreme and shocking. While we might abhor and have an aversion to horror, we are also attracted to it. We want to read about horrors, and some of us want to write horror.

When it comes to the erotic, well, Freud said it all. As much as most people have a desire to move into the sexual arena, human beings also have quite a bit of resistance to actualizing their erotic fantasies. This is compounded by serious health concerns of our time—like AIDS, hepatitis C, and herpes, to name a few. Some have said that the surge of cyber-sex—who doesn't know somebody having an online affair?—and the proliferation of erotic writing seen in print is a direct result of our struggling to satisfy carnal desires in safe ways. If you put "horror" and "erotic" together you end up with one of the most intriguing and fastest-growing subgenres in fiction: erotic horror. The ultimate in safe, edgy sex!

As with any other creative pursuit, the erotic horror writer has a wide range of expression to choose from. Horror can be about real-life serial killers, or supernatural beings like werewolves. It can be soft, psychological, reality-based, hard-edged, new weird, or what used to be termed splatter—graphic, in-your-pretty-face writing. Erotica, likewise, can be soft and gentle, sensual, romantic writing reminiscent of nudes photographed in artistic poses through a gauze-covered lens, all the way to what is deemed pornographic—blatant descriptions of "the act" in all its permutations, using graphic language, and can include bondage, fetishism, and sado-masochism. Erotic horror, blending both worlds, creates a complex mosaic of styles and angles on its fire-and-ice subject matter.

Of course, one person's dreadful horror is another's lengthy yawn. And what's erotic to you (as a writer) might leave a reader, shall we say, "non-plussed." In other words, your idea of erotic horror may not be a reader's idea of erotic horror, which begs the question: *How do you write erotic horror that will leave readers shivering with conflicting feelings?*

The answer: Work with archetypes.

The Monster With a Thousand Faces

I'm going back to the dictionary one more time before I close it. The word *archetype* is in vogue and consequently is frequently misused. Clarity is everything in writing, so here's a definition (emphasis mine):

The *original* pattern or model *from which all things of the same type are copied or on which they are based*; a model or first form. Prototype.

To encourage even more precision, here's how the word is used in Jungian terms, since this is specifically how I'll be using it:

A collectively inherited unconscious idea, pattern of thought, image, etc., universally present in individual psyches.

To understand *archetype*, let's work with the familiar image of much erotic horror: the vampire. What is the *archetypal* vampire? If you could persuade all the vampires that have ever existed in fact, fiction, and mythology, in artwork, film, and print to congregate in the same mausoleum, and if you could convince each to let you superimpose them, one on another, the elements that they all have in common would comprise the archetypal vampire.

Certainly, vampires have changed from century to century and differ from culture to culture. Arguably, the first vampire who ever saw print was in the *Epic of Gilgamesh,* circa 2500 B.C.: the death-bringer. Ancient Chinese vampires are not Baltic vampires. The vampires of the Middle East are not the same as those of South American cultures. But whether the vampire is a disembodied spirit or a corporeal being, whether the Nosferatu sucks blood or brains or air or souls—I wrote one in *Freak Show* that sucks dreams!—there is at least one element that they all share. They may prey on strangers or family members, or be thwarted by the symbols of any and all religions or be utterly unthwartable; they may or may not be allergic to sunlight and garlic or repelled by crosses and mirrors. They can be romantic seducers—aka Good Guys with Fangs—or repulsive grab-'em-and-suck-'em-dry reanimated corpses. Bottom line: Vampires are out *to take something from us.* All vampires are predators, parasites that live off humanity.

Here, then, is a definition of erotic horror as it pertains specifically to vampires from *The Kilpatrick House Dictionary of the English Language* (first edition, unabridged, uncensored, unpublished): "A predatory being that preys on human beings in a sexually arousing or satisfying and/or sexually repulsive way."

Voila! Vampire: the erotic horror archetype! Coming soon to a bookstore near you! Archetypes are not just important in terms of writing erotic horror, they are the crucial raw energy on which all powerful writing of any genre is based.

Inside Us All

According to the psychologist Carl Jung, archetypes dwell in both our *personal* psyche and within the *collective* psyche. We know that these powerful energies have come to the fore, meaning our consciousness, when we feel an emotional "charge." Likewise, when we get charged by a piece of writing, it is because the archetype imbedded in the work is affecting us. What we read on the page mirrors a universal energy each of us carries within, and that syn-chronicity between inner and outer reality reverberates through us.

It's easy to see that the image of the vampire that the fictional tropes em-ployed varies from era to era, culture to culture, and writer to writer. Some titles illustrate this well. Sonja Blue, the female vamp in Nancy Collins's books *Sunglasses After Dark* and *In the Blood*, is a different being from Deirdre in Karen E. Taylor's ongoing series that began with *Blood Secrets*. The former writer's works present a hard and cold vampiress, but that is exactly what makes her alluring. The latter's work involves a romantic figure, close to a Harlequin heroine. Both *femme fatales* live on blood, prey on men, and fit the definition of erotic vampire.

On the male undead side of things, Chelsea Quinn Yarbro's long-running vampire anti-hero in her Count Saint-Germain series retains a high level of empathy for the human females he seduces and upon whom he preys. In my own grittier novels in the *Power of the Blood* series, André, David, Karl, and Julien all employ their individual style when approaching blood-stocked women, ranging from aggressive to tender to intellectual, but that style is always highly sensual.

More extreme versions of the erotic vampire can be found in Poppy Z. Brite's gay vampire novel *Lost Souls*, and also in a pansexual pastiche I penned under the *nom de plume* Amarantha Knight, *The Darker Passions: Dracula*, a retelling of Bram Stoker's classic. In my scenes behind the scenes, where Victo-rian skirts are lifted, the Prince of Wallachia, Dracula himself, becomes a full-blown sexual being with no inhibitions to temper his severe appetites. (Didn't we always know he had it in him?)

What is important about all of the above vampire examples, and what they all have in common, is that they utilize the essence of the archetypal vampire. None are stereotypes. Stereotypes are basically *dead* archetypes. The power of the archetype is in its freshness and universality, because it spans time and culture. This means that the energy embedded in the image resonates with all readers because it taps into and stirs up the collective unconscious.

This does *not* mean all readers will love every one of these books or authors. Nobody can guarantee that. Reaching some of the readers some of the time is as good as it gets. The reader might be excited or repelled, horrified or aroused, by any or all of these archetypal vampires—some even bored by them. But pro-vided the writing itself isn't doggerel, if a bored reader is honest with him- or herself, the realization *might* dawn that what seemingly is not of interest is actually unsettling in some way, provoking feelings and responses the reader would rather not know about. As Franz Kafka said, "I think we ought to read only the kind of books that wound and stab us ... A book must be the axe for the frozen sea inside us." And although you, as a writer, cannot control readers by forcing them to face what they cannot or will not face, still, if you write the most powerful story or novel you can, unearthing the archetypal energy and working with it through imagery, you will elicit a reaction, which many people believe is what writing is all about.

When you work with an archetype, it's important to figure out what the past holds, as well as the parameters of current cultural images. That way, you don't repeat what's been done, and you can get a jump on the next step in the archetype's evolution. Literate readers know what has been written, even if they haven't read everything ever published in their favorite genre. They can *feel* the freshness. If the writer hasn't bothered researching the past and consequently and unwittingly rehashes it, the work smells *stale*.

Weaving Erotica and Horror

Another important point about writing erotic horror is that any fiction in this subgenre must work as both a piece of erotica *and* as a piece of horror. Lucy Taylor has an intriguing story in *Flesh Fantastic* called "Love in the Age of Ice." In this tale, a porn star is cryogenically frozen and brought back by her loving husband. You can see the thrust, as it were, of both the erotic and the horrific elements, and I won't spoil the story by giving away the climax. Most of Lucy's stories can be read in either light, which is why they are so effective.

Another writer of well-crafted erotic horror is Nancy Holder. Check out her "Blood Gothic" in the anthology *Shadows 8*. She takes the vampire victim to an extreme here, where we see a woman wasting away with erotic fantasy.

Elizabeth Massie's amazing southern gothic tale "Abed" in *Still Dead: Book of the Dead 2* is a ghastly portrayal of how a matriarch deals with a zombie in the family. Sèphera Girón, one of Canada's leading erotic horror writers, uses spurned lesbian love to create a deadly erotic-horror romance in "Rael," from *Sex Macabre*.

To ensure that your story succeeds on two levels, try this: Forget the horror element for a moment. Read the story as if it were strictly erotica. The simple question: *Does the writing turn you on?* Do all the parts fit? Now, reread the story as if it were placed in the horror section, shelved next to the latest Stephen King. Does it creep you out? Does the plot hang together strictly as a good horror read? If you must answer no to *either* of these sets of questions, you have not written an effective erotic horror story. You will need to go back and strengthen weak elements so that the story can stand alone as either erotica or horror. The story needs to perform on both levels equally.

Erotic horror is a fine line. If you can tap into the archetypal power of your images, if you can balance the erotic and the horrific, you will be giving the reader what he/she wants, whether you're aiming for a soft touch that gently brushes the reader's psyche, or the deep, razor's-edge cut that pierces to the soul and does what Kafka says, and breaks up "the frozen sea inside us."

Writing for the New Pulps: Horror-Themed Anthologies
—John Maclay

During the first half of the twentieth century, pulp magazines, such as *Weird Tales,* provided a ready market for horror, occult, and supernatural short fiction. H.P. Lovecraft himself contributed to these periodicals, and such writers as Ray Bradbury and Robert Bloch got their start in their pages as well. But, with the advent of television, the quantity of magazine fiction in all genres fell off drastically. Indeed, one often hears the comment that the commercial short story is dead.

Those who would say so are simply not looking in the right place. They need to go beyond the periodical racks of their favorite full-service bookstore and study the paperback section instead. Or, they need to go on the Internet to Matt Schwartz's often amazing "all things horror" Shocklines (www.shocklines.com). There, they'll find many anthologies, printed on rough stock and (usually) bearing sensationalistic covers. They'll also find limited edition and trade paperback anthologies from the specialty presses. Here are the new pulps—and often not even in disguise!

What can you expect when you sell a story to a themed anthology? Payment varies from three to ten cents per word (for those anthologies which are truly professional!), typically as an advance against royalties—and royalties can be significant. Anthologies, such as *Stalkers,* have sold so well that they returned more than two thousand dollars to each contributor. Stories from these books have been nominated for awards and included in subsequent "year's best" volumes, so your efforts have the potential of being highly worthwhile.

Advice From the Pros

Let's hear from some other writers, editors, and publishers of horror anthologies.

J.N. Williamson

J.N. Williamson says, "My approach to editing the five Masques anthologies, the latest with the editorial assistance of Gary Braunbeck, was primarily twofold: First, to try to get stories by several writers whose appearances tend to sell copies for the publisher and also earn reviews; secondly, to find several underrated or even unpublished writers of talent-coming-to-fruition and introduce them—give them a boost.

"And in all instances," Williamson continues, "I sought work that was original, well constructed without logical problems, and proved to be genuine stories, not vignettes. I want a beginning, middle, and satisfying ending and can recall just one piece, nominated for a few awards, which violated these principles, but got in anyway. (No, it was not written by a so-called 'household name.')

"When the first Masques anthology was published in 1984, I was primarily a novelist and had placed just twenty-nine short stories. Since then, operating on the same (but opposite) premise, I have written and sold well over 125 more works of short fiction, the majority directly to anthologies."

Williamson touches on another feature of horror anthologies that appeals to me: one's ability to appear among famous names. "For example, my own stories have been published in volumes that have included work by Stephen King, Dean Koontz, Joyce Carol Oates, and John Cheever. It's also been my pleasure as an editor and publisher to work with a multitude of writers, veterans and newcomers alike."

Richard T. Chizmar

"Editing an anthology is essentially a juggling act," says Richard T. Chizmar, respected publisher and editor of *Cemetery Dance* magazine and CD Publications. "First, you have to find a balance with your contributor list, a successful mixture of well-known, commercial authors (whose name value will help sell the book) and newer, lesser-known (but certainly no less talented) writers who can carry their weight. Then there's the actual editing …

"A few stories arrive in perfect shape and your job is easy: Simply file the story and mail the check. Most stories, however, need a little fine-tuning—some punctuation changes, a few deletions or additions to help pacing or flow; nothing too intrusive. And, of course, a few stories need more significant work, such as major changes in structure, plot, or characterization. These tales go back to the author for rewrites. Finally (and unfortunately), there are usually a few stories which are just dead-wrong for the anthology, and in that case you have no choice but to return them to the author with your regrets.

"As I said, it's a juggling act. You have to balance your publisher's needs with your own editorial tastes along with the author's personal feelings and ego. Hard work, but fun."

Jeff Gelb

"Don't expect to get rich writing for anthologies," says Jeff Gelb, co-editor of the long—running *Hot Blood* series. "It is true that you can ride the coattails of established writers like Stephen King to antho royalties. But contributions by the likes of King are rare indeed. The *Hot Blood* books all earn royalties based on healthy additional printings, book club, and foreign sales. Generally, though, no one writes short fiction for anthologies for the money; they do it for the love of writing and the love of the subject matter.

"If you're a young writer," Gelb says, "anthos offer you the opportunity to share the stage with the pros, to bask in their glory, and help establish yourself with their fans.

"It's a great way to get noticed. And these days, with the dwindling (magazine) short-story market, it's one of the best ways to escape the ghetto of small-press magazines (as good as they may be) and hit the bookstore shelves. And hey, it looks great on your writing résumé, too!"

Michael Garrett

Michael Garrett, co-editor of the *Hot Blood* series, offers additional practical insight. "Prospective anthology authors must keep in mind that publishing is a business," he says. "As business people, publishers intend to make a profit on every published collection. This, in turn, places the anthology editor in the 'middleman' position of simultaneously meeting the needs of both the publisher and the anthology's intended audience.

"Restrictions imposed by the above condition prevent me, as an anthology editor, from simply selecting the submissions I personally prefer most, or from accepting the first twenty or so reasonably good submissions. In order to please the publisher, I must secure a large percentage of stories from known authors whose recognizable names will help sell the book. This places me in the unfortunate position of occasionally rejecting a better story from a lesser-known author in order to accept something by a name author. This equates to a business decision, pure and simple. I would obviously prefer to accept the very best stories submitted, regardless of the authors' names, but that simply isn't possible.

"Within the above boundaries," Garrett says, "I must also consider the wide interest range of a series' readership. Because of varying tastes of readers, I must sometimes accept stories targeted to a certain audience segment, even when a story doesn't especially interest me. Obviously, it would be impossible to produce an anthology wherein all readers thoroughly enjoyed all stories.

"With an ongoing series such as Hot Blood, quality is of utmost importance to assure consistency from volume to volume," Garrett says.

"I prefer to work with authors who understand and appreciate the author-editor relationship and are willing to perform requested rewrites to make their stories the best they can be."

Well, there you have it, from some people who've been there.

Now, as it should be, the rest is up to you. If you're not a self-starter, you won't sell to horror anthologies, our "new pulps"—or anything else for that matter. But if you are, anthologies can be a most exciting and rewarding market.

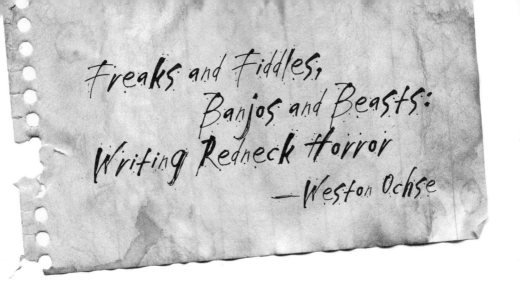

Freaks and Fiddles, Banjos and Beasts: Writing Redneck Horror
— Weston Ochse

Redneck horror or Southern Gothic or rural horror—whatever name you use, backwoods horror has been around since before Washington Irving's headless horseman terrorized the Hudson River Valley. But backwoods horror lacks the glitz of its big city counterparts. Urban horror looks sharp—all dressed up with glass and marble settings of skyscrapers and neon lights. Erotic horror has that sex appeal that arouses us while simultaneously making us squirm. Supernatural horror makes the hairs on your arms stand up.

This leaves backwoods horror, the inbred redneck of fiction.

So, why is backwoods horror so popular and so successful? Why do authors like Joe Lansdale, Ed Lee, Poppy Z. Brite, Ray Garton, John Farris, Tom Piccirilli, Allen Lee Harris, Robert McCammon, and Beth Massie continually produce best-selling novels? Why are Flannery O'Connor, Tennessee Williams, Truman Capote, William Faulkner, and Carson McCullers, all recognized Southern Gothicists, staples of American literature, taught at institutions of higher learning throughout the land? Why do we love movies like *Cabin Fever, Wrong Turn, The Evil Dead* series, *Deliverance, The Hills Have Eyes*, and *The Texas Chainsaw Massacre*?

Is it our guilty pleasure, our more or less shameless indulgence in "low-brow," or even "no-brow," mindless entertainment?

Regionalism and Setting

No matter the setting, backwoods horror is not about *a specific locale*, but about *isolated locations*. Any place will do. Although much backwoods horror is set in the American South, the setting can be any rural area, inculcating local myth, legend, and character. Tennessee doesn't own a patent on rednecks. Pennsylvania, Florida, Washington, Iowa, and even California have their remote and barely accessible terrains as well—each with its own unique inhabitants.

When asked about the setting of his novel *November Mourns*, Tom Piccirilli, a Colorado author whose writing has been described as Southern Gothic, had this to say:

> I haven't lived or visited the Appalachian region, but it's obvious in our modern society that the South has not been as homogenized as other places. There are still isolated areas untouched by the rest of America, places that remain unique and aren't immersed in the melting pot. In terms of setting, this made it a natural area for me to put a story that deals with superstition, history, the fear of change, the effect of religion versus science, etc.

Piccirilli chose the South as a setting, but could have easily selected one of a thousand isolated places throughout the land. Lansdale writes of East Texas. Ed Lee writes of Florida. Ray Garton's characters populate the many backwoods places of California. Says Garton:

> There will always be backwoods, rural areas. They'll never go away, and they will never change. They are inherently creepy—to me, anyway—and people will always be writing about them in one way or another, and people will always be reading about them. I think they're a staple in the genre.

What is a Redneck?

So what is a redneck?

Asking and answering that question launched the comedy careers of more than a few of television's most popular comedians.

The stereotype includes, as *Wikipedia* says:

> … lives in a trailer or old weather-beaten farmhouse in a rural area … drives a beat-up pickup truck, possibly adorned with the Confederate flag and a gun rack in the rear window …
>
> … blue jeans, a baseball or trucker hat … prone to swearing, perhaps not as much as the stereotypical Yankee, but more than other Southerners or Appalachians.

We've all seen this redneck. Most times, you'll find him to be the antagonist, chasing, devouring, or stalking an upwardly mobile protagonist, who happens to be in the wrong place at the wrong time. But, if this is all there is to it, then why all the hoopla?

The answer is because good writers will surprise you every time. A good writer won't "people" his story world with "hard-drinking Irish cop types" and "space-brained, blonde bimbo types." Likewise, he can't offer a non-dimensional redneck type—and there is certainly no need to! Rednecks can be women, too. Rednecks can be young children. A redneck can be the preacher who holds the baby beneath the baptismal font a few minutes too long. A redneck can be Grandma who bakes lye into her Christmas cookie recipe. A redneck can be the innocent, cross-eyed kid across the street who lost his arm to the industrial auger on his pappy's farm last summer. A redneck doesn't have to be bad. A redneck can be sympathetic.

What of the poor, out-of-work fellow with terminal cancer who wants nothing more than to secure the future of his family? What of the little boy who disappears and whose older brother and friends search for him? The former is Brian Keene's novel *Terminal* and the latter is Dan Simmons's novel *Summer of Night*, both some of the finest writing I've ever had the privilege to read.

Rednecks think differently. If they lack in "book-learning," they have a more intuitive way of knowing.

Young Cory Mackenson of Zephyr, Alabama, Robert McCammon's point-of-view character from his glorious novel *Boy's Life,* has this to say:

> See, this is my opinion. We all start out knowing magic. We are born with whirlwinds, forest fires, and comets inside us. We are born able to sing to birds and read the clouds and see our destiny in grains of sand. But then, we get the magic educated right out of our souls. We get it churched out, spanked out, washed out, and combed out. We get put on the straight and narrow and told to be responsible. The truth of life is that every year we get farther away from the essence that is born within us.

Young Cory's got it. We've had the magic educated out of us.

But the redneck, fiercely independent, holds on to his sense of mystery as he copes with life and the world around him.

Characterization

> My brothers face one another with no need to move their lips, conversing inside the single, massive, bald head and fractured mind. Silently they argue and debate and agree, lying in bed, nostrils flaring and their hands flapping. Since birth they've stared into each other's eyes, sharing the same blood flow and coursing neurochemicals.

From *A Choir of Ill Children*

Tom Piccirilli's introduction of these conjoined triplets doesn't fit any known redneck stereotype, yet these are the sorts of backwoods characters that inhabit his fiction.

If anything, backwoods fiction begs for dynamic characterization.

In *Appalachian Galapagos,* the sequel collection to *Scary Rednecks,* I took pains to develop vibrantly unique characters. In "Pitfighter Serenade," arguably the darkest piece of fiction I've ever written, my protagonist allows different parts of his body to be removed so that he can be allowed a chance to kill the thing that murdered his best friend. Not only is the character voluntarily deformed, but the story deals with the state of mind necessary for such a masochistic mechanism for revenge.

Style

Something that I want to make perfectly clear is that backwoods horror is not a genre, nor is it a subgenre. *Backwoods horror is a style.* It is a construct within which writers can craft plot and conflict. Create an isolated place, inhabit it with vivid characters, and then unleash your nouns and verbs, sprinkle with adjectives, and … *poof.*

But you'd better do it well. If not, that note of condescension that rings throughout your narrative will turn horror into comedy—unintentional comedy.

Tom Piccirilli's work has been described as "gorgeously written Southern Gothic, lush with grotesques and grotesqueries." Poppy Brite's work is considered stylish and provocative. Flannery O'Connor and Truman Capote were no slackers either, and although they each approached backwoods horror differently, their best-selling results serve as exhibits to polished prose.

As a big fan of Ed Lee's writing, I've noticed through the years that his strong prose is the result of active voice and transitive verbs. From *The Bighead* to *Goon* (co-written with John Pelan) to *Monstrosity,* the power of his writing affects the reader as much as the writing itself.

In the time I've been writing hardcore and simply harder-edged horror, I've become convinced that the imagery fails as sentence structures expand. The gross-out becomes convoluted and contrived when the writer gets overly descriptive.

But one still has to "describe" what's going on adequately enough to convey the activity to the reader. This is done with short, declarative sentences and strong transitive verbs. The reader gets the image in one-two punches instead of a long visual wrestling match. I often invent my own verbs for these critical scenarios, and I don't give a damn if they aren't in the dictionary. Creative license lets me say what I want to say in the most effective manner possible.

He walked into a bathroom cornered black with fungus.

Isn't that better than "When he walked into the bathroom, he saw that it had black fungus in the corners?"

Backwoods Creatures

Why is it that zombies and rednecks go hand in hand? Is it because no one can imagine a downtown coffeehouse Wi-Fi absconder, a hip-hop cell phone salesman, or an Ivy League med student ever being ensnared in the clutches of the undead, as if income and Starbucks coffee acumen is a barometer of one's mortality?

I asked actor and writer Sean O'Bannon for his take on the apparent zombie-redneck relationship. "I think we're all one zombie attack or natural disaster away from sitting in our living rooms on a pile of bricks, holed up with an AK-47 on our laps. And this may be just me, but I also believe Bubbas (rednecks) are a throwback to the rugged individualist formerly seen in Westerns. They're simple, unpretentious, and uncomplicated folk who aren't afraid to let the shotgun barrel help 'em prove a point, especially when it comes to defending their families and/or their principles."

Besides *El Zombo* as a backwoods horror mainstay, there's Chupacabra, Bigfoot, Pumpkinhead, scarecrows, and a virtual never-ending queue of creatures that are more than willing to inhabit your tale, most of which just wouldn't fit in on the bustling city streets of New York City. For monsters, there is one master catalogue, an exquisite encyclopedia of the uncanny: *Weekly World News*. Thumb through its pages and see what creatures are sharing the pages with the ever-present Batboy. There's enough grist in there for anyone's monster mill.

Conclusion

If backwoods horror were a vehicle, it would be a jacked-up 4x4 pickup: scarred bumpers; dented quarter panels; three different colors of paint, one of which is bondo; tinted windows; NASCAR bumper sticker; Playboy mud flaps. Although it appears grimy and rundown sitting next to the powerful 450hp Corvette of urban horror, it is no less dominant. Who needs a new car smell? Who needs a sunroof? Who needs leather seats? Let me ask you this: When you go out into the cornfield spotlighting zombies with your Remington 30-30, which one would you prefer to be driving?

Yep … see … there's even some redneck in you. So write about it already, and when you do, just remember to do it well because the tradition of backwoods horror is as old as America. In fact, back then, they called it literature.

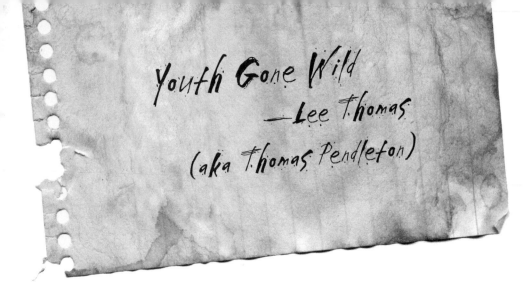

Youth Gone Wild
—Lee Thomas
(aka Thomas Pendleton)

As a marketing category, teen fiction (aka young adult) has blossomed over the last decade, thanks, in great part, to a kid named Harry and a young woman named Buffy. The category encompasses adventure stories, mysteries, romance, chick lit, literary, science fiction, fantasy, and, yes, horror.

Editors are eager for fresh takes on the teen experience, and horror is an extremely popular genre for this category. It's easy to see why.

A good horror story will take a relatively normal individual, Our Hero, and pit them against a malevolent, often mysterious enemy, The Monster. Our Hero must struggle to understand this monster, its strengths and weaknesses. Then he must face it. Often, Our Hero conquers the unknown beast, sometimes not, and until some understanding of The Monster is found, Our Hero is powerless against it. Every day, teens are placed in the position of Our Hero, faced with the unknown and often powerless against it. They deal with parents, teachers, peers, and a world full of rules they have yet to fully understand.

Teen fiction, at its best, examines these confusing emotional issues; therefore, the coming-of-age theme is essential. Characters face the unknown and take steps to gain power over it. They are forced to make life-defining decisions by examining who they are and taking actions that set the stage for the adults they will become.

This is what makes horror so compelling for a teen audience (besides the *cool* monsters, of course). Horror looks at issues of death, alienation, insecurity, physical changes, loss of faith, and the inherent fear of the unknown. On some level, horror fiction shows teens that even the greatest obstacles can be faced and survived. The most well-known example of this comes from the television series *Buffy the Vampire Slayer*, in which the idea presented is that high school is, quite literally, *hell*.

The good news is we've all been there. Few of us have been vampire slayers or burgeoning wizards, but we've all enjoyed and *endured* the teen years. We know the angst, the fear, and the self-consciousness. Most of us have felt completely out of place at one time or another; dreamed of the life ahead, feared the things we couldn't control. Sure enough, similar things happen to adults, but for young readers, these are daily struggles amplified by surging emotions and made all the more difficult because teens lack enough personal history to properly process what is happening to them.

Know What I'm Sayin'?

Most writers know that *how* you tell a story is as important as the story you're telling. It is imperative to find the strongest point(s) of view from which to tell the story and to create an accurate and engaging voice for the work. You will want the details and observations woven into your prose to sound authentic.

For instance, if you were writing a medical thriller without doing the proper research, you might fudge some of the hospital descriptions or a bit of key lingo. If you're clever and make it sound good, a general audience may read right over the mistakes, but doctors will read them and cringe. Now, imagine your audience is comprised solely of medical professionals. This is what you're facing when you write for a teen audience. Do your research. Observe current trends in fashion, entertainment, and technology, because these all play strongly into how your readers view the world (at least if you're writing about contemporary teens). Don't try to fake them out, especially when it comes to spoken and internal dialogues. The lexicon changes frequently, so be observant if you have teens of your own. If not, don't worry; research is easy to come by.

Hollywood has done a lot of the work for you. With the abundance of youth-focused media—magazines, television, films, music—you can jack into teen-speak just about any time you want. Listen to the cadence and content of what is said and respect the meaning of the words. If you're just jotting down phrases, all you'll accomplish is a parrot act. This leads to forcing "hip" phrases and creating a clunky, inauthentic voice.

With that noted, use slang sparingly. Like regional dialects utilized for effect, a little goes a long way.

This Rocks! This Blows!

People enjoy an exciting story featuring characters with whom they can identify; that's a given. But, you may see writing for children or teens as an opportunity to teach them something about the world.

Including educational material in your story may help sell your book to teachers and librarians, but tread softly. If you want to make the book a learning experience with historical data, science, sociology, or any other subject of study, weave the information subtly into the plot, and make it relevant to the story you're telling. Your first goal should be to entertain. A detailed explanation of the economic ramifications of the Civil War is hardly necessary to the plot of a kid confronting a Confederate ghost, although it may prove to be a great way to get your readers to see what's on television.

Similarly, issues of morality—sex, underage drinking, drug abuse—all have their place in teen fiction, but nobody likes to be lectured or preached to. If you have a moral theme to your story, let it come out naturally through the storytelling. Edicts of right and wrong are just going to make your reader roll their eyes and say, "Whatever!"

They may be younger than you, but your teen readers aren't stupid. If you approach a work of teen fiction with the notion of "dumbing it down," you're doing a great disservice to your work and to your audience. Yes, you are writing for a different reading level, but teens will pick up a condescending tone quickly. Try to remember you are writing from their point of view. You're in their world. Comment on that world as they would, not as you, many years (perhaps decades) removed, would comment on it.

Also, don't be afraid to use difficult words. They are fine when used sparingly. Your audience wants to be challenged, but overuse of "ten-centers" is a good way to lose your reader.

That's Just Nasty!

Writing horror fiction can be incredibly liberating in that it often addresses taboos and pushes social boundaries for effect. This doesn't change when writing for younger audiences; however, the way the material is presented does. So, how far can you go with sexual and violent content directed at the younger reader? A good rule of thumb to follow is the Motion Picture Association of America's (MPAA) PG-13 guidelines. Needless to say, if you're writing for children, you'll want to dial that back even more. Since each publisher has different criteria, an editor will tell you if you've gone too far with a particular scene. Avoiding overt gore and sexual content is not likely to hurt the impact your work has on teen readers. It may actually help, as their imaginations will take them places you can't.

Save the detailed descriptions of beheadings and disembowelments and focus your skills on building an atmosphere of dread and highlighting the emotional impact the plot is having on your characters. If you've done your job, your readers will feel every bit of the sorrow and disgust your characters do.

But kids like the gross stuff! Indeed, many teens and even children groove on the nasty and disgusting details of a good horror story, but there are a lot of things that kids like that they really shouldn't be exposed to. And guess what?

Parents won't be thrilled with a book marketed to teens, containing age-inappropriate content. Publishers, while serving the interests of their young readers, are also very conscious of the parents' role in the economic equation, as you should be, too.

The 411

What are editors looking for?

In today's marketplace, much of your success writing for a teen audience will likely come down to one or two sentences: the commercial hook. Yes, you must still write a great story with interesting characters, but the hook is your book's own advertisement. It has to pop and intrigue with only a handful of words.

As a writer, you are in constant competition with television, video games, the Internet, and a myriad of other entertainment media. Editors know a book must get a reader's attention fast and make them want to part with money they could be spending on *Resident Evil 4* the most recent *Scary Movie* film, or a grande Frappuccino at Starbucks. So, make your hook sharp and short and teen focused.

Here are some guidelines to keep in mind, but remember every publishing house is different. The age demographics for children's books are not always set in stone, but they are fairly consistent.

- Teen (Young Adult): 12–18 years of age
- Middle Grade (Tweeners): 8–13 years of age
- Chapter Book: 7–10 years of age
- Picture Book: Newborn–6 years of age

Word counts can also vary, but a typical teen title will run between 35,000 and 60,000 words.

In the end, a book of teen fiction requires what any good book requires: a strong, original story; three-dimensional, realistic characters; and effective prose. It's that simple, and it's harder than it looks.

Cool?

Writing Horror Comic Books— And Graphic Novels
—David Campiti

Why write horror comics? As a horror writer, you can do things in comic books that you can't do in any other storytelling form. While comic books don't sell the way they used to in the medium's Golden Age (or even Silver Age), since they are distributed in far fewer outlets than in past decades, still more than two dozen comics publishers are buying and publishing horror comics right now. That's a greater number than the past five decades.

Hollywood has its eye and checkbook on comics like never before, thanks in part to such horror comic-based successes as *Blade* (and its sequels), *The Crow* (and its sequels), *Constantine*, *From Hell*, *Road to Perdition*, *Sin City*, and so many more.

Many a horror writer can make *more* money writing professional horror comics than by writing short stories or novels. A fairly typical, professional page rate is $100 per page as an advance against royalties. That's $2,200 for a standard twenty-two-page issue; a six-issue "mini-series" story arc would pay $13,200 up front, plus potential royalties, plus additional reprint money when collected into a "graphic novel" trade paperback, and even more when reprinted overseas, for decades to come. Compare that with typical advances for a horror novel, or that nickel a word for short stories.

Contemporary Horror Comics

Naturally, before writing your first comic horror story, it pays to take the time to learn why contemporary horror comics are written the way they are.

Brian Augustyn, a former DC Comics editor who edited Joe R. Lansdale's early comics foray *Blood and Shadows*, and who freelance edits and writes such properties as the teen-vampire chiller *Crimson* and the adaptation of the Christian post-apocalyptic scare series *Left Behind*, explains his take on it.

"First and foremost, we have a weighty specter hanging over what we try to accomplish in horror comics in the new century," Brian told me. "After twenty years as the Gold Standard of comic-book horror, DC's Vertigo imprint casts a long and influential shadow across all modern endeavors. Thanks to editor Karen Berger's singular and wide vision, writers such as Alan Moore, Grant Morrison, and especially, Neil Gaiman, raised comic-book horror past the tricks and twists of the mystery comics era, and transformed the genre into literate dark fantasy. At the very least, we need to strive to approach their accomplishments and literate depth.

"[But] current horror comics can trace much of their current success and preeminence to a slightly more recent pop-cultural phenomena: Kevin Williamson's *Scream* films brought us to a wide-eyed awareness that anything taken too seriously, or treated as too sacred, atrophies and dies ... *Scream*, in all its iterations, and the films that it spawned are ... hyper-ironically self- and culturally aware. Those films and the television success *Buffy the Vampire Slayer* made it okay to laugh at our own fears—even while they made us shiver. Both films and television shows contributed another, more noticeable advancement to modern horror: the notion [that] gore-horror is good horror ...

"This postmodern splatter-horror, which transcends the splatter-horror of the Freddy Krueger era by being so self-aware, led to such laugh-and-shriek filmfare as *28 Days Later* and *Shaun of the Dead*, which, in turn, lead inexorably to true twenty-first-century horror comics such as *30 Days of Night*, *Wake the Dead*, and pretty much everything else the great Steve Niles gets himself up to. "

Market Research

As should the writer for any medium, a horror comics writer must undertake market research. Nice guy that I am, here is some I've done to get you started.

Paul Levitz, publisher and president of DC Comics, Inc. (www.dccomics. com), has a unique perspective on comic horror.

"I think horror comics are in their third phase, the first being the EC period (of the early 1950s), which seemed defined by the O. Henry snap endings and visual, visceral horror 'money shots' (*Tales-from-the-Crypt*-style horror); then the tamer mystery comics which supplanted them in the marketplace, were served mainly by irony and monsters which didn't get to do anything too monsterous ... [and] now concept-driven horror, drawing on mythology, society, and the world of ideas (*30 Days of Night*, the Vertigo ouevre from Alan Moore's *Swamp Thing* through Neil Gaiman's *Sandman*, and *Hellblazer*). I came in during the middle period, worked on a lot of the mystery titles as an assistant editor and editor, and even wrote a few stories for them (I recall having an ending changed by the [Comics] Code [Authority] on one of my tales because it was 'too gruesome').

"The current phase is more fun for writers, since you can explore ideas at length, and because of royalties/participations, you stand to make real money from a good idea. The second-phase mystery comics were doomed to mediocrity because the economics for the writers was so poor—a typical story then might have paid one hundred dollars or so and, even adjusting for inflation, it still wasn't worth much thought. Today we have writers earning six figures a year in royalties on previous years' work still in print and earning for them (and for us, of course) ... an upside that provides significantly better motivation for originality and effort."

See? And you thought I was kidding about the bucks.

Comics writer and novelist Neil Gaiman has talked about his own market research: "When I decided I wanted to write comics in 1985, I went out and bought Will Eisner's *Comics and Sequential Art*. If I were doing it now, I'd also buy Scott McCloud's *Understanding Comics*. I'd look at some comics scripts ... [and] then I'd read a lot of comics and try to figure out what works and what doesn't—and why.

"And then I'd start drawing some comics for myself, not for people to see, just to figure out how to get from one panel to the next, one page to the next. If you're going to work with an artist, now's a good time to go and meet artists.

"... There is a lot to know. Most bad comics are written by people who don't know that there is anything to learn ... (Many of them were written by writers who are successful in other fields.) Having something to say is fairly essential, too. "

30 Days of Night is one of many impressive horror properties from IDW Publishing (www.idwpublishing.com). Editor-in-chief Chris Ryall said to me, "We're actually doing some books that hearken back to the classic EC horror stories of the '50s. I think horror stories, more than many other genres in comics, are timeless, and the things that scared us or creeped us out then aren't so different from what affects us now.

"That said, when I look at new horror properties, I look for new approaches to old concepts. Even ... vampires, werewolves, and ghosts. I think there are ways to approach these ideas with a fresh eye, and find all-new ways to evoke horrific feelings in people. So I look for something that I haven't seen before. The past decade, the focus of horror comics seems to be more and more gore, and while the visual nature of comics lends itself to shockingly graphic images, I look more for atmosphere than I do gore. Scares are more effective in the build-up, not in the actual depiction of horror."

Scott Allie, veteran editor at Dark Horse Comics (www.darkhorse.com), who edited *Buffy the Vampire Slayer* and its spinoffs for more than half a decade, offers, "I'm looking for variety, to be honest, but even if it's in the vein of gore or schlock, I want some style and brains to it. The main thing is that any horror comic should have a strong visual element. Too many writers try pawning off their novels in the form of comics, with no attention to the fact that this medium is predominantly visual.

"Study the medium. You wouldn't walk into Hollywood without making sure you understood the difference between prose and a script. Or you won't get far if you do. Play to the strengths of this medium, but bring whatever you can from the other. If you have really impressive credits from another medium, it counts in this one, but simply having a résumé won't help much."

Horror Comic Concepts

Just as poets and photographers and musicians discover, the horror comics writer must recognize that ideas are all around us. Compelling horror comics stories can be created in many ways.

I once knew a family of four in which the mother, a nurse, shot herself to death over grief of being unable to care for her always-sick little boy Kenny. Her five-year-old daughter, Lisa, discovered the body. For years, Lisa insisted her mom kept coming back to visit her and would tell her things that Lisa could not possibly have known otherwise. Her father, fed up with the "stories," finally moved them away after Kenny died.

But the things Lisa said stayed with me.

Years later, after I had edited comics adaptations of Anne Rice's *Interview with the Vampire* and related projects, I found myself writing for *The Vampire Companion* as well as new comics stories for *Dark Shadows* and even a vampire story for a superhero-team book called *Hero Alliance*. (Premise: A flirty female vampire uses her abilities to pose as a super-heroine and become part of the group until the death toll rises.) Although I'd enjoyed writing both projects from the perspective of "fixing problems" in continuity or in concept, I'd had it with vampires.

Then I got to wondering why certain religious trappings surrounded much vampire lore: why the crucifix and holy water burned them; why they could be staked to death with wood; why, in certain instances, blessed silver could hurt them; why they were often buried for three days before rising from the dead; why they slept in the day and rose at night; and so on.

I put on my "solving problems" chapeau and wondered, "What if the first vampires were the Roman Centurion guards who put Christ to death and were splattered in his blood? " Then it all began to make sense: The crucifix and wooden stakes were obvious; the holy water was Christ's tears; the silver was the fifty silver coins given to Judas; the rising from the dead after three days matched Christ's resurrection on the third day; and since he arose in the morning, vampires were doomed to hiding from the light. It all came together … almost.

The premise needed one more piece. I realized that every culture, every group that's been around long enough, has its own legends. So I added the concept of the vampires having a legend *they* believed: If all the original fifty pieces of silver could be returned to the church, they could be cured and redeemed.

I took those ideas, remembered the little girl with the sensitivity to her mother's spirit, and made her a primary character in the story. After carefully developing three other characters, I had a series that I wrote, and Brazilian artist Al Rio drew, for Image Comics during the '90s. The series was called *Exposure*. It made a lot of money, both in the U.S. and internationally, and we received more fan letters about it than any other series I've written.

I guess the ideas had merit—a few years later, someone produced a Dracula movie that adapted the same origin of vampires (and making Judas into Dracula) and, even more recently, Johnny Depp fared pretty well with the return-the-coins-to-lift-the-curse-and-find-redemption idea in *Pirates of the Caribbean*.

Show, Don't Tell

The "show, don't tell" mandate of good prose is one that might well be the prime rule for horror comic writing. You need to think visually.

As Brian Augustyn told me, "Truly effective writers of prose horror are already on top of something many other prose writers don't 'get' about comics. To truly engage the reader, horror writers know they must be incredibly visual to makes us see and feel the shocks and screams. That visual sense, the ability to 'paint' a word picture of an action or a moody portrait of a creepy place will translate well to comics, of course. The evolution of that skill, however, is to convey much of that mood and atmosphere to the artist, and then trust the artist to deliver ..."

But that's not all. Horror comic writers can control time by indicating the size and number of panels (not frames) on a page; control dialogue cadence by the way they break up dialogue into multiple balloons (not bubbles); and control the entire pacing, intercutting of scenes, and more by skillful crafting of their scripts.

A comic book script most closely resembles a movie script. It describes the action scene by scene, panel by panel, and all the narration, dialogue, sound effects, and so on are complete, with each element of text numbered. Specific layouts, special types of panel borders, and other details are clearly identified.

As Neil Gaiman wisely mentioned, studying comic scripts will allow you to learn proper formatting. Among many Web spots offering sample scripts, you can check out:

Dark Horse Comics: www.darkhorse.com

Robert Weinberg: www.robertweinberg.net/cablescript.htm

My Glass House Graphics: www.glasshousegraphics.com

Movie Magic Screenwriter, a software program, includes a comics script-for-matting template.

A general rule of thumb: Clarity is your guideline. There are times to be ambiguous in your art—but never in providing word pictures for your artist.

Finally, now that you've been introduced to writing horror comics, we can tackle writing for graphic novels: "Graphic novels" are just big, fat comic books with a grandiose name and a square spine.

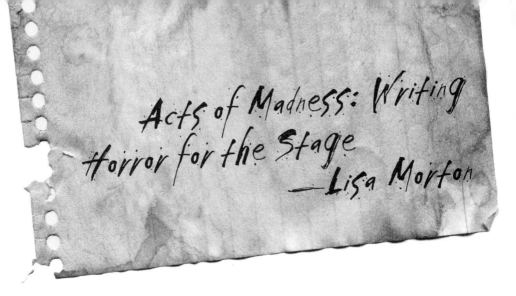

Acts of Madness: Writing Horror for the Stage
—Lisa Morton

The horror play is our oldest surviving form of dramatic entertainment (*Medea*, anyone?), and it offers many unique rewards to the contemporary dark-fiction author: the chance to see your prose come to life, participation in a social group of like-minded artists, instantaneous recognition (hopefully in the form of screams and applause), and the possibility of reviews from major newspapers.

Although it bears some resemblance to screenwriting, playwriting involves considerations that neither fictive prose nor screenplays need worry about: *Can you find the right theater company to work with? Will your idea work on a stage with a minimum of sets and characters? Does it involve a large cast or special effects? Are you the fool who'll get stuck with scrubbing the fake blood from the stage every night?*

I recommend starting your grand leap into theater by asking yourself this question: *How deeply do you want to be involved?* Maybe you're not interested in anything beyond just optioning your story or novel to a theater company (meaning one has already approached you), in which case, you can expect the company to offer you anything from zero to twenty-five to fifty dollars per performance, with slightly more for opening night, and you can stop reading here.

Maybe you'd like to try directing, to guarantee the most accurate translation of your script to stage; although the script is held in higher regard in theater than it is in film, a director's vision can still jar badly with a writer's, even if he doesn't change a single word of text. If you're working with an existing company and they're amenable to the idea of letting you direct, great. If you end up deciding you can only direct if you produce the play yourself, you'll probably put a great deal of money into the production, because theater rental isn't cheap, especially in urban areas. Your chances of making even a fraction of your money back are, well … call it an expensive hobby.

The unlikeliest event would be to have your horror play produced in a large (meaning more than one hundred seats) theater. These venues are true money-making propositions that turn a profit and need to. They're probably likelier to choose yet another production of *The Odd Couple* or the new play by Tony Kushner (*Angels in America*) over your stage adaptation of *Bride of the Monster*. If you hope to reach Broadway, you need to start small first and work your way up.

Finding a Good Company

So all roads lead back to finding a company to work with. This can be surprisingly easy. Most urban areas have at least a handful of small companies; Los Angeles and New York, of course, have dozens. Many small companies prefer to perform new plays rather than pay for rights to something that's already been done.

Start going to plays. Notice the names of the theater companies staging these works and check out their Web sites. Talk to the ticket-taker at the door; you'd be amazed how often she's also the producer, director, or the company's artistic director. Find out if the company has monthly meetings or workshops. The group may require you to pay dues or join the company (especially if you want to direct as well), but dues are normally reasonable, and you'll have fun in the workshops. If you have publishing credits, you'll probably find that the company will be thrilled to work with you (really).

Let us assume you've found your dream company. There's a little theater, seating anywhere from forty to ninety-nine people, and it's what is typically called a *black box* (meaning the walls are bare and painted black).

Before you write your play, make sure you see several productions at the space, and look for the following: How big is the stage? Maybe it's a narrow, tall space with a two-story stage, in which case, you might want to incorporate that into your play. Maybe it's wide enough to accommodate two different sets at once, which might make it easier for you to write scenes that take place in different locations. Although it's unlikely that the stage has anything as fancy as a trapdoor, overhead flying rigs, or even curtains, it might have something else fun you can use, like a stairway.

Does the theater have any existing sets? Even small companies often have a *flat storage* area to keep parts of old sets. Flats may include working doors or windows, or a particular wallpaper or paint job. Incorporating an existing set into your script, rather than writing for a set that needs to be built from scratch, will save the your company money and effort.

What kind of actors will you have to choose from? This can be a particularly prickly question; many companies limit the number of roles that can be cast from outside their group. If you've written a play for five teenage girls and the group has only *one*, with no outside casting permitted, you've already sunk yourself.

What kind of lights, sound, and other technical effects does the theater offer? If your play depends on slide projections, for example, you might find out the theater can't handle it.

What special skills do members of the company possess? Maybe they have musicians, special makeup-effects wizards, magicians, whatever. You might want to consider working in whatever they have to offer.

Okay, you've scoped out your company, and you've got an idea. It's time to ask that classic horror writer's question: *Is this a great idea that's going to scare the pants off everyone? Will that story that worked so well in prose form still terrify onstage?*

Chances are the answer is yes—a good story is a good story, for the most part. However, here's one possible drawback: Your audience will be primarily *theatergoers*, not *horror readers*. They're coming for a good chill, yes—but they're probably too sophisticated for a haunted house, jump-out-and-go-boo cheap thrill. Assume the last horror play they saw was *Dracula*, and they enjoyed it—as campy spectacle, with more tittering than shuddering.

Given this, you're best off if your story is contemporary and well-plotted; even if your play is a short one-act, building dread will win over your audience more than a barrage of shrieks. There's certainly nothing wrong with a good, old-fashioned monster or two, but if there's not a solid, even thoughtful, story surrounding your creature, you're liable to find yourself the comedy hit of the season.

Now you've got a story that you're convinced will frighten even the most jaded theatergoer, and it's perfectly in synch with what your company has to offer. It's time to start the actual writing. Great, except ... you have no idea how to write a play.

On the Scene

Here's the *single most important thing you need to know*: Plays are broken up into little chunks called *scenes*, and slightly bigger chunks called *acts*. A scene will take place entirely on one set during one span of time, although actors may exit and enter during the scene. A new scene will occur at a different time, but major location changes are probably best saved for an act change. This is theater, so changing location will mean that stagehands actually have to come onstage and physically move a set around in front of the audience. Hopefully, your chosen company is experienced at doing this; they'll appreciate you if you've saved any major changes for an intermission between acts.

How many scenes and acts does your play incorporate? If it's a short play, intended to be part of an evening of similar short plays (each running ten to forty minutes), it'll be one act, and preferably no more than a couple of scenes (the theatrical equivalent of a short story, in other words). If it's long, the play can run up to three acts. Although there's no limit on the number of scenes, over-usage of short scenes is likely to jar an audience. Try to keep the number of scenes per act to no more than three or four.

How should the script be formatted? Here's where you get a break: There is no one right or wrong format for plays. I've seen plays formatted to look like screenplays, and I've seen them formatted to look like plays in book form (wherein a character's name typically goes on the left margin). Try to look at a play script that's been previously created within your company and follow that format. Basically, as long as dialogue is plainly separated from scene description, you're fine.

How much technical lingo do you need to put into the script? Again, there's a big advantage over screenplays: You don't need to know much more than *Lights fade up* to open a scene, *Lights fade to black* to close a scene, *Enter* when a character first appears, and *Exit* when he leaves the stage. You shouldn't need to indicate much blocking (the movement of the characters/actors) in the script, since that's the director's job.

How far can you go onstage? Well, you'd be ill-advised to try that "Great Splatterpunk" story onstage. Why?

Violence: Unless your company has a trained and experienced fight choreographer, you'd best avoid physical violence onstage. Nothing looks worse to that guy in the second row than the actor who pretends to fall back from a blow that's plainly come nowhere near him. Guns are also a bad idea; if you want something that actually fires, you'll probably be limited to cap guns or starter pistols, and even those can be deafening in a small, enclosed space. You might be able to cheat a gunshot with a prerecorded sound effect played over the audio system, but it's stylistically risky.

Gore: Gore is certainly possible onstage, and it has a fine pedigree in theater (remember the Grand Guignol of early twentieth-century Paris?). Even if your company lacks a skilled makeup-effects person, basic gore effects are possible and just require a little clever thinking. Does that victim who has fallen behind the couch need to come up covered in blood? No problem: Hide a bucket of blood and a sponge behind the couch. Does a werewolf need to shred a victim live? Have the attack happen slightly offstage; the victim's screams will electrify the audience, and the werewolf can easily re-enter covered in blood and even gnawing on a bone. Just be careful of any effect that calls for *serious* splatter; stage blood is usually made from something sticky (like Karo syrup), and it's not easy to clean off walls or fabrics.

What are some other tricks you might put into your script to create tension and dread in your audience? Theater can be a wonderful medium for horror. After all, it's happening live in front of your audience, probably no more than ten feet from the front row. If you exploit the theater's full potential, you'll leave those ticket buyers remembering your play for years.

Don't forget to use lights and sound. Although the company will have a technical director who sets the lights, there's nothing wrong with indicating certain simple lighting effects in your script. Virtually every theater, for example, has a *dimmer board*, which means any light can be dimmed to just a slight glow above darkness, or can be flashed suddenly to simulate lightning.

Likewise, your theater will have a sound system, possibly with a mixing board that might even allow more than one sound at once to be played. Spooky music, screams, growls, crashes, thunder, creaks, footsteps ... sound effects CDs are plentiful and cheap, and can add instant production value.

Play Acting/Reading

So now you've written a play that you think both smart and terrifying, but you're a little nervous about handing it over to your company. Try to get some friends (or maybe a few discrete actors from the company) together for a reading, just to hear the words out loud. Maybe you can even schedule your small reading in the company's theater on an off-night.

Great! The reading sent chills up your spine, the company adores your work, and they're ready to start rehearsals. What can you, the revered playwright, expect?

If you're acting as your own director, you can expect lots of missed rehearsals, failed effects, and actors who can't remember blocking. If you've opted to simply be an involved writer, the director may or may not allow you to sit in during rehearsals (don't be surprised if she doesn't). If you are a part of the rehearsal process, you may watch in your own paroxysm of horror as an actor stumbles repeatedly over a simple line. It would be bad form to bypass the director at this point to give new words to the actors; it'll be up to you to gauge how accessible the director's going to be to receiving your input.

One final warning: If your company is well established, critics will turn out for opening weekend, so you can expect reviews within a week. If the reviews are great, maybe your show will play to packed houses and even have its run extended. If not, well ... you've just discovered possibly the scariest part of writing horror for the stage.

Fear Spins Off: The Tie-In Novel Comes Into Its Own
—Yvonne Navarro

For years, people have been prophesying that computers and digital media would be the stone at the head of the grave dug for books by television and movies. From the perspective of a writer and a reader, it was hard not to feel a twist of apprehension, but ultimately, books are not only strong, they seem to be getting stronger. And one of the more telling indicators that the written word is holding its own, and will continue to do so, is the media tie-in novel.

Once tucked here and there on the shelves at the bookstores and seldom noticed, tie-in novels have moved to the front of display space and prominence. They represent everything from genre movies such as *Hellboy* and *Elektra* to books set in science-fiction worlds such as *Star Wars* and *Aliens*, and, of course, all those wildly popular television series like *Buffy the Vampire Slayer, CSI, Smallville,* and *Monk* (to name only a few). The market for tie-in books has expanded to include gaming (*Resident Evil*), graphic novels (*MirrorMask*), every possible area of children's books, romance and comedy movies, and general suspense. The possibilities are literally endless—and notice, horror writer, how many of these tie-ins are *directly* tied in to our calling: horror.

Many bookstore customers who pick up a media tie-in for the first time don't really understand what they are holding. The common misconception is that the movie is based on the book and that somewhere at the end of the credits is the author's name. Despite the dreams of thousands of writers, that's just not the case—in fact, a book that spawns a movie is never called a tie-in. A tie-in novel is just that: a book *tied* to a soon-to-be or recently released movie, television show, comic or graphic novel, or sometimes a role-playing or regular game. These two elements are inextricably linked—*tied*. Without the first, there would never be a book.

So You Want to Be a Tie-In Writer

How do you get to write a media tie-in?

A lot of fans think they can sit down in front of a computer and bang out a book to go with their favorite television series, but that's not the case. Generally speaking, the publishers who contract for these projects look for writers with solid experience. Tie-in books mean tight deadlines—for some reason, these books are seldom contracted for until the last couple of months before a movie is set to be released.

If a writer is lucky, he's given three months to write the book—start to finish. More often, he gets only two, and deadlines even shorter than that are becoming disturbingly familiar. A publisher needs to be certain that a writer will not only make that deadline, but has the wordsmith experience to tell a good story. From the publisher's point of view, the best way to judge the writer's ability is to see a publishing history that includes a couple of novels, preferably in a genre related to that of the spin-off/tie-in project. (Established horror writers wrote many of *The Crow* and *Nightmare on Elm Street* books, and this book's editor—Mort Castle, established horror short story and novel writer— got the nod to do the *Texas Chainsaw Massacre* comic book tie-in.)

You should know that tie-in novels are "work for hire." Work for hire is an entirely separate industry, quite different from the route of publishing that a "regular" novel takes within the publishing field. Writers are typically paid a flat fee (usually half on signing of the contract, and the remainder on approval of the edited and revised manuscript), and royalties on book sales are seldom included. Once the book is completed and published, the writer has no more rights under the contract and won't be paid any additional amounts. Very few tie-ins make the best-seller lists, and even when one does, the writer won't see any more money. This is something tie-in authors know and accept from the start.

While the work-for-hire aspect of writing a tie-in novel can be a downside, tie-ins are still a lucrative business. Some authors work on tie-in novels to supplement their incomes, while others move into this arena of publishing and end up building their entire careers.

Words on the Page

With a movie tie-in, the writer gets the movie script from which to work—and there's no waiting around after that. The script is the writer's outline for the entire novel, and the writer essentially fills in all the "good stuff." For a writer to snag a pre-screening copy of the movie is rare, so turning this script into a book isn't as easy as it might seem. Scripts have little set description other than day, night, interior, or exterior, and almost no emotion. The writer's idea of how a scene looks can be quite different from the movie director's, and there simply isn't any way (or time) to reconcile the two. It's rare indeed for an author to have any contact with anyone involved in the movie, such as the scriptwriter or actors, although once an author has written several books in a specific universe, he's somewhat more likely to have these contacts.

One of the frustrating and stressful aspects of tie-in writing transpires when the writer receives an "updated" version of the script a few days before the submission deadline and realizes that major scenes have been deleted or added or significantly changed. Tie-in writers thus become very, very good at last-minute revisions.

Come to Our Universe

Tie-in writing has also come to offer opportunities to create original novels based on a film or television world that already exists, such as the *Aliens* or *Buffy the Vampire Slayer* novels. More and more of these novels are appearing as publishers see their popularity and the profits they generate. It is not unusual to have a line of books ready to hit the bookstores along with the debut of a new television series.

What makes a writer successful in this arena is a solid knowledge and fondness for the world in which she is writing. A project that entails an original novel does not come with a ready-made script to follow. The process starts with the author pitching an idea to the editor in charge of that venue; once the pitch is accepted, the writer usually writes an outline. That outline has to be approved by the editor and a representative of the movie or television property.

The Bottom Line

Payment for tie-in books depends on many factors, and there is no set amount. The project itself can influence what a writer might be offered, especially if it's set in one of the more popular universes such as that of *Star Wars, The Crow*, or *Nightmare on Elm Street*, but that's only a piece of the payment puzzle. The author's background and book-sales history, the difficulty of the project and whether the deadline is going to be a hardship, and whether the book is a novelization of a script or an original novel are only a few factors that play a part in determining the final dollar amount.

Again, in the tie-in/spin-off field, contracts that include a percentage for royalties are rare and becoming rarer. Books that earn out their advance and actually pay royalties are the rarest.

An advance is exactly that: an advance against royalties. A typical tie-in book that gives its author 1 percent in royalties needs to sell forty thousand copies just to earn out its standard advance amount. Such sales figures are scarce in an era where any given weekend might see four new movies and their accompanying tie-ins released. Because of this, many tie-in authors accept flat fees and move on to the next project.

Tie-Ins Get Respect—Now

As more and more tie-in novels hit the shelves, the medium itself has emerged from the unofficial category derided as "hack," a subgenre frowned upon or sneered at by "real writers" and the literati.

Today, best-selling and well-reviewed authors such as Elizabeth Hand, Poppy Z. Brite, and Kevin J. Anderson, as well as many, many others, have written exceedingly popular tie-in books. In the world of today's writers, there is even support for the tie-in author, whether this person is someone who's just snagged a first-time project, or a seasoned writer looking for suggestions or support from fellow tie-in authors. The Internet has brought all these writers together and given them day-to-day, real-time communication, advice, and networking. A brand new organization doing just this is the International Association of Media Tie-In Writers, or IAMTW. The organization has a Web site, www.iamtw.org, and it has a wealth of information to offer for members and non-members alike.

With its demand for high-quality craft, its increased respect and dollar-generating potential, and an opportunity to take one's imaginings to the familiar worlds of *Nightmare on Elm Street, Halloween,* or *Resident Evil*, the media-based novel has more than a few enticements for today's horror scribe.

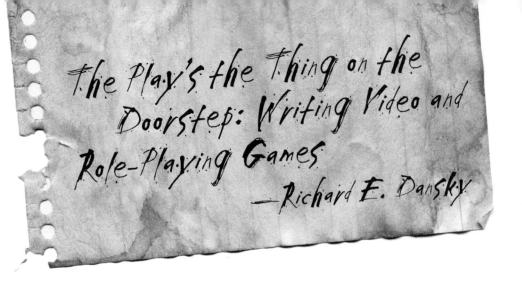

The Play's the Thing on the Doorstep: Writing Video and Role-Playing Games
—Richard E. Dansky

Do you want to write for games?

I have a question for you:

Do you *play* games?

Think carefully before you answer. It's not an idle question. Games, particularly writing-intensive, role-playing games (or RPGs, as we'll call them to save word count) or video games, aren't just novels with rules added to them. They are new forms, each decades old now and evolving faster than the last generation of creators likes to think about. They have their own demands and restrictions, their own unique benefits and techniques and vocabulary.

If you don't play games, you cannot have a feel for that stuff, for what's been done before and how to avoid repeating the mistakes that have already been ironed out a thousand times over. Most importantly, you won't know what makes a good, fun game from your *own* experience; you won't have that experience to instinctively draw on.

And that can lead to one heck of a mess.

The Story That You Do Not Write

In game writing, you are *not* writing the story. You are providing the tools necessary *for someone else to write the story*. In a traditional role-playing game, that someone is the game master, who creates the story with the cooperation and collaboration of his players. In a video game, that someone is the player. However, you are never writing for yourself. The temptation to pick the player up and carry them along on your story can be difficult to resist, but doing so eliminates the *sense of play*, the choices players make that provide the real sense of accomplishment in any game.

Diametrical Opposites

Tabletop RPG and video-game writing are, as far as horror is concerned, diametrically opposed in their shape. RPG writing is concerned with creating possibilities, hooks that players can use to shape their characters and that game masters can use to craft their scenarios. It is open-ended writing, designed to promote exploration, experimentation, and an outward motion to the game. To put it another way, sooner or later, everyone stops using the premade dungeons or setting books as anything more than a jumping-off point, and starts to create their own characters, settings, plotlines, and, God help us all, campaign soundtrack mix CDs.

Video-game writing, on the other hand, is close-ended. Everything that the player does, sees, acquires, talks to, says, or otherwise interacts with must be accounted for, created, and built. There's no on-the-fly improvisation with video games, no "Oh, I didn't think of that." Everything goes onto the disc and into the box, and whatever's in there had better stand up to any combination of moves, maneuvers, and button mashes. The writing must serve not only the narrative, but also the purpose of gently steering the player away from the hard walls of the game's reality. Have the player smack up against those walls too hard and too often, and you lose the sense of immersion that makes a great game.

Thus, you do not tell the player that the reason they can't go through the locked door is that there's no virtual space behind it and the door is actually nothing more than a door-like texture slapped onto a random chunk of wall. You tell the player that when his in-game avatar reaches for the doorknob, he feels a blast of unearthly cold that makes him draw back. Or you trigger a stentorian voice announcing that the way is forbidden. Or ... well, you get the idea. You don't say "You can't go that way" or, even worse, leave the player standing there, frantically making doorknob-turning motions in midair until he gets frustrated and goes home.

Strange Mixture

On the creative side, horror-RPG writing is an odd mixture of narration, description, character sketch, and technical writing. Odds are that any given RPG assignment is going to consist of some combination of world setting (tell the players what happened here, with these people, and make it interesting for gaming), character creation (these are important characters in the setting; sketch them out well enough that anybody who picks this book up can drop them into a campaign without skipping a beat.), role-playing advice (tell the kids what kind of game they can play here, and don't be snotty about it), and rules (you've got six ten-sided dice and a beanbag to play with; explain how someone can use that to make acid blood jet out of their eyes).

What all of these elements are directed toward, however, is allowing the game master and players to collaboratively tell a scary story. It doesn't matter if they're playing a variation of *Vampire, Call of Cthulhu, Kult,* or any other horror game; the intent is the same. Everybody gets together and has a good time scaring the bejesus out of one another. What you do as a writer is give them everything they need to do that. The history and setting? That's where you establish where the gruesome murders happened, what the mystic artifacts are that vampire lords have warred over for a thousand years, why an undying hunter has pursued a single bloodline—now represented by a player character— relentlessly through the centuries. Characters created for the game master are supporting actors, setting the stage and providing the opposition for the *real* stars, the players' characters. Rules provide a structure for conflict resolution, but, more importantly, provide a mechanism for players and non-player characters to interact and create effects, setting the boundaries for the world.

The Rules You Make, The Rules You Cannot Break

Writing for RPGs is similar to writing for any licensed property. There's an existing and extensive canon: who lives where, who did what to whom, who's dead or off-limits, and so forth. There are rule sets to consider, the skeleton on which the rest of the game is built. If your writing doesn't mesh with the mechanics of the game, it's going to get tossed back or tossed out. It behooves anyone who wants to do RPG writing to learn a prospective employer's setting and rules. Once you're on board, most companies will send you research materials in the form of various books published for the line, but you generally need to know what you're talking about *before* they'll let you in the door.

It's hard enough for the line editors (often called developers) to wrangle writers who know the rules and setting intimately. Paying for the privilege of bringing someone up-to-speed isn't something the breakneck pace of RPG publishing generally allows. Fortunately, most companies post comprehensive writers' and submission guidelines on their Web sites, so you can get an idea of what is sought in terms of both content and style. Line editors generally respond well to polite query letters or having samples handed to them at conventions or other personal appearances, and once your foot is in the door and you prove yourself reliable, you'll have line editors beating down your door to offer you work.

Very few role-playing books are single-author creations. Usually, sections get doled out an author at a time, to prevent any one author from carrying too heavy a burden. It's therefore imperative to keep in touch with the other writers on your book so you don't step on each others' toes.

In many ways, creating horror content for RPGs is much easier than it is for video games. After all, an RPG is played entirely with words, allowing you to use anything and everything that's setting-appropriate. It's always easier to have blood suddenly start dripping from the walls when you don't need to worry about "animated textures," "specular mapping," and "soft-body physics," all of which are concerns for the tech folks, and can simply say (or write) "blood starts dripping from the walls." The trick, of course, is to remember that you're not going to be the one scaring the player with this—the game master is. That means fewer long speeches about evil for the main villain, and more development of the character so that—when the moment comes for that speech—the game master in that role can speak naturally and confidently off-the-cuff. It means less loving description of the Count's throne room, and more thought about what can be done there when the player-characters decide to make a break for it.

Remember, this is stuff that the players can and have to interact with. They can't sit back and smart-ass it as if it were a movie, because the game's still going on for their friends and a smart-alecky comment taken in-character can get them all killed. It's not happening to someone on the screen or on the page, it's happening to an extension of themselves, a portion they've chosen to put out there, and that means they're involved. They're attached. They're risking a little teeny tiny self-something—and that's what's ultimately really scary.

The Art of Collaboration

Writing is frequently a solitary exercise. Not so in video-game writing. You can't just say, "And then the hero rides his horse into the castle." Someone has *to build* that castle and texture it and make sure the game allows for riding. Someone has to make and texture the horse, and texture it, and capture and attach the motion. Someone has to make sure the main character can get on and off the horse, and that his feet won't go through the floor when he does so. *Nothing* a game writer does happens in a vacuum.

Instead, you work with a team. You work with the designer—who's responsible for mapping out what the game is and what everything in it does—and you work with the artists—who build every single aspect in the game. You work with the engineers—who make it all happen—and with the QA folk—who make sure everything works right. If you're writing dialogue, you also work with the actors and voice-shoot directors and sound engineers—who put the voice files in the game. And all those relationships create dependencies, so you can't go back and "just change a word here and there." Doing so can create all sorts of unintended consequences, ranging from the need for expensive re-recording to altering the length of a line so that, when it gets translated for the German version, it doesn't fit onscreen any more.

Because, as a writer, you are part of a team, you are facing definite limitations. First and foremost, you don't get everything you want. Second, there are technical constraints to deal with.

This, however, is also the great strength of video-game writing. Your dialogue meshes with the artists' images and the designers' vision and the engineers' features to give you a multi-pronged attack on the players' nerve centers, combining sound and vision and even the tiny little rational part of an immersed gameplayer's brain.

At least, that's what happens when you do it right.

Saying It Right

Game dialogue has particular needs. There's always a game going on, which means that even when you're writing exposition, you want to "keep it snappy." You never know when a gunfight's going to break out or a zombie's going to erupt, so you don't want the player to be stuck listening when they could be, well, playing. Good dialogue serves the purposes of gameplay, driving and informing and rewarding the player, increasing the immersion, and developing emotional attachment to the game characters. However, it doesn't replace gameplay.

Furthermore, game writing isn't just the writing of a straightforward narrative. There are repeated game events that need to be written out, which is another way of saying you're going to need twenty variations of "Get it off me!" and "It's eating my brain!" for each character, not to mention a full slate of death screams, howls of agony, and moans of fear. Every one of them will be heard during the game, and a single one that comes across as goofy can wreck your player's immersion permanently.

"Cut scenes," or cinematics (also known in some cases as scripted events), allow for a little more breathing room. These moments occur when the game comes to a temporary halt for a pre-arranged scene, usually to illustrate a plot point, provide a vital piece of information, or show off bitchin' special effects. Here, there's more room to stretch, but even then there are limits. Cut scenes, particularly polished, pre-rendered ones (those are the ones that look really shiny), cost a small fortune. Every second racks up thousands of dollars, and every word can take up valuable *and expensive* seconds.

The Horror Game

Now, the horror, the horror ... What makes a horror game different to write than, say, a run-and-gun first-person shooter?

Horror-game writers get to work more with mood and ambience than do other game writers; the genre leans heavily on devices like character diaries and discovered documents.

There are more than just words that a horror-game writer can bring to bear. Working with the team to realize the full effect—everything from camera angles to sound design to character and onscreen monster motion—can be put to the service of giving the player a good jolt. A camera that's locked so the player can't see the source of the ominous growl coming from the darkest corner of the room can scare the pants off even the most jaded gamer, if timed and focused and, most of all, written right.

Conclusion—The Future

The business of video-game writing is evolving as you read this. If you are a gamer, if your writing talents lie in horror, if you can contribute to a team, you can be part of this new and rewarding medium.

Now Fear This: Writing Horror for Audio Theater
—Scott Hickey and Robert Madia

Old Radio Now

The room is dark, save for the glow of the stereo dial.

Five people sit and listen as dozens of tiny creatures escape from the mind of a struggling horror writer and begin to wreak havoc on his unsuspecting neighbors. Screams echo throughout the neighborhood as the writer comes to the realization his ideas ... have escaped.

The year? 1939? 1945? 1950? No to all three. It's 2001.

The locale is in upstate Maine, and the show is our production of an episode of *The Grist Mill* entitled "Pandora's Head."

This is audio theater.

Audio theater is sometimes referred to as "old-time radio" because of the rich legacy of dramatic productions during radio's Golden Years. Horror shows like *The Witch's Tale, Lights Out, Hall of Fantasy,* and *Inner Sanctum* established what the theater of the mind could do.

Although dramatic radio is heard only occasionally on U.S. airwaves, the medium has continued as an entertainment art form in Great Britain, Canada, and Australia. Indeed, the BBC solicits submissions of scripts for dramatic radio. Moreover, the Internet seems to be creating a new venue for audio theater. Over one hundred production companies have sprung up over the last five years. While the Internet market for audio drama—audio horror!—still has a lot of growing to do before it becomes truly lucrative, it might well be at the point at which we found video games ten to fifteen years ago.

Sound Challenges

Writing audio horror does present the author with big challenges, but it also provides for great artistic rewards. Special effects for your stories are accomplished with no expensive pyrotechnicians, automobile wranglers, or stunt coordinators. Your creatures from the Pit Number 666, Lowest Level of Hell, are created with neither liquid latex nor CGI programming. Let 'em *hear* the right clues—and the listeners' minds take over.

Of course, there's a difficulty in describing the action to your audience. With a screenplay, you know the audience will see what you've written as brought to life by a director, a set designer, and actors, but with audio theater, the script has to describe what's happening so your audience can imagine it for themselves.

Screenplay:

> INT. NIGHT. ABANDONED HOUSE.
>
> JOHN and NADINE enter the basement. Lighting is at a minimum.
>
> NADINE: We'll never find it here.
>
> JOHN: Sure we will.
>
> JOHN turns on his flashlight, illuminating the basement. The beam falls on an old, rusted chest in the corner.
>
> JOHN (excited): There it is!

Now see how the same scene could be done for audio theater.

> JOHN and NADINE enter the old house. Their FOOTSTEPS
>
> ECHO in the abandoned building. The basement door
>
> CREAKS as they open it.
>
> NADINE (nervous): It's down here in the basement.
>
> Sound of FOOTSTEPS descending stairs.
>
> NADINE: It's too dark to see anything. We'll never find it.
>
> JOHN: Sure we will. I brought my flashlight. Let me turn it on.
>
> Sound of CLICK as flashlight is turned on.
>
> JOHN: There! That's better. Now we can see everything.
>
> NADINE: Uh-HUH! In the corner. It's the old chest, but look at ALL the rust. Can we even open it?

An audio script must spell it all out for the listener. Yes, there's an artificiality of dialogue here, sometimes clumsy-seeming when simply *read* and not *heard*. Of course, no one talks this way in real life.

But contrived language is necessary to provide the clues that cannot be given alone with sound effects, music, etc. The totality of the "aural information" has to provide the sense of place, the mood, the tone—the plot. And dialogue is a great part of that totality.

The average script for a modern audio-theater program runs between twenty-five and thirty minutes (which averages a minute a page), consists of at least three acts, and contains specific indications for sound effects and music. To assist the producer, a list of sound effects should be submitted on a separate page that can be used as a check sheet when the script is in production.

Though the horror genre generally has few taboos, or sets out deliberately to violate them, writers of audio horror will probably want to avoid using foul language. In our first two episodes of *The Grist Mill*, we used language that was perhaps not quite appropriate for the entire family. When these shows were picked up by a local radio station, scenes with swears and even pseudo-swears had to be re-recorded. It was a hard lesson, but one worth learning, because it taught us something about reaching a larger audience.

In true American tradition, *violence* and *gore* are not only approved, but encouraged. With special effects being staged in the listener's mind, the right audio cues will allow Mr. Listener to envision a scene as tame or as gory as he wishes.

Creak, Squeak, and Slam

In scripting sound effects, you need to be as specific as possible. CREAK is not always enough. A creaking door sounds different from a creaking window or a creaking floorboard. Try to use sounds that are recognizable.

To be sure your sound effects (SFX) person and actors know what to expect and where to expect it, put sound effects directions in all capital letters. This makes it easy to locate them in the script.

It's an axiom of radio drama—or radio, period—that you want to avoid "dead air," so use silence sparingly. If a character needs quiet while hunting the vampire in his lair, make it a momentary silence: five seconds of dead air will seem like three eternities.

A "musical transition" (written as—what else?—MUSICAL TRANSITION) indicates a passage of time or a switch of location. Production companies typically have their own libraries of royalty-free music for these transitions, as well as for creating mood from scene to scene.

Modern audio producers are well aware of what's been done before. They've been fans of "old-time radio" for years, and they agree the time is ripe for a comeback of the genre in new and emerging media.

That means would-be scripters have to do their research of audio as it is—and as it was—to successfully write audio horror (or audio anything). Listen to the older shows.

Then re-listen to them. Then listen *again*, but this time mentally discard the story and listen solely to the dialogue.

It's the dialogue that keeps the story moving, isn't it? The classic radio dramas use narration sparingly. Your lesson: Steer clear of narration. "Show, don't tell" is the rule for all good writing. Dialogue is showing for the ear. Narration is telling.

Your script is ready. Now it's time to get it produced. A good starting point for your market research is brought to us by the new old standby, the Internet: www.audiotheater.com lists other Web sites and offers production advice and information about today's (and tomorrow's) audio theater. You'll find *The Grist Mill* listed, and, yes, we do occasionally buy unsolicited scripts, although we are currently working with bigger-name horror writers. There are many production companies with Web sites you learn from with a mouse-click, among them the Great Northern Audio Theater and the Atlanta Radio Theater Company.

And now …

The Audio Team

Congratulations. You have sold your audio-horror script. And in a very real way, it is no longer *your* script. Sure, the writing was initially all you—but the interpretation is a different matter.

Let's make that *interpretations*. From the producer. From the director. From the actors. What you heard in your head while you wrote the script might be somewhat different, really different, as a finished production. *Your* script has become *our* script—and the collaborative nature of audio drama is simply a given.

Since the dawn of storytelling, people have been unable to resist the frightening tale told in the dark. It still comes down to spooky stories told by flickering firelight in the dead of night.

And even in our high-tech, super-cyber times, that's just the mental playhouse audio theater provides as the curtain rises on sounds of dread and grue and you quietly whisper, "Good evening, friends and fiends … Now fear this!"

Resources for Audio Theater Information

Old radio programs: www.otrcat.com

Old radio programs: www.radiolovers.com

All about today's audio theater, including markets and contest info: www.audio theater.com

Radio without Boundaries, airing Jerry Stearns's Sound Affects, featuring audio drama from around the world: www.kfai.org

Home of The Grist Mill: www.amfmtheater.com

Good Characters and Cool Kills: Writing the Horror Screenplay
—Brendan Deneen

Every film-development executive is looking for the same thing when it comes to horror movies: an original idea with good characters and cool kills. More importantly, however, I want you to scare the hell out of me. I'm speaking for myself, in my role as director of production and development for Dimension Films, but I'm also speaking for ever so many others with similar positions at the numerous, worldwide, independent production and film studios.

You've no doubt heard that for the novel or short fiction, "Story is king." That maxim applies to the horror film as well—with the scares serving to bolster the story's strengths. "Story" and "scares" are true co-dependents: Scares for fright's sake aren't enough. The fright moments should evolve organically from story (and the story world you've created), so that your narrative would not even exist, let alone move forward, without them.

What Scares Us

Where do good scares come from? Gore alone is not necessarily scary; neither is a creepy basement filled with cobwebs. What scares us is a feeling that the terrible events we're witnessing on the screen could happen to *us*, the idea that when we leave the theater, that horrible killer might be lurking in the backseat of our safer-than-safe Volvo.

To get beneath an audience's collective skin and scrape nerve endings, certain elements are absolutely essential in a horror screenplay. They are: premise, protagonist, villain, kills, second act, and conclusion.

Premise

As you've heard about every creative endeavor since you were first encouraged to color outside the lines, "originality counts" when an acquisitions exec considers your premise. Just as so many other chapters of this book have stressed, you absolutely *must* familiarize yourself with what's come before. If you suddenly get the impulse to write a movie about a guy who dresses up as his dead mother and kills people in the shower at his motel, you're probably not doing your job. However, once you've watched everything from *The Cabinet of Dr. Caligari* to *Saw II*, you'll have a clearer sense of what not to write.

Then comes the hard part: finding an idea that is original, has logical story sense, and will be commercial enough to lure in an audience.

That premise doesn't have to be outlandish to be original. Sometimes simplest is best. "Write about what you know" is another slice of advice you've found in this book, but that's not always easy when you're talking about horror.

Instead, take something you know and extrapolate. If the people in the apartment above are constantly making noise and waking you up, perhaps—in your movie version—you get up the nerve to go up there and complain.

You knock. You find the door already open.

You step in.

The silence is louder than any noise they've made.

It's the silence of the dead.

And that's what they are.

And then you see ...

Even if you cannot always create a premise we've never before encountered, you can strive for originality by introducing a new twist. By the time the *The Wizard of Oz* hit the screen in 1939 (and tell me that film doesn't have its horrors with flying monkeys and melting witches), the story elements were so familiar as to border on cliché—but that doesn't mean *Wicked*, with its new take on the old premise, isn't a current Broadway killer.

Protagonist

While pretty much everyone acknowledges that a good horror movie lives or dies on its villain (Hey, Leatherface, Michael Meyers, and Dr. Hannibal!), your protagonist is almost as important. A classic example is Jamie Lee Curtis in the original *Halloween*. She had all the essential ingredients of a great horror-movie protagonist: female, pretty, strong-willed—and she had a *direct connection* to the villain. Repeat: a direct connection. While it's possible to have a protagonist who's completely unrelated to the action or the villain, it's always much more intriguing when our hero is directly linked to the *why* and the *how* the villain has emerged as its monstrous self. (Let's hear it for that protagonist professor who gave Dr. Jekyll an "A" in chemistry and encouraged his innovative experiments!)

Everything Tina Jens has to say about characterization in this book's "Such Horrible People" applies to creating your film's protagonist. Good kills and scary situations don't mean much if your characters are cardboard cutouts.

No matter how creative your set-up with feral pigs, cannibals, and demon dust-bunnies from outer space, a situation is not dire unless the audience is rooting for your protagonist.

Make sure, then, that you take time early in your movie to introduce your protagonists and the world they inhabit. The opening of your movie should introduce your characters and their conflicts rather than jumping right into the bloodletting.

Further, the audience should never get ahead of your protagonist (story-wise). Do not reveal an important plot point to the audience while the protagonist is left in the dark. It disengages the audience from your character and makes the protagonist seem unintelligent. (The day of the "dumb protagonist" who does things only because the plot dictates he must has ended.)

The protagonist is the audience's gateway into the world of your horror movie and should therefore be just as shocked as the audience when gruesome and terrifying things happen.

Villain

How important is the villain? The right bad guy can lead not only to a successful movie, but to franchise possibilities that could make both you and the studio that discovers you millions of dollars.

Thus, your villain must be ... unique. You want the "Wow! Now that's a villain!" response. Consider recent examples that connected with the audience—and the studio accountants: the skeleton-masked killer(s) from *Scream*. The spooky little girl from *The Ring*. And that sadistic but oddly playful killer from the *Saw* movies. Each villain brings something new and different to the horror movie canon.

If, as I've implied, it's wise that your hero have a direct-connect link to the villain, your villain also profits from such a relationship with the protagonist or other people who populate your film. Oh, there's nothing wrong with a random psycho killing whoever he comes into contact with, but the most engaging bad guys often have a motive, albeit sometimes a mad one, to hunt and murder specific story people.

For instance, in our story about the loud upstairs neighbors who have been discovered brutally murdered in their apartment, perhaps our protagonist goes on to discover that there is a crawlspace between the apartments—and someone has been living there. This clues both the protagonist and the audience in;

the murderer is somehow linked to the people who died, and there is probably a damn good reason (perhaps an utterly logical one—if you're a psychopath) that those people had to be dispatched.

Kills

The right kill can separate *your* movie from whichever popcorn slasher flick will appear and disappear from the theater within a week of its release. That "good kill" will be discussed on horror-oriented blogs for years and years:

> *Gurgle!* And Kevin Bacon gets an arrow through the neck in the original *Friday the 13th!*

A cool kill. Definitely.

A key to finding good kills is to know what kind of deaths we've seen in previous horror movies. In a well-done screenplay, there's no such thing as a "senseless killing;" the death is organic to the storyline. So, don't try to shoehorn in a cool kill that makes no story sense.

The kills must become even cooler and more intense as the movie progresses. If you blow people away in the first fifteen minutes, then what will you do to keep them in their seats the next seventy-five? That's not to say your opening kill shouldn't be a nasty and gripping one; just make sure you have something lined up for the finale that will have people scared to go to sleep that night.

Second Act

The second act is probably the hardest part of any movie to write. Once you have your premise and your protagonists, it's almost easy to figure out how the movie is going to end: your hero will triumph over the murderous psycho in some grand fashion. (Or maybe the reverse …!)

The second act, however, is where a lot of scripts run out of steam and, as a result, often lose the interest of the executive reading them.

One of the ways to avoid the "second-act slump" is to map out the trajectory of your entire story. A story meriting ninety or more minutes of screen time has to have several layers, and it's the second act in which those layers begin to reveal themselves. Seeming facts that the audience has been led to accept can prove false. The protagonists' motivations should be questioned by one another— and by the audience as well.

Basically, you attack the second act (and the larger story as well) almost as if you're *not writing a horror movie at all.* Your characters and their stories must exist *independently* of the horror element that you've introduced into their lives. The second act is the perfect place to explore their lives—so that we understand and *feel* the effect the horror element has on them.

Back to our "apartment murderer:" In the second act, our protagonist discovers the person living in the crawlspace used to be the superintendent of the building. Our protagonist could then investigate the history of the apartments and why the murderer has chosen to hide himself within the walls of a place he used to manage. As he learns the history of the "crawlspace creeper," the protagonist discovers a personal connection to either the killer or the building—or both!—that he never knew about.

Conclusion

Your conclusion shouldn't be one big sloppy showdown; instead, this is the point at which *all* the narrative threads should come together—the third and *final* act. Now is the time to write the final segment of the arc you created for each and every one of your characters, from the first act all the way through to this point—at least for the characters who have survived this long!

Now is the time for all the things that the protagonist has learned to lead him right back to the villain and the villain's motivations, making the final confrontation an *emotional* as well as a physical battle.

The conclusion must also have a spectacular end for the villain at the hands of our protagonist (or vice versa). Audiences demand it, and so does the old rule of "don't build us up for a letdown." This is the *culmination* of the protagonist's suffering throughout the film; it must be a convincing and exciting demise for the character we love to hate or for the protagonist we hate to see killed.

If an audience has its demands for the conclusion, so does a profit-minded studio: The conclusion must be open-ended enough so that there is room for and the possibility of a sequel. Nothing excites a development executive more than a franchise waiting to happen.

A Film Formula

Formulas become formulas because they give results. I've provided a formula above that can enable you to do what a screenwriter of horror films must do: Scare me (or someone not all that different from me!).

The formula equals … Scary.

This formula might equal … A contract from a major movie studio.

But …

If you send me a screenplay about those noisy neighbors and a killer living in the crawlspace of a spooky apartment building, you may just be hearing from me.

Or my lawyers.

Part Eight

Horror Business: Selling, Marketing, Promoting

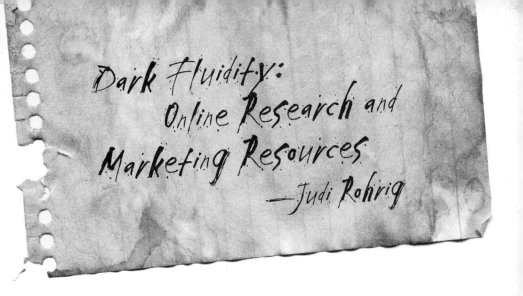

Dark Fluidity: Online Research and Marketing Resources
—Judi Rohrig

In the twenty-first century, here, on the other side of Y2K, the Internet is no longer the new-fangled curiosity or flashy gizmo to be lobbed in the ol' writer's toolbox and plucked out if need be. Having an up-to-date computer and access to the vast resources available via the World Wide Web is now as essential as that first feather sharpened into a pen and something dark and fluid to dip the tip in once was.

The Internet provides a big, wide window offering, quite simply, well … everything: e-mail addresses, author Web sites, message boards, name generators, electronic publishing, writing classes, market reports, convention listings, maps, bookstores, and instantaneous acceptances or rejections. You can also do detailed research, from charts listing when the moon was full from 1700 to 2035 (http://aa.usno.navy.mil/), to the manifests from Christopher Columbus's Nina, Pinta, and Santa Maria (www.immigrantships.net), to the last meals of executed prisoners, to … well, dig inside your own imagination.

Access to all this information means there is a good, a bad, and an ugly to utilizing the Internet. What was good last week may have morphed into one of the others in the time it took you to sign on this morning; things can happen that fast. In fact, anything or everything in this article could be totally outdated by the time you read this.

Or not.

We live in, ah, interesting times.

Let's take a look around at *some* of what the Internet offers writers.

Stop, Drop, and...

Research is an integral part of a writer's life, and there are two basic approaches: A writer can develop an outline, flesh out character backgrounds, tape up his maps, and trim his nails all in preparation for cobbling his story, or he can jump in and let the character/location/plot dictate what he needs to discover. Either method requires a careful hunt for precise information.

Yes, it's fiction, but we live in a post-*CSI* world in which even minute details require spot-on accuracy. You can't risk losing the reader simply because you didn't know the difference between a rifle and a shotgun or that, unlike rifle cartridges, revolver casings are not ejected after each shot.

The Internet allows immediate access to information that once mandated a drive across town to the local library, even longer (and expensive) travels to distant locations, or an exhaustive hunt for an expert.

It's possible the Internet may replace all those writing reference books on your shelves.

William J. Strunk's *The Elements of Style* is a must-have, classic reference guide. Though I would recommend a copy of the most recently released version—fourth edition (Longman) by Strunk, E.B. White, and Roger Angell—the 1918 edition (W.P. Humphrey) has fallen into public domain, and is available online (www.bartleby.com).

Google. There, I've shoved the word under your nose. Google is probably the most recognized search engine these days, because of its recent appearance and rapid rise on the New York Stock Exchange. Of course, there's also Yahoo, Lycos, Alta Vista, MSN Search, Teoma, Wisenut, Gigablast, or Dogpile (www.dogpile.com), which piles all the best engines into one. I prefer Dogpile, but "Stop, drop, and Google" sounds more like what a writer wants to do to find information.

Googling *Hellnotes*, a weekly electronic newsletter I edit and publish, brought about a number of hits. Several actually had to do with the newsletter itself and not the Chinese currency called "hell notes."

Whichever search engine you use is wonderfully timesaving for doing exploration and examination of your subject. Recall above when I provided the link for the ships' manifests for Christopher Columbus's historic voyage across the Atlantic? I wanted to write a story about what really happened to the sailors left stranded at La Navida (cannibals were on my mind!) and found a wealth of information about the indigenous tribes Columbus met when he hit land in 1492. (There were indeed cannibals and a whole lot more.)

Oftentimes, clicking on links takes you further than you might have hoped or imagined. It certainly impacted my story.

A trick of the trade: It's a good idea to occasionally Google your own name or Web site to make sure someone hasn't copied a story of yours, pasted his name on it, and offered it out as his own. Or that some admiring fan hasn't plastered your copyrighted story on her own page so everybody can read it for free instead of buying a copy of the book or magazine it appeared in.

Book 'Em, Dano...

Of course, it's at this point where those of us who've been doing this for a little bit steer writers to all the places online where growth as a writer is the focus.

Unfortunately, quite a few writers choose to skip this step and move right into publishing what words they have managed to rub together, so we'll forge ahead into the online steps to getting published because in a lot of cases, a writer doesn't actually have to know anything about writing to get published. Indeed, in this Cyber Age, a publisher doesn't have to know anything about publishing either. (Remember that part where I mentioned bad and ugly?)

P.T. Barnum wisely advised that there's a sucker born every minute. Sadly, a percentage of those chumps are no doubt writers—horror writers.

Very few things move quickly in publishing. Editors must wade through stacks of submissions, considering the stories. Manuscripts that have been submitted following the editorial guidelines and proper format have the best chance of allowing editors a chance to read the story rather than grumble about rank amateurs wasting their precious time.

Getting stories into print also takes time. Then there's marketing and …

Oh, there's just so frustratingly much you have to *actually do* as a horror writer to succeed.

But one cyber-second! The Internet provides all sorts of ways around the traditional, wearisome publishing model.

Scenario: Joey (not his real name) does … Web sites! Cliff (also a protected innocent), the new friend Joey met online, hasn't been able to sell his stories. Is this a marriage made in heaven or what? Joey puts up a fresh new Web site, www.Zith ering-Zombies.com, where he can publish his friend and all his other new friends and to hell with those haughty editors (or those who don't have Flash-Googleplex).

Of course, Joey can't *pay* Cliff and the other writers for their work. And Joey doesn't know much about punctuation and grammar either—but they are all feeling the love of the genre.

What does the genre gain? What does the author gain? (Consider this cautionary tale in a few years when some real editor advises that she thought your story "Babbling Blood," published in Joey's *Zithering-Zombies* would have been a good fit for her paying anthology. But that editor wants only original, not reprint, material, and "Babbling" has been published. More or less. Sort of …)

The horror genre has seen more than a number of Web sites dedicated to publishing fiction come and go. A few have actually stood the test of time, in no small part because of the dedication of those behind the keyboards.

In 1999, Chiaroscuro's *ChiZine*, with Brett Alexander Savory at the helm, saw two Bram Stoker Awards affirm its existence and excellence. The first award was for Brian A. Hopkins's short story, "Five Days in April," which was one of the first stories published at the site (and the first electronically published story to win a Stoker), and the second went to the site itself in the Alternative Forms category. Even today, thanks to a partnership with Dorchester Publishing's Leisure Books and the skills of its editorial staff, *ChiZine* continues to set the bar on online publishing for both story quality and author remuneration.

There are other Webzines that do offer homes for good writing—and some of them, good horror writing. It is essential to research these cyber markets—and to deal only with those that are "the real deal."

Writers still need to look at print publications—magazines and anthologies—for their stories. They can do that online, as more and more magazines and anthologies begin to accept electronically submitted stories. Some are even abandoning snail-mail submissions altogether.

A caution, however: Those publications seeking electronic submissions usually have specific guidelines about formatting such offerings. If a story is to be pasted into the body of an e-mail, with asterisks replacing italics, then a writer had better use the find and replace to get rid of italics and substitute asterisks and use the "cut and paste" function to put the story into the e-mail. An e-mail-accepting editor is still an editor, and the editor is always right.

Who's on First

Shopping a story leads to the crossroads for every writer. For the horror writer, it's the midnight encounter with the devil. (And, no, I haven't forgotten the section on honing a writer's craft!)

Online locations and the searching writer are a match made in a cooler place than expected. In Edo van Belkom's "Sharing the Creeps," later in this book, you'll find such superb resources as www.ralan.com and www.gilaqueen.us. I just want to add my praise for what Ralan Connelly does at his Web site. For me, Ralan C is the number one stop, the Hertz Rent A Car for market listings.

I'd also be remiss (ahem) if I did not mention *Hellnotes* (www.hellnotes.com); after all, I've been extremely close with the editor and publisher for years.

Not to be overlooked or dismissed are the numerous message boards where friendships and information on markets are traded in a flash. Such bulletin boards as can be found at www.shocklines.com and www.horrorfind.com can help an aspiring writer become part of a vital and real horror-oriented community of fans and authors.

As in any networking venue, the more "positive visibility" you maintain on message boards, the better you can market and promote your work.

The Road to Hell

All the resources a writer needs for research and marketing can't possibly be covered in a mere chapter. This is but a beginning: The Internet is a window, remember? Go take a look around, and see what "Welcome" and "Warning" signs it can offer you.

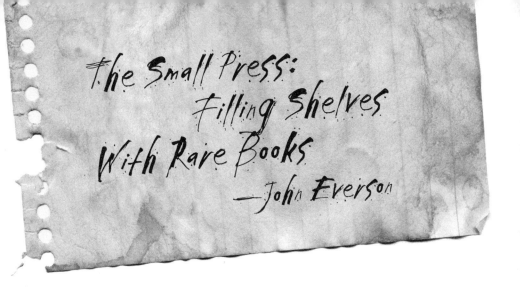

The Small Press:
Filling Shelves
With Rare Books
—John Everson

If you've only frequented the paperback-packed shelves of the mall bookstore, chances are you've never even heard of the "Small Press." Larger bookstores might have some titles that weren't published in New York—but not many. You need to do a little homework to find these publishing purveyors of classic and new out-on-or-over-the-edge genre releases. Once you start, though, you'll find a treasure trove.

The Small Press consists largely of mom-and-pop publishing operations. They're presses often run by a harried guy who sits down after dinner every night to don the multiple hats of publisher, editor, marketing director, and circulation manager. Given this intensely *sole* proprietorship, small presses tend to have very distinct personalities, and often work with a small list of core writers.

Some were formed simply to keep older works in print, generally in beautifully designed and sometimes slipcased hardcover editions. Some exist to put out newer limited editions of both established name authors and newcomers. And there is also a growing cadre of small-press owners who are putting out trade paperbacks of works by new writers.

As many in the publishing world will attest, issuing a paperback has gotten easier over the past few years than running a magazine. While the 1990s were the age of upstart magazines, the 2000s seem to be the age of the instant book publisher. That's a good and bad trend; it's certainly helped more authors get their names on book spines, but like the magazine frenzy of the 1990s when titles exploded and then imploded in an issue or three, having a book contract doesn't mean you'll ever see your book appear. Small presses come and go like the wind. And if the publisher has no lines of distribution, it's unlikely that anyone beyond a few of the author's friends and family will ever see it.

The following are some small presses that have proven themselves as viable, lauded publishers of limited edition and trade paperback, small-press horror books. This chapter of *On Writing Horror* is not, however, meant to be a current market guide. (You can check *Novel & Short Story Writer's Market* for that.) Rather, it provides a look at the diversity and individual cachets of these decidely non-mainstream publishers, and thereby offers suggestions as to how to approach, submit to, and successfully publish with a small house—a house that can often provide boutique treatment for your book that a bigger press, driven by needs for bigger profits and bigger audiences, might not be able to give you.

Ash-Tree Press
www.ash-tree.bc.ca

Barbara Roden and her husband, Christopher, started Ash-Tree Press in 1995, when they saw an open niche for quality reprints of difficult-to-find classic supernatural tales. Ash-Tree has published 110 titles and currently averages eight to ten new books a year.

Ash-Tree's niche centers on the supernatural: "We supply titles that are difficult, if not, impossible to find; books that aficionados of the ghost story have long wanted to be able to read but have not been able to find or afford in their original editions," Roden says.

Ash-Tree publishes limited editions of 500 copies, generally single-author reprint collections, since the press specializes in classic authors. Ash-Tree also has three high quality paperback imprints: Classic Macabre (reprints of older, classic genre works, mainly novels), New Century Macabre (contemporary work that is somewhat outside the normal Ash-Tree range), and Vampire Classics, which reprints works in that genre.

Ash-Tree will consider new authors, as long as they take the time to understand what the press is about.

Bloodletting Press
www.bloodlettingbooks.com

"I never really went into publishing thinking about what I could contribute to the small press, but what I would like to collect," says Bloodletting Press founder Larry Roberts.

Roberts started Bloodletting in January 2003 to cater to the dark, hardcore horror market. Bloodletting has published 17 titles to date, mostly hardcover or leatherbound novels and novellas. Key titles include Steve Gerlach's *Rage,* Edward Lee's *Ever Nat,* and less graphic works like Douglas Clegg's *Neverland* and Elizabeth Massie's *The Fear Report.*

Roberts says, " Books like *Ever Nat* by Edward Lee would never make it into the large press due to their graphic descriptions, but that doesn't mean that they don't deserve to be read."

Bloodletting was originally open to unsolicited submissions, but, after being buried in manuscripts, now accepts submissions by invitation only.

On Writing Horror

224

Tips for writers from Larry Roberts: I read a lot of small-press horror magazines, and if I read someone I like, I'll hit them up for a story.

Borderlands Press
www.borderlandspress.com

For the most recent edition of their popular *Borderlands* anthology series, Tom and Elizabeth Monteleone received more than 1,700 stories! That's why, outside of submissions to anthologies, Borderlands Press remains closed to unsolicited submissions.

The Monteleones say Borderlands is more traditional than many of the small horror presses. They call it a "Boutique Press," because "we still make our books with hand-wrapped linen and leather, and our traycases have an old-world look and feel to them. Our niche is the serious collector who wants high quality."

The press offers classic reprints, like F. Paul Wilson's *Repairman Jack* and *Adversary Cycle*, as well as newer titles like *Lost Boy, Lost Girl* and *In The Night Room* by Peter Straub. Borderlands will occasionally choose newer writers to work with.

Cemetery Dance Publications
www.cemeterydance.com

Founded in 1988 to publish the seminal horror magazine *Cemetery Dance*, Richard Chizmar's press has grown over two decades to become one of the kingpins of the independent horror press. CD has published almost everyone who's anyone in the genre, from Stephen King, Dean Koontz, and Clive Barker to Peter Straub, F. Paul Wilson, and Joe R. Lansdale.

CD is not currently considering any unsolicited manuscripts for the book imprint, but will read query letters (no e-mails, please).

Darkside/Midnight House
www.darkside.com

John Pelan says Midnight House is basically "what I'd do if I were editor of Arkham House, with Darkside Press covering the more S-F side of things." He "prints books for [him]self and the five hundred people who share [his] tastes." He has published around 50 titles to date.

The press is not open to unsolicited submissions, and is largely focused these days on reprinting classic works from the likes of Fritz Leiber, Charles Birkin, and Mark Hansom and classic science fiction from Clifford D. Simak, Daniel F. Galouye, and Cleve Cartmill.

Pelan says the small presses can serve numerous purposes, but, as for the small press being a perfect place for non-commercial projects, "I hate to sound crass, but if it's really non-commercial, that means I can't sell it, either!"

Delirium Books

www.deliriumbooks.com

Like many publishers, Shane Ryan Staley ventured into the book business after editing a magazine called *The Twilight Garden.* "I started out in this genre as an author," Staley says, "but I felt, at the time, that the genre needed a publisher who would take chances on newer authors. So I put my writing on hold and started publishing zines, and then books."

Since launching the Delirium imprint in 1999, Staley has published 80 titles, now averaging 15 a year. The average press run of Delirium titles is 200, though some titles have been printed in pricey, rare editions of fewer than 40. The press found its niche in publishing a wide range of horror for the collector's market, producing low-print-run, highly collectible books. Delirium has also had great success introducing new authors to the collector's market, Staley says.

While Delirium began as a proving ground for newer writers, like many small presses, Delirium was overrun by submissions and is now an invitation-only house.

Tips for writers from Delirium Books: Be willing to market yourself not only to publishers but to readers as well.

Earthling Publications

www.earthlingpub.com

Paul Miller started Earthling in 2000, out of a love for finely crafted books and quality dark fiction.

The press currently averages six titles a year, mainly novellas, but also some novels and single-author collections. Generally, Earthling works in hardcover, but has also issued perfectbound paperbacks and has just launched a line of slipcased classic novels.

"More Tomorrow & Other Stories" by Michael Marshall Smith was a key book for us," says Miller, "not only because it won the International Horror Guild Award, but also because it was Earthling's highest print run and sold out relatively quickly."

Earthling is no longer open to unsolicited submissions, because "the amount of unsolicited work grew exponentially ... and, sadly, I could no longer keep up with it."

Gauntlet

www.gauntletpress.com

Gauntlet started life as a magazine in 1991, and released its first book the following year. While the press has published newer writers like Jack Ketchum, F. Paul Wilson, and Poppy Z. Brite, Barry Hoffman says his main interest is in enhancing the legacy of some of the masters like Ray Bradbury and Richard Matheson. "There is an awful lot of unpublished material from both authors, and it has been a privilege to be able to print this work—material that is often better than the best of what is being published today."

Gauntlet publishes novels, screenplays, and short story collections and will offer its first anthology in 2006.

Gauntlet is currently closed to submissions as its list is full for the next three years.

Tips for writers from Barry Hoffman: Persevere. If you're new, you'll get more rejections than acceptances. Submit in a professional manner. I get too many e-mails basically saying "Do you want to read my manuscript?" Some are mass mailings, and that's unprofessional. And some authors send an entire manuscript before finding out if we're open to submissions.

Necessary Evil Press
www.necessaryevilpress.com

Donald Koish started Necessary Evil in June 2003 after a long apprenticeship as an avid reader and book collector. Jobs as copyeditor and proofreader led to his interest in launching an imprint. His goal is simply to publish beautiful books that contain fabulous stories.

The press produces signed, limited hardcovers as well as trade paperback and chapbook-type projects. One of its most recent titles, and its first novel, was Tim Lebbon's *Berserk*.

NEP is not open to unsolicited submissions. "Being a one-person show, I just don't have the time to read a lot."

Necro Publications
www.necropublications.com

After publishing five issues of the extreme horror magazine *Into The Darkness*, David Barnett faced the fiscal realities of magazine publishing and switched to books. Twelve years later, he's created one of the most respected, well-designed, hardcore-horror book lines out there. A series of hardcover editions of Edward Lee books form the cornerstone of Necro, which has issued upwards of three dozen titles, including short-story collections from Charlee Jacob and Mehitobel Wilson and novels from Jeffrey Thomas and Patrick Lestewka.

Necro has also spun off a Bedlam imprint for more general horror fare, and Little Devil Books, a children's imprint, was launched in 2005 with a young adult Edward Lee book.

Barnett has watched many presses come and go, but says there is a glut of small presses today. "Digital printing has made it much more accessible to everyone who wants to publish books. Sadly, just because you can, doesn't mean you should."

Necro is currently not open to unsolicited submissions.

Night Shade Books

www.nightshadebooks.com

Night Shade released its first book at the 1998 World Fantasy Convention, and has since issued sixty titles, one-third of them in 2005 alone. Jeremy Lassen says whenever and wherever mainstream presses fall short, independent presses can and should fill that gap. Night Shade was started because there were too many good projects, marketable projects, that needed to be done that were not being done by major publishers.

Lassen describes his press as a publisher of upscale literary horror. Lassen states, "Leisure fulfills the meat-and-potatoes, monster-mash side of things, and there are a number of publishers that specialize in fancy limited editions, and do a nice job. Night Shade is all about the trade hardcovers and trade paperbacks of titles that Leisure would probably never touch. Conrad Williams, Joel Lane, M. John Harrison ... these are hard-hitting names that appear in the year's best anthologies each year but aren't represented by either the mass-market presses or the collector's presses."

Night Shade is open to queries for novels only.

Tips for writers from Night Shade Books: Write what you think is your best book. Put it in a trunk and write another one. Do this four times. Then start sending your novels out for submission.

Raw Dog Screaming Press

www.rawdogscreaming.com

Raw Dog Screaming Press is the youngest press in this survey, started in October 2003 as an outgrowth of the online zine *The Dream People.* Founder John Lawson says he realized there was an interest in the bizarre literature of his zine, but that—to be taken seriously—it needed to appear in a more substantive form than pixels. The press has released seventeen titles, including Jeffrey Thomas's *Everybody Scream!* and the Stoker-nominated, flash-fiction collection *100 Jolts* by Michael Arnzen.

RDSP tries to publish the works that are "too weird" for the conventional horror scene. "We're fond of books that mix genres and challenge the usual labels."

Unlike many of the presses listed above, RDSP's mission is less to produce collectible books and more to break new authors.

RDSP will accept unsolicited submissions. Check guidelines at its Web site.

Tips for writers from RDSP: Patience and persistence are key, but the main thing is to get out and meet publishers and other authors.

The Overlook Connection Press

www.overlookconnection.com

Overlook's Dave Hinchberger launched his press with a signed, limited edition of *The Shape Under the Sheet: The Stephen King Encyclopedia* in 1989.

Overlook Press is a natural extension of his bookstore. "I found myself in the position of reading many authors, and getting to know quite a few of them in the process. I was already promoting their works extensively in our bookstore catalog with interviews, news, etc. The natural progression was to continue my interest in promoting books, and start producing some of them as well."

Overlook averages press runs of 500 copies in hardcover and trade paperback formats, and has issued around 30 titles to date. Hinchberger says Jack Ketchum's *The Girl Next Door* has been a key title for the press. "It's like the Energizer bunny, it just keeps going, and going, and ..."

Overlook considers unsolicited submissions, but rarely. "If it does make it to my desk, I request a synopsis and the first two chapters to peruse."

Tips for writers from Overlook Connection Press: Short fiction submissions to magazines and open anthologies seem the best way to get out there and get noticed. Just keep writing, and keep submitting.

Twilight Tales

www.twilighttales.com

Twilight Tales probably has the most unique birth story on this list; the press began as an outgrowth of a live, weekly, fiction-reading series. The writers' collective issued its first chapbook in 1998 and, these days, prints trade paperbacks. "Our books reflect the same mix of authors as our show; spanning the genres and spanning experience range," says founder Tina Jens. "We mix best-selling novelists with never-before-published writers. We enjoy discovering new talent and grooming young authors."

Twilight Tales keeps its catalogue in print, but its first runs for anthologies range between 250–400 and from 100–300 copies for single-author collections. The press has issued 22 titles, including chapbooks, trade-paperback anthologies, and single-author collections.

Submission to Twilight Tales requires participation in one of the group's many reading venues, or previous publication in its webzine. Single-author collections and podcasts are solicited by the editors.

Tips for writers from Tina Jens: Always act professional. I'll choose a story by a less-talented author who is easy to work with over a story by a more-talented prima donna. I don't have enough time or get paid enough money to work with difficult authors.

Wildside Press, LLC

www.wildsidepress.com

John Betancourt started Wildside as a hobby in 1989, to publish one book for a science fiction convention. Some 3,000 titles later (with 500 titles scheduled a year), you might guess that Wildside is a hobby no longer. The press has four additional imprints (Prime Books, Cosmos Books, Point Blank, and Borgo

Press), and the bulk of its output focuses on mainstream classics. Wildside publishes one to two new horror titles a year, along with classic horror reprints. It also publishes six magazines, including *Weird Tales, Strange Tales,* and *Fantasy Magazine*. The press issues both trade paperback and limited hardcovers, with print runs from 600–1,200.

Recent titles include *People of the Dark*, the third in a series of short-story collections by Robert E. Howard, Andrew Lang's classic epic poem "Helen of Troy," and newcomer Holly Phillips's *In the Palace of Repose* short-story collection.

Wildside takes on few original book projects, but will consider queries via e-mail. See their Web site for directions on where to submit short fiction.

Tips for writers from Wildside Press: Write short stories well. Establish a unique voice.

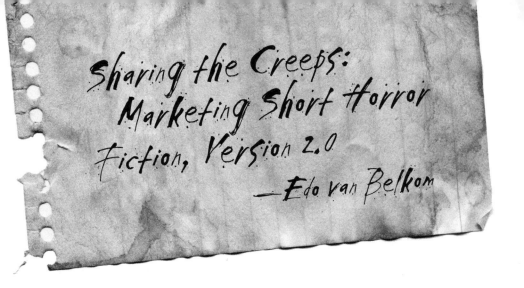

Sharing the Creeps: Marketing Short Horror Fiction, Version 2.0

—Edo van Belkom

The conventional wisdom for marketing short stories is to create a list of the best-paying markets and submit to them from the top down, sending the story to the highest-paying market first. If and when the story is rejected, you send it to the second highest-paying market, gradually working your way down the list until the story finally sells.

Unfortunately, there aren't the same kind of high-paying, prestigious markets in the horror field as there are in say, science fiction and fantasy. Horror currently has nothing comparable to *Asimov's Science Fiction, Analog Science Fiction and Fact,* or *The Magazine of Fantasy and Science Fiction,* long-established magazines that pay professional rates and maintain a solid circulation base.

Still, there are several highly-regarded magazines publishing horror. In the recent *Writer's Digest* "Fiction 50"—a regular list of the top fifty fiction publishing magazines in the United States—three "horror" magazines are included. *The Urbanite* was ranked number eight, *Weird Tales* was ranked number twenty-six, and *Fantastic Stories of the Imagination* (formerly *Pirate Writings*) came in at number forty-six. There are, then, good markets out there publishing horror, even more if you consider that a publication like *The Magazine of Fantasy and Science Fiction* (number four on the list) will publish the odd horror tale, as will other mainstream publications.

Remember, however, that the markets listed in the "Fiction 50" are judged on a number of criteria, from "rate of pay" to the "number of stories published in a year," from "personalized rejections" to "range of interest." Therefore, some highly regarded, albeit low-paying or low-circulation, magazines in the horror genre did not make the list.

These magazines are generally known as semi-professional and small-press magazines. Some prestigious horror magazines such as *Cemetery Dance* and *Talebones* are considered semi-professional, but nevertheless publish some of the best short fiction in the field. For example, Jack Ketchum's "The Box," first published in *Cemetery Dance*, won the 1994 Bram Stoker Award for best short story, so exclusion from the *Writer's Digest* list need not be an indication of the quality of a magazine's contents, or even rate of pay. *Cemetery Dance* has published over fifty issues and currently pays the HWA professional minimum of three to five cents per word.

Marketing Resources

The horror genre is blessed with many excellent sources of market information, covering everything from small-press magazines to anthologies from major publishers.

One regular print newsletter featuring market information is the *Gila Queen's Guide to Markets*, published by horror writer and reviewer Katherine Ptacek. Each issue focuses on a specific genre—romance, Western, mystery, erotica—in addition to providing up-to-date information about new and established markets.

Other worthy publications that sometimes provide market info for horrorists are *Locus* and *Science Fiction Chronicle*. Their focus is, of course, on science fiction, but with genre overlap—if not always crossover—seeming to be a trend, these monthlies are helpful.

Each print publication also has a Web site, and newsletters like *Gila Queen* are also offered in an electronic version. There's no better way in this day and age to get up-to-the-minute market info than in the form of a weekly electronic newsletter such as *Hellnotes*, or on a Web site like www.ralan.com, that is dedicated to nothing other than listing paying markets for fiction. Any decent search engine will be able to find other market sites with a list of key words geared to the horror or any other genre.

These newsletters and Web sites are invaluable if you have several stories to market, or if you feel more comfortable breaking into the horror field at the ground level and working your way up to the professional ranks.

Small Press

If you've sent your story to all the top markets without any luck, or have been discouraged by countless impersonal rejection slips, you might consider lower-paying markets or even those that pay in contributor's copies. You might even consider publishing your story on a Web site.

Publishing in small-press magazines can be an excellent starting point: First, there are many small-press horror magazines, most of them eager to publish new writers. Second, the contact you have with editors is quite often more personal than can be had with editors at top magazines. And finally, making a sale, even to a pays-in-copies magazine or to a Web site, can give you some much-needed confidence as you work toward more professional markets.

Not so much of a digression: My first story, "Baseball Memories," was published in a pays-in-copies literary magazine called *Aethlon*. After the story appeared there, it was selected by Karl Edward Wagner for the twentieth installment of his *The Year's Best Horror Stories* series.

Aethlon was not the first place I sent the story, but rather the fourth, after it had already been rejected by some of the major magazines of the day. Would it have sold to a top market if I had continued to use the "top down" method of marketing? Perhaps, but selling to small-press magazines, with the occasional submission of a story I thought had superior merit to the top markets, seemed the best route for me early in my career.

WWW

Another publishing outlet for horror stories that has opened up in recent years is the World Wide Web. There are countless horror-related Web sites out there that "publish" fiction. Web sites are hungry for content, and more and more people get their fiction fix via the Internet every day. However, be aware that while there are some truly professional Web sites that publish horror fiction, such as the horror site *ChiZine*, which pays a respectable seven cents a word for fiction, there are so many amateur horror sites out there, it's sometimes hard to identify the quality markets for your fiction. And a page-long list of Web site publishing credits won't impress a magazine editor as much as one or two fiction pieces published in highly regarded print magazines.

Pro Markets

While the small press and the World Wide Web might be great places to learn the craft of writing, they are not the place to forge a professional horror-writing career. The "big press" might prove frustrating, with its greater likelihood of rejection, but when a story is accepted, it will mean something serious for your wallet and your résumé.

Information about professional markets is just one of the advantages of joining a profressional-writers' organization such as the Horror Writers Association. As well as providing new writers an opportunity to make contacts within the field and learn from established pros, the HWA's Web site and regular newsletter include listings for horror markets paying professional rates for fiction.

Mainstream Markets for Horror

But if the horror-focused magazines all reject your story, what then?

Submit to mainstream or other *non-horror* markets.

Obviously, some mainstream markets like *Redbook* or *Ladies' Home Journal* won't be receptive to stories about zombies and ghouls, but some other top magazines might. For example, contemporary horror often finds its way into *Alfred Hitchcock's Mystery Magazine*.

Many professional magazines outside of the top fifty will also consider horror fiction. For years, the slick men's magazine *Cavalier* routinely published the horror fiction of Stephen King, Dennis Etchison, and Mort Castle. Sadly, *Cavalier* is no more, but there are still countless other magazines that will consider publishing a horror tale if it conforms to the overall needs of the magazine.

I once read a posting on an electronic bulletin board about a magazine for truckers called *RPM*. The magazine, I learned, published fiction, and that got me thinking: *RPM* ... trucks and trucking ... my story, "Death Drives a Semi." Why, yes, *RPM* wanted my story, my horror story, and paid me five cents a word, eight contributor's copies, and (all right!) an *RPM* baseball cap for one-time rights. To top it all off, the magazine had a circulation of 120,000.

Study the Market

An excellent source for finding alternative horror markets is the annual *Novel and Short Story Writer's Market* published by Writer's Digest Books. Each year, that guide lists hundreds of professional, literary, and little (small-press) magazines and journals, as well as contests, agents, and book publishers. You'll have to spend some time studying the reference book to find markets for your horror, but once you do, you'll have a great list of possibilities.

Remember, too, the kind of first-hand market research done at your local newsstand or bookstore.

Say yours is a literary horror story, heavy on atmosphere and mood. Take a look at several of the literary magazines on the shelf and give them a try. And if your horror story features a serial killer, you might try sending it to a mystery or crime magazine. Of course, the best way to learn what kind of fiction a magazine publishes is buying a copy and reading it from cover to cover.

This last point you've probably heard before, but it bears repeating: The best way to market your short fiction is to know your short fiction markets.

Resources Cited

Gila Queen's Guide to Markets: www.gilaqueen.us

Locus: www.locusmag.com

Hellnotes Newsletter: www.hellnotes.com

Science Fiction Chronicle: www.dnapublications.com

Novel and Short Story Writer's Market: www.writersdigest.com

Horror Writers Association: www.horror.org

Ralan's Guide to Speculative Markets: www.ralan.com

Speculations: For Writers Who Want to be Read: www.speculations.com

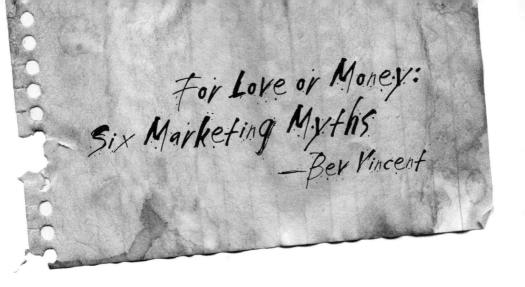

For Love or Money: Six Marketing Myths
—Bev Vincent

Because getting published is so difficult, novices desperate for that first break, that first short story in *print,* sometimes fall prey to misleading schemes that do nothing to further their careers. They're addicts seeking a fix, and publication is the drug. In return for empty promises, they give away print rights instead of getting paid for their efforts.

Thanks to the Internet, the horror community has become tightly knit. Published and aspiring writers network with each other and with readers. Inspired by this sense of community, upstart editors with little experience and less capital launch magazines and anthologies. Usually well-intended but occasionally misguided, these individuals might more properly be called "story collectors," because they seldom offer serious editorial feedback beyond proofreading, and sometimes not even that.

Since the editor often can't pay much—or anything—in advance, he trots out one or more of these six myths to entice amateur writers to submit:

1. Your payment is in exposure. Countless amateur Webzines are devoted to publishing horror fiction. You are led to believe that a story slapped up on a Web page with a black background and a border of skulls and blood will enhance your name recognition. Professional editors will automatically give a story more consideration the next time you submit something because they've heard of you through this appearance.

However, editors rarely pay attention to such "publications"—if they even learn about them in the first place. Since these markets accept almost anything they receive, the overall quality tends to be poor. You might as well write your story on the men's room wall and hope people are exposed to it there. One story in a pro market, with a circulation in the thousands, will garner more attention and name recognition than a hundred stories posted on Webzines.

2. I'm going to publish your story on my Webzine, but you can still sell it elsewhere. True, but you can only sell that story again as a reprint, which limits potential markets and income. Posting a story anywhere on the Internet (other than on a password-protected critique site that requires members to register) is generally regarded as exercising your first serial publication rights. You also run the risk that the person running the site won't honor requests to remove the story after the agreed-upon term, which virtually eliminates any chance of selling it even as a reprint. No editor is going to pay for a story that is freely available on the Internet.

3. You'll receive a pro-rated share of a percentage of the royalties accrued by the anthology. The concept of royalty-only anthologies exists in other genres, but seems especially popular in horror. My largest royalty payment for one of these projects is seventeen dollars, and I've received checks worth less than the postage stamp on the envelope. If an editor can't pay an advance, he likely has no money to market the book, either. Copies are printed on demand, which means they won't appear on the shelves of your neighborhood bookstore or on the racks at the airport. The potential audience: contributors' friends and families, especially since these books tend to be more expensive than mass–published ones. Reviewers rarely cover these books because of the recent proliferation of poorly produced, poorly edited anthologies.

4. I don't have a publisher yet, but I'll pay an advance once I do. Horror-anthology ideas are a dime a dozen, but getting a publisher to buy the concept is a tough sell, especially with a slate of unknown writers and an unproven editor. If you sign a contract for a story with an unsold anthology, you risk tying it up indefinitely. Even if promised a pro rate, you won't see a dime until a publisher buys the book, and the editor may later be forced to renegotiate the advance because he was overly optimistic about the book's potential. Until the anthology comes out, you can't market your story elsewhere, even as a reprint. Numerous projects wither because an enthusiastic but naive editor couldn't find a publisher. The editor's fallback position is sometimes to self-publish the anthology in a deluxe, signed/limited edition that is so expensive, even your family and friends will think twice about buying a copy.

5. We don't need a contract—this isn't a book sale, after all. Every time you let someone else publish your work, you need to specify in writing what rights you are granting and for what duration. Should you ever decide to publish a collection, the contracts establish whether you actually have reprint rights to your own stories. Contracts should have escape clauses that return rights to you if a certain period elapses without the work being published. If an editor acquires your story and then vanishes without printing a single copy, your rights to that story end up in limbo. You might sell your story somewhere else, assuming the book or magazine will never appear, but you end up in an awkward position if the editor suddenly resurfaces and produces the book. Remember, too, that part of any contract is a consideration, so if you don't get a realistic promise of compensation, the contract may be unenforceable.

6. It's not about the money, anyway; you're writing because you love to write. If you're serious about being a professional writer, then you should expect to be treated professionally by your editors, and that includes getting paid. The editor and publisher are benefiting from your work. Even a free Webzine is probably using banner ads to support the site, and your story attracts traffic. You can love what you do and still be paid for it—the two are hardly mutually exclusive.

The motto oft quoted by professionals is that money flows *toward* the author. There are exceptions. Some literary magazines have a certain cachet associated with being published in them. Donating stories to charity anthologies is a well-regarded practice. However, in general, you should follow the top-down approach to marketing your stories. If you end up in a situation where the only market left is a royalty-only anthology or a lavish limited edition where yours in the most familiar contributor name, maybe it's time to give that story a second look instead of simply giving it away.

One Reader at a Time: Promoting Your Horror Novel
—Scott Nicholson

A Perfect World—Not

In a perfect world, the author writes the book, the publisher produces the book, the bookstore displays the book, and the consumer approaches the shelf knowing which book is the one to buy.

We don't live in a perfect world. If you get a large advance, then your publisher will probably invest some time and money in promoting your book. Chances are good you're not reading this book, if that's the case. A full-page ad in *The New York Times Book Review* or even a quarter-page ad in *Fangoria* are not in the cards. If you want to reach your core audience and beyond, you'll have to shoulder some of the responsibility. The bad news is self-promotion takes away from your writing time, and you still have to build your audience one reader at a time. The good news is you can get a decent return without spending a lot of money.

Ideally, you should have some sort of product before you start promoting. Your name itself is a product, so the best starting point is to secure a Web site domain that matches the name under which you publish. Your Web site should serve as the focal point for all your promotional endeavors. All press releases, bookmarks, biographies, and interviews should mention your Web site. Your virtual home is a twenty-four-hour billboard that anybody in the world can reach for free.

Web Promo

The Web offers many other opportunities: Start a blog and share your view of the world. Hang out on message boards such as Horror World, Shocklines, or

Horror-Web, which discuss genre books with like-minded people. Subscribe to a variety of newsgroups and participate in online discussions. This will make your name visible and help you meet new people who might be interested in your work. If you join, though, be sure you participate as a community member, not just as someone who shows up every year or so to crow about your new book release. That won't win you any respect—or readers.

Many writers launch their own newsgroups or newsletters, allowing people to sign up for free and receive updates at regular intervals. Banner ads are another way to promote your books online, though it will take some work and maybe some money to have them posted where they will get decent exposure. You might try trading an article for ad space or agree to a banner swap with another site.

Home Base

Do not rely solely on the Internet for promotional efforts. Traditional media is still powerful, and while most writers can't personally fund a national advertising campaign, you'd be amazed at the coverage you can get for free. The key to print and broadcast media is to start close to home. Smaller towns usually have a radio station that would probably love to have a local author as an interview guest on the morning show. Most large cities have a talk station that books a variety of guests. Cable networks often carry locally produced television news shows. Don't think of any media outlet as too small. If nothing else, think of appearances on smaller stations as practice for the "Big Time."

Just as you start with local stations, your local newspaper should be the first to receive a press release about your book. From there, you can take a regional approach. Remember: Your press release must read like an interesting story.

Some papers will call you for an interview and feature story, while smaller papers will often run the press release as is. Don't overlook newspapers in former hometowns, trade magazines in your profession, and alumni publications from your old colleges.

When sending press releases to radio and newspapers, you'll have to decide how you want to send them. It's tempting to send blanket e-mails to all of your potential media outlets, but snail mail gets far more attention in busy newsrooms. Some newspapers make placement decisions based on the availability of good cover art. If you have a nice author photo, you might find it and the cover of your book on the front of the arts and entertainment section. You can have color photographs duplicated for about twenty cents a copy, though a professional photographer may run you hundreds of dollars. However, you might find a local photography student to take a photo of you in exchange for a credit line. Environmental shots, where you are at your desk or in a setting representative of your genre, are more interesting and will likely earn you better page placement.

Ideally, your publisher will send out review copies for you and will probably let you supply a list of reviewers and publications. You can also ask the publisher to provide you with extra copies to distribute on your own. Include books with your press kits if you can. If your publisher is miserly, you might choose to buy some at discount or send out your free author's copies, but in that case, you should be more selective and send books only to the places most likely to be interested.

Once you have a press release, create a media area on your Web site. Post a high-quality (minimum 300 dpi) JPEG electronic image of your author photo on the site along with your press release, book cover image, links to reviews and interviews, and links to any real-life research or subject matter connected to your book. This gives reporters and producers a central location to learn about your work and easily retrieve any material they need. If you have published multiple books, you should have a page, or even an entire Web site, for each book. Some authors launch flash animation book trailers that resemble movie ads. As with all promotional efforts, your level of sophistication depends on your available time, energy, and money, but your site says a lot about you and your work, so don't skimp. If you have Web-design skills, then make your site a showcase. If you have to hire someone else, aim for the basics while still providing comprehensive information to your visitors. No-frills professional Web design averages about one hundred dollars per Web page.

Printed matter, such as bookmarks and postcards, has a stronger physical presence than a Web banner, but distributing it can be costly. Places like www. brochure.com can print postcards in bulk for three cents apiece, but if you mail them out individually, add twenty-nine cents to the cost (as this is written—with an increase likely soon). Bookmarks cost about a fifth of a cent to print, and you can mail them directly to stores, pass them out at signings, or put them on giveaway tables at conventions and libraries. If you have multiple books out, feature all of your titles and simultaneously promote your Web site on the bookmarks.

What about simply buying ads in magazines and on the radio? They are usually not cost effective below the best-seller level. Radio ads count on repetition to build familiarity, and you're unlikely to reach your core audience. Print ads are often gone too quickly to have much impact, but you can target your audience better by seeking genre publications.

You'll want to focus the bulk of your efforts to coincide with the first month of your book's release. This means you probably need to start planning the moment your book is scheduled for publication, even if it's a year down the road. Bookstores generally place orders three or four months in advance, so if you want to try to influence them, you'll need to mail material about your book or drop by in person before your book's publication date. A decent portion of your material will go directly in the trash, but most booksellers seek new books and authors to share with their customers. Besides, you never know who is opening the mail. The bookstore clerk of today may be the chain store buyer or major book editor of tomorrow.

Send press kits and review copies a few months early to the magazines because they have longer lead times. Your publisher may send out advance review copies. If not, ask for extra copies of the book to send out on your own. Get them all in the mail as soon as you receive them, and keep a few around for the reviewers who contact you. The first month is the most important in the life of your book; that's when it receives the most notice and the best shelf display. If you're published in hardcover, you have a longer shelf life, but unsold mass-market paperbacks are stripped of their covers after ninety days, and the bookstores return the covers to the publisher for credit. Every book you move through your own efforts will increase your sell-through (the number of copies that are bought by customers at bookstores) percentage and improve your profitability to your publisher—which means new book contracts and increased support.

If you are a people person, then store signings, library talks, and convention panels create instant connections with an audience. Some authors have no trouble roaming a bookstore and telling strangers about their work. Others, even if sitting meekly at a table, feel like the salespeople they have always loathed and avoided. If you travel a lot, make bookstore stops part of your routine. This habit also gives you a chance to meet the store employees who can tell readers about your books.

Just as your media efforts begin close to home, don't forget those who are already in your corner. Let your family and friends help whenever possible, and once you find a fan or reader, treasure that person. Sponsor giveaways through your Web site or newsgroup, let your newsletter subscribers distribute bookmarks for you, and make people feel they are part of your success. Because they are. Without readers, you have no career.

Good Publicity

Good publicity is the cumulative effect of a sustained and spirited effort. Promoting your work takes as much, and possibly more, creativity than writing a book. Don't view it as drudgery and cold marketing. View it as a chance to share your passion, your words, your life. Whether you invest only paper and stamps or thousands of dollars, you are the master of your own fate. You will reap the rewards when your book is in the hands of hundreds of new readers.

Resources

Bookmarks and postcards: www.brochures.com; www.custompostcards.com

Newsgroups: http://groups.yahoo.com; http://groups.google.com

Press releases: www.stetson.edu/~rhansen/prguide.html; www.sfwriter.com/prindex.htm

Online media kits: www.hauntedcomputer.com/media.htm; www.josephnassise.com/press.htm; http://tobiasbuckell.com/wordpress

Book signings: www.writerswrite.com/journal/jan00/james.htm; www.writing-world.com/promotion/booksigning.shtml

Good examples of author sites: www.jakonrath.com; www.neilgaiman.com; www.kelleyarmstrong.com; www.michaelconnelly.com

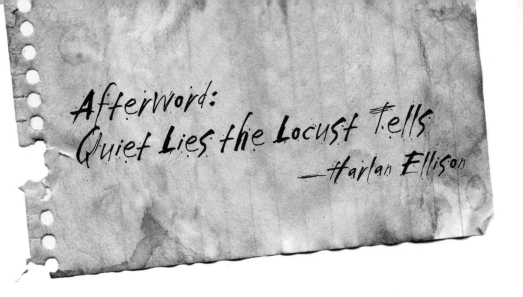

Afterword:
Quiet Lies the Locust Tells
—Harlan Ellison

She thinks we were all killed when they made the Great Sweep, but I escaped in the mud.

I was there when the first dreams came off the assembly line. I was there when the corrupted visions that had congealed in the vats were pincered up and hosed off and carried down the line to be dropped onto the rolling belts. I was there when the first workmen dropped their faceplates and turned on their welding torches. I was there when they began welding the foul things into their armor, when they began soldering the antennae, bolting on the wheels, pouring in the eye-socket jelly. I was there when they turned the juice on them and I was there when the things began to twitch.

No wonder She wanted all of us dead. Witnesses to their birth, to their construction, to their release into the air—not good. The myrmidons were loosed on the Great Sweep.

I think I am the last one left alive. The last one who can create dreams and not nightmares. I am the locust.

The reversal is sweet. What we always knew to be nightmares—the empty lives, the twisted language, the squeezing of the soul—they now call dreams. What we looked high to see as dreams—silliness, castles in the sky, breathing deeply on windy afternoons—She has commanded be termed nightmares, lies. I am the locust. I tell quiet lies. Called nightmares. That are truly fine dreams.

I swam in the mud till I was the color of the land. And made my escape. Overhead I saw the corrupted things soaring off to spread their rigor of obedience and fear and hatred. For many days I lay there, hidden, turning on my back for the rain, trapping small fish and insects for my food. Finally, when the Great Sweep was done and all my brothers and sisters were dead or locked away in madhouses, I went to the forest.

But like the locust that the Middle Ages saw as the symbol of passion, I will live forever. I will tell my quiet lies and no matter how blindly the people follow their instructions, in every generation there will be a hundred, perhaps a thousand, if chance is with them, even a hundred thousand, who will keep the quiet lies alive. To be told late at night to the children. With their bright eyes they will pay attention, and the dreams that have been outlawed, now called nightmares, will take root and spread.

And fifty years from now, a hundred years from now, when She thinks all courage has been drained out of the people, the children of the locust will be retelling the quiet lies. We will never be eradicated.

Decimated, yes, but still we survive.

Because in us lives the noblest part of the human experiment. The ability to dream.

I've watched, since the Great Sweep. Oh, what wonders She has given them in place of what they had. They have no real freedom, they have no genuine control of their lives, their days and nights are set down for them though they don't even perceive it that way. But She has given them endless flickering images on screens: surrogate dreams (the real lies, the true nightmares) that make them laugh because they hear laughter behind the flickering images, and scenes of death and destruction that they think are representations of the real world that She commands be termed "news." She has given them more and greater sporting events, young men and women hurling themselves at each other in meaningless contests She tells them represent survival in microcosm.

She has given them fashions that obsess them—though they do not understand that the fashions are one more way of making them facsimiles of each other. She has given them acts of government that unify them into hive groups, in the name of removing responsibility from their daily lives. She has taken control completely, and now they believe that the grandest role they can play is that of cog in the machine of Her design. In truth, what they have become are prisoners of their own lives.

All that stands between them and the shambling walk of the zombie are the quiet lies the locust tells.

Because I keep on the move, I have come to miss two aspects of human congress more than all the others combined. Love and friendship. Before the Great Sweep I never had the time or the perseverance to discover what raids love can make on the boredom of silent days spent alone. Nights are worse, of course.

I long to share confidences with a friend. But because I have placed myself outside the limits of their society, I fear striking up acquaintances.

Who would be my friend, in any event? I live in the last of the forests and I sleep in caves. The countryside is best for me. The cities are like the surface of the sun: great flares blast off the concrete; there are no places to hide, no cool corners in which to wait. Geomagnetic storms, sunspot occurrences, enormous air masses. I am wary of the cities. She rules without mercy there. And the people do not touch each other. Like those who are terribly sunscorched they avoid each other, passing in silence but with their teeth bared.

A day's walk from the forest, there is a small town. I began going to the town innocently, making myself known by showing only that edge of myself that would not alarm anyone. And after a time I came to know a small group of young people who enjoyed hearing my stories.

Now they come to the small cave where I sit cross-legged. They do not tell their parents where they're going. I think they gather roots and herbs as a cover for the afternoons in which they sit around me and I tell them of transcending destiny, of the three most important things in life, of true love and of my travels. They lie about having gone on many picnics. And each time they bring one of their friends who can be trusted—one of the ones with that special sly, impish smile that tells me the flame burns steadily. Inside. Where She cannot snuff it out. Not yet. (I do not believe in Gods, but I ask God never to let Her discover a way of reading the inside of the people. If She ever finds a way to probe and drain the heart, or the head, then all hope will be lost.)

The young people surprised me. The last time they came, they brought a much older woman to the cave. She was in that stretch of life somewhere between seventy and the close of business. For an instant I cursed their enthusiasm. It had blurred their judgment. Now I would have to run again and find a far place to begin again.

But the sly smile was there on her wrinkled face as she stooped to enter the cave. Firelight caught my wary expression as she entered, she drew a pinback button from the pocket of her padded jacket and clipped it on the left breast. It read: *Étonne-moi!*

She grinned at me as she sat down on the other side of the fire.

"I read French imperfectly," I said.

"Diaghilev to Jean Cocteau in 1909," she answered. "*Astonish* me."

I laughed, as the children settled down around us. How long had this woman kept her badge of defiance secret? Surely since the Great Sweep. Fear dissolved. The old woman was not one of Her subjects. This dear old woman, corpulent and cat-eyed, pain in her joints, was determined to live every moment with sanctification until the end. So I spun spiderwebs about looking for true love, about transcending destiny, about the three most important things in life, about times before the Great Sweep, and about just desserts.

"You're a Calvinist," she said. "Irreducible morality." But she said it with humor, and I shrugged, feeling embarrassed. "I don't think you really like shouldering the burden, even if you do it."

"You're right," I answered. "I would gladly lay it down; if I knew others would carry it."

She sighed. "We do, friend. We do."

I learned later that She had sent myrmidons against the old woman and her brother; and they were killed. They had tried to lead a strike. No one joined them and they were caught out naked in the daylight. And were killed. The children told me. The terrible sight of it had not been wasted on them. They were angry when they told me.

I loved her, that old woman. She was the locust.

I heard the sound of the locust from the hills one night. It was a man with an alto saxophone playing all alone, long after midnight. He was playing the kind of music I haven't heard in years. It was jazz. But it was the kind of sky-piercing jazz that long ago I had resisted, wondering if it was jazz at all. It had been rooted in the old order of what "Negroes" were lauded for playing, but as intense as steel, passionately soaring, the breaker of the circle. It had manifested radical inclinations; and I had refused to hear it.

But hearing it now, a solitary corner of one man's loneliness, afloat in the night, I longed to hear more. To return in time to that place where the music had been new, and I swore if the miracle of transport could be done, I would listen without insisting memory be served. I would hear it without narrow judgments. The locust played "Green Dolphin Street" and "Since I Fell For You." I remembered the name of the man who had played those tunes, years before the Great Sweep. His name had been Eric Dolphy, and I wished he would come down out of the far hills and travel with me.

I miss friendship. I miss music. What She gives them now, what She has led them to believe they want to hear, is as empty of human concern or enrichment as the fury of a thunderstorm.

It made me so sad, hearing him up there against the sooty night sky in which no stars had shone for a time beyond my recollection; a sky through which Her myrmidons flew to find old women and their brothers; a sky that would soon enough drop on the man with the horn. So sad I packed my few belongings in the rucksack … and I went away from the forest; from the cave, from the hills, and from the children. They would either hoard the quiet lies the locust had told, against the day when such tales would be needed, or they would follow their parents into the mouth of the machine She had oiled and set running.

Even I grow tired.

I warned them not to follow me. I am not the Pied Piper. They said, "We'll go with you. We can trust you." And I said, "Where I go there is no following. Where I go there is no mother, and no father, no safe days and no safe nights;

where I go I go alone, because I travel fast." But they followed. They hung back and I threw stones at them, then ran as fast as I could to lose them. But they kept coming. Three of them. Two boys and a girl. I wouldn't let them sit with me when I rested, and they stayed out of range and yelled through the forest to me.

"Our parents stood by and watched. They didn't lift a hand. When those things fell out of the sky and took the old woman and her brother, they didn't do a thing. When they set fire to them, no one tried to stop them. We can't live with people like that. You told us what that means."

I tried not to listen. I am not their leader. I am just the locust. I cannot even lead myself. I cannot do what they think must be done. All I can do is tell them quiet lies.

That isn't enough.

Some among them have to take the strength upon themselves.

Some among them must rise up from their midst to lift the real burden.

Must I do all the work?

I can tell them of the night of black glass, and of the hour that stretches, and of the visionary ... but I am no one's hero.

I waited behind a tree and when they passed I stepped out and explained my limitations, the amount of burden I was prepared to carry. They smiled the impish smiles and said I was better than that; I could beat off myrmidons with my bare hands; I was their inspiration. I slapped one of the boys. He took it and looked hurt, but they wouldn't leave me.

A man hides in the far hills and plays slow soft melodies. Nothing more is asked of him. Until he goes to the final sleep. That is a peace greatly to be desired. Why can't they hear the message? Do any of them really listen?

I struck out again and let them fend for themselves.

And when She sensed our movement, because there were four of us, unauthorized, moving at random, She sent the nightmares on their night flight, like bats that see in the dark, and they fell upon us. I did not stay to help them. In the chaos I escaped, went into the ground and hid. I tried not to think about the sounds the children made. And finally there was silence.

There are no leaders. There are only terrified souls trying to live till the day when She loses control and the machine turns on her. Until that day, unless I find a distant hill where the final sleep will free me, I will tell my quiet lies. There is nothing more to it than that.

There are no heroes of my generation. That role has yet to be filled. For my part, I am just the locust.

I speak of dreams called nightmares. No more should be expected, at risk of driving the reflection so deep into the mirror it will never emerge again.

The ability to dream is all I have to give. That is my responsibility; that is my burden. And even I grow tired.

The HWA Members Who Contributed to This Book

C. Dean Andersson is the critically acclaimed author of thirteen novels, including such horror books as *I Am Dracula* and *Raw Pain Max*.

Michael A. Arnzen teaches Writing Popular Fiction at Seton Hill University. His trophy case contains two Bram Stoker Awards, an International Horror Guild Award, a Ph.D. in English from the University of Oregon, and a severed limb. His latest books are *Freakcidents* and *Play Dead*. Arnzen lives at www.gorelets.com.

Jay Bonansinga has been called "one of the most imaginative writers of thrillers" by the *Chicago Tribune*. His novel *Frozen* was a national best-seller. He has worked with film director George Romero (*Night of the Living Dead*) and has been a Bram Stoker Award finalist. Find him online at www.jay bonansinga.com.

Ray Bradbury, the author of more than thirty books, is one of the most celebrated fiction writers of our time. Among his best-known works are *Fahrenheit 451*, *The Martian Chronicles*, *The Illustrated Man*, *Dandelion Wine*, and *Something Wicked This Way Comes*. In 2000, Bradbury was awarded the National Book Foundation's Medal for Distinguished Contribution to American Letters.

Ramsey Campbell has been described by *The Oxford Companion to English Literature* as "Britain's most respected living horror writer." He has been given more awards than any other writer in the field, including the Grandmaster Award of the World Horror Convention and the Horror Writers Association's Bram Stoker Lifetime Achievement Award.

David Campiti is the owner of Glass House Graphics, the largest talent studio/agency for comic artists and graphic designers on the planet. He has written such comic book projects as *Superman, Beauty and the Beast*, and *Dark Shad-*

ows. Teaching Creating Comics seminars all over the world, Campiti lives in Wheeling, West Virginia, with his *FHM*-model wife and baby daughter.

Mort Castle's books include the short-story collection *Moon on the Water* and the novel *The Strangers*, optioned for the screen by Jeff Balis of Whitewater Films. Cited as one of "21 Leaders in the Arts for the 21st Century in Chicago's Southland," Castle has directed an annual writing workshop at the World Horror Convention since 2002.

Jeanne Cavelos has gone from NASA astrophysicist to senior editor at Bantam Doubleday Dell to best-selling writer. Her books include *The Passing of the Techno-Mages* and *The Many Faces of Van Helsing*. Jeanne is the director of Odyssey, an annual six-week workshop for writers of science fiction, fiction, and horror. Visit her at www.jeannecavelos.com.

Joseph Curtin, a struggling artist for most of his adult life, wrote his first novel, *Daughters of the Moon,* on the cusp of age forty. Deluded by his initial success, Joe penned *Monsterman*, a werewolf/coming-of-age/teenage angst tale for Five Star/Tekno Books (September 2006).

Richard E. Dansky is the Central Clancy Writer for Ubisoft and the manager of design at Red Storm Entertainment. You are saved from reading anything further about him, due to the fifty-word limit on author bios for this book—unless you visit his Web site at www.richarddansky.com.

Brendan Deneen is Director of Production and Development at The Weinstein Company/Dimension Films. He is also the author of the comic book *Scatterbrain* as well as the *New York Times*-reviewed children's play *Mortimer, The Lazy Bird*. Brendan currently works in New York City, where he lives with his wife, Kim, and two cats.

Harlan Ellison® has been called "one of the great living American short-story writers" by the *Washington Post*. He has won the Hugo eight and a half times, the Nebula three times, the Stoker five times, the HWA's Lifetime Achievement Award, the Edgar Allan Poe Award twice, and many, many more such honors. Ellison has won more awards than any other living fantasist for the seventy-five books, the more than seventeen hundred stories, essays, articles, and newspaper columns, the two dozen teleplays, and the dozen motion pictures he has. He lives with his wife, Susan, in Los Angeles.

John Everson won a Stoker for his debut novel *Covenant*, and, under the watchful eye of his cockatoo, has authored two horror short-story collections: *Vigilantes of Love* and *Cage of Bones & Other Deadly Obsessions*. He copyedits, designs, and performs other "odd jobs" for various small presses. Visit www.johneverson.com.

Gary Frank is the author of many things, including the new supernatural thriller, *Forever Will You Suffer*.

W. D. Gagliani's novel *Wolf's Trap* was a finalist for the Bram Stoker Award in 2004 and was reissued in mass-market paperback by Leisure Books in 2006. His fiction and nonfiction has been published in various print and on-line venues since 1986. Visit his Web site at www.williamdgagliani.com.

Richard Gilliam, educator, journalist, and fiction writer, began writing full-time in the early 1990s. Employing an investigative reporter's research skills to inform his fiction, Gilliam has co-edited a number of acclaimed antholo-gies, including *Phantoms of the Night,* and has been a finalist for the Bram Stoker Award.

Scott Hickey is the creator and producer of the horror audio series *The Grist Mill,* now in its fifth year of production. He has worked with Brian Price and Jerry Stearns of Great Northern Audio Theater and Jeffrey Adams of Imagi-nation-X. He lives with his father in Lowell, Massachusetts.

Gerard Houarner is fiction editor of *Space & Time* magazine and has a career working in mental health. He is the author of the novels *The Beast That Was Max* and *Road to Hell* and the short-story collections *Black Orchids from Aum* and *I Love You and There Is Nothing You Can Do About It.*

Tina Jens is a two-time Bram Stoker Award nominee. Author of the award-winning novel-in-stories *The Blues Ain't Nothin': Tales of the Lonesome Blues Pub,* she produced "Twilight Tales," the live weekly reading series at Chicago's Red Lion Pub for ten years, recently having left that post to focus on her work as editor of the *Twilight Tales* line of anthologies.

Nicholas Kaufmann's stories, including *City Slab, Cemetery Dance,* and *The Mammoth Book of Best New Erotica* (Vol. 3), have appeared in numerous magazines and anthologies. He's received several honorable mentions in *The Year's Best Fantasy and Horror* and has served on the HWA Board of Trust-ees. He lives in Brooklyn, New York.

Nate Kenyon is the author of *Bloodstone* (Five Star/Tekno Books, 2006), and his fiction has appeared in various magazines as well as in the horror anthol-ogy *Terminal Frights.*

Jack Ketchum is the writer of *Crime and Punishment, To Kill a Mockingbird,* and *Under the Yum Yum Tree,* co-authored with Slappy White. (Oh wait, that's somebody else ....) No, he's the four-time winner of the Stoker Award and au-thor of eleven novels and three short story-collections. Sorry, it's *that* guy.

Nancy Kilpatrick is the award-winning, scream-queen author of thirty books, including novels, story collections, one nonfiction volume, and anthologies she has edited. She works in the horror, dark fantasy, mystery, and erotica genres, and also teaches writing. Check out her Web site for her latest endeav-ors at www.nancykilpatrick.com.

Stephen King is acknowledged by his peers and his readers as the most successful horror writer of modern times. His novels and short stories have been translated into virtually all of the world's languages and have been presented in every medium. Among his honors are nineteen Bram Stoker Awards, as well as the HWA's Lifetime Achievement Award, numerous World Fantasy and International Horror Guild Awards, and the National Book Award. Perhaps more than any other contemporary, King has climbed over or knocked down any walls that might exist between "popular" and "literary" writing.

Tracy Knight is a clinical psychologist and university professor whose short fiction has appeared in over twenty-five anthologies. He also is the author of two novels, *Beneath a Whiskey Sky* and *The Astonished Eye*, the latter of which was nominated for Best First Novel by the International Horror Guild.

Joe R. Lansdale is the author of a number of novels and many short stories. His most recent novel is the widely acclaimed *Sunset and Sawdust*. His short story "Bubba Ho-tep" became the cult film of the same name, and *Masters of Horror* on the Showtime network has filmed his story "Incident On and Off a Mountain Road."

John Maclay has sold more than one hundred horror and fantasy stories, twenty of them in the past three years. He was the original publisher of J.N. Williamson's *Masques* horror anthology series. He lives in Baltimore, where he is also active in the Freemasonry fraternal organization and in historic preservation.

Bob Madia has published short stories, plays, and comedy, and is senior scriptwriter for *The Grist Mill*. Several of his screenplays have been optioned and a short feature has been produced. Bob works as a reporter for Russell Publications in Chicago's south suburbs. His wife, Dawn, and daughter, Sarah, are a constant source of encouragement.

Nick Mamatas is the author of the Lovecraftian-Beat road novel *Move Under Ground*, which was nominated for both Bram Stoker and International Horror Guild Awards. He lives in Vermont.

Michael Marano is a writer and critic whose reviews appear in *Cemetery Dance* and on the public radio program *Movie Magazine International*. His novel, *Dawn Song*, won the International Horror Guild and Bram Stoker awards; his short fiction has appeared in numerous high-profile anthologies. Reach him at www.mindspring.com/~profmike/.

Michael McCarty is a former stand-up comedian and musician. Currently a staff writer for *Science Fiction Weekly*, a weekly newsletter, *Hellnotes,* and the supernatural horror Web site *Dark Krypt*, he is the author of the books *Giants of the Genre, More Giants of the Genre*, and *Dark Duets*. His Web site is www.geocities.com/mccartyzone/.

Mark McLaughlin, a Bram Stoker winner, is the author of *Slime After Slime Motivational Shrieker* and the co-author of *The Gossamer Eye* and *At The Foothills of Frenzy*.

Tom Monteleone sold his first short story in 1972. Since then, he's sold a whole lot more.

David Morrell is the award-winning author of *First Blood*, the 1972 novel in which Rambo was created. To date, he has written twenty-eight books and has been translated into twenty-six languages. His *Lessons From a Lifetime of Writing* distills what he has learned in his long career.

Lisa Morton has authored six produced feature films, two nonfiction books, and dozens of short stories. She has also written, directed, and produced numerous small theater productions, including the highly acclaimed collection of horror one-acts, *Spirits of the Season*. Find out more at www.lisamorton.com.

Joseph Nassise, a Bram Stoker and International Horror Guild Award nominee, is a past president of the Horror Writers Association. He is a current member of the Horror Channel's Creative Advisory Board, and the author of the recent dark fantasy series *The Templar Chronicles*. Visit him at www.josephnassise.com.

Yvonne Navarro lives in southern Arizona with her husband and two huge Great Danes. She works on Fort Huachuca, a major military installation in the Southwest, and does way too much other stuff. Recently completed projects include *Ultraviolet*, *Elektra*, and *Hellboy*. In total, she's written twenty novels and almost one hundred short stories. Visit her at www.yvonnenavarro.com.

Scott Nicholson is the author of *The Farm*, *The Home*, *The Manor*, *The Harvest*, and *The Red Church*. He lives physically in the Appalachian Mountains of North Carolina, mentally in a martian asylum, and electronically at www.hauntedcomputer.com.

Joyce Carol Oates is the renowned author of many novels, including *Big Mouth & Ugly Girl*, *Freaky Green Eyes*, and *The Falls*. Her novel *Blonde* was a National Book Award nominee and *New York Times* best-seller. A recipient of the National Book Award, the PEN/Malamud Award for Excellence in Short Fiction, and the HWA's Lifetime Achievement Award. Ms. Oates is the Roger S. Berlind Distinguished Professor of the Humanities at Princeton University.

Weston Ochse lives in the Arizona desert, constantly dodging the border patrol, illegal aliens, and tarantula wasps. His novels include *Scarecrow Gods* and *Recalled to Life*. Sometimes mistaken for a redneck, Weston co-authored the collections *Scary Rednecks and Other Inbred Horrors* and *Appalachian Galapagos*, nominated for the Pushcart Prize.

Tom Piccirilli is the author of fifteen novels, including *Headstone City, November Mourns*, and *A Choir of Ill Children*. A four-time winner of the Bram Stoker Award and a finalist for the World Fantasy Award, Tom makes his home in Loveland, Colorado. Learn more at his official Web site, www.tom piccirilli.com.

Bruce Holland Rogers is the author of nearly two hundred short stories, some of which have won a Pushcart Prize, the Bram Stoker Award, and a World Fantasy Award. He teaches fiction writing in the Whidbey Writers Workshop MFA Program and in writing seminars in Italy and Greece. More info is available at www.shortshortshort.com.

Judi Rohrig, though merely an Indiana housewife with a computer in her kitchen, manages to edit *Hellnotes* (a Bram Stoker Award-winning weekly newsletter) and to sell a few tall tales—stories published in *Masques V, Cemetery Dance* magazine, and in an upcoming DAW anthology, through contacts made via the Internet.

Michael Romkey is the author of nine horror novels including *American Gothic, The Vampire's Violin*, and *The London Vampire Panic*.

Wayne Allen Sallee's credits can be found by "googling" him, which will, in turn, make his ears ring. In 2006, Midnight Library is releasing a fifteenth anniversary edition of his *The Holy Terror* and Annihilation Press will publish a collection of his stories, entitled *Fiends by Torchlight*. He is still quite understandably single, and his tombstone will read "The computer remained his nemesis to the very end."

Steven Savile's novels include *Inheritance, Dominion, Retribution*, and *Exile*, the first in a series of novelizations of the cult comic strip *Slaine*. Savile has been a runner-up in the British Fantasy Awards and has been awarded the Writers of the Future Award.

Harry Shannon has been an actor, a singer, and an Emmy-nominated songwriter. His novels include *Night of the Beast, Night of the Werewolf*, and *Eye of the Burning Man*.

Peter Straub is the winner of six Bram Stoker Awards and the author of two classics co-written with Stephen King, *Ghost Story* and *Black House* (the sequel to *The Talisman)*, in addition to his own classic, *In The Night Room*.

Karen E. Taylor is best known for *The Vampire Legacy* series. "What can I say? I start out to write a story and, before I know what's hit me, the main character turns spectral, or grows fangs, or wings. It's what I do and what I love," says Taylor.

Melinda Thielbar started her writing career with two short stories, one of which was published in *Weird Tales* magazine and received an honorable mention in *The Year's Best Fantasy and Horror*. She currently lives in North Carolina with her husband and her two cats.

Lee Thomas is the Bram Stoker Award-winning author of *Stained, Parish Damned, Damage*, and *The Dust of Wonderland*. Writing teen fiction as Thomas Pendleton, he is the author of the forthcoming book *Mason* and co-author (with Stefan Petrucha) of the series *Wicked Dead*, both from HarperCollins.

Paul Tremblay is a fiction editor with *ChiZine* (www.chizine.com) and author of *Compositions for the Young and Old* (Prime Books), and he's tall.

Bev Vincent is the author of *The Road to the Dark Tower*, the authorized companion to Stephen King's *Dark Tower* series. With short-story appearances in *From the Borderlands, Corpse Blossoms*, and *Shivers IV*, he's a contributing editor to *Cemetery Dance* magazine and *Accent Literary Review*. His Web site is www.bevvincent.com.

Edo van Belkom is the author and editor of more than twenty-five books and two hundred stories of horror, science fiction, fantasy, and mystery. A Bram Stoker Award winner, he has also been honored with two Aurora Awards (Canada's top prize for speculative writing) and, in 2006, the Silver Birch Award. His novels include *Lord Soth, Teeth*, and *Scream Queen*.

Robert Weinberg is the author of more than thirty books, many of them horror and dark fantasy. He has twice won both the Bram Stoker Award and the World Fantasy Award, and has also served as the grand marshal of a rodeo parade.

Stanley Wiater is a highly acclaimed, multiple-award-winning writer, creator, and commentator on popular culture. In exploring "the fantastique," Stanley has profiled more fantasy, horror, and science fiction authors, artists, and filmmakers than any other writer. He has been hailed as the "the world's leading expert on horror authors and filmmakers" and "the master journalist of the dark genres."

J.N. Williamson shared the HWA's Lifetime Achievement Award honors with Stephen King for 2002. The author of many short stories and highly regarded novels, including *The Longest Night* and *Affinity*, he might well best be remembered for editing the *Masques* anthologies, which featured prominent writers and offered many promising newcomers their first important publication. Jerry Williamson died in December 2005, and we miss him.

Douglas E. Winter edited the celebrated horror fiction anthology *Prime Evil*. His books include the definitive critical biography *Stephen King: The Art of Darkness*, the World Fantasy Award-winning *Faces of Fear*, and the suspense novel *Run*. A member of the National Book Critics Circle, Winter lives in Oakton, Virginia.

Index